SOUND THEOLOGY

WORSHIP AND WITNESS

The Worship and Witness series seeks to foster a rich, interdisciplinary conversation on the theology and practice of public worship, a conversation that will be integrative and expansive. Integrative, in that scholars and practitioners from a wide range of disciplines and ecclesial contexts will contribute studies that engage church and academy. Expansive, in that the series will engage voices from the global church and foreground crucial areas of inquiry for the vitality of public worship in the twenty-first century.

The Worship and Witness series demonstrates and cultivates the interaction of topics in worship studies with a range of crucial questions, topics, and insights drawn from other fields. These include the traditional disciplines of theology, history, and pastoral ministry—as well as cultural studies, political theology, spirituality, and music and the arts. The series focus will thus bridge church worship practices and the vital witness these practices nourish.

We are pleased that you have chosen to join us in this conversation, and we look forward to sharing this learning journey with you.

SERIES EDITORS:

John D. Witvliet
Noel Snyder
Maria Cornou

SOUND THEOLOGY

Pipe Organ Power Plays among Protestants,
Pulpits, Professors, and Peers

Randall Dean Engle

CASCADE *Books* • Eugene, Oregon

SOUND THEOLOGY
Pipe Organ Power Plays among Protestants, Pulpits, Professors, and Peers

Copyright © 2024 Randall Dean Engle. All rights reserved. Except for brief quotations in critical publications or reviews, no part of this book may be reproduced in any manner without prior written permission from the publisher. Write: Permissions, Wipf and Stock Publishers, 199 W. 8th Ave., Suite 3, Eugene, OR 97401.

Cascade Books
An Imprint of Wipf and Stock Publishers
199 W. 8th Ave., Suite 3
Eugene, OR 97401

www.wipfandstock.com

PAPERBACK ISBN: 978-1-6667-1006-9
HARDCOVER ISBN: 978-1-6667-1007-6
EBOOK ISBN: 978-1-6667-1008-3

Cataloguing-in-Publication data:

Names: Engle, Randall Dean, author.

Title: Sound theology : pipe organ power plays among Protestants, pulpits, professors, and peers / Randall Dean Engle.

Description: Eugene, OR: Cascade Books, 2024 | Series: Worship and Witness | Includes bibliographical references and index.

Identifiers: ISBN 978-1-6667-1006-9 (paperback) | ISBN 978-1-6667-1007-6 (hardcover) | ISBN 978-1-6667-1008-3 (ebook)

Subjects: LCSH: Organ (musical instrument)—Europe and America. | Organ (musical instrument)—History. | Church music.

Classification: ML553 E2 2024 (print) | ML553 (ebook)

All Scripture quotations, unless otherwise indicated, are taken from the Holy Bible, New International Version®, NIV®. Copyright ©1973, 1978, 1984, 2011 by Biblica, Inc.® Used by permission of Zondervan. All rights reserved worldwide. www.zondervan.com The "NIV" and "New International Version" are trademarks registered in the United States Patent and Trademark Office by Biblica, Inc.®

For North Hills Christian Reformed Church
Troy, Michigan

For we are co-workers in God's service;
you are God's field, God's building.
1 Corinthians 3:9

Tot psalmen en gebee'n wort 't orgel recht gebruycket,
O Salich welcker keel des Heeren roem ontluycket!
—JACOBIUS REVIUS

The organ is properly used for psalms and prayer
Oh bliss whose throat opens the glory of the Lord!

Soo dat het eene is een sieck Wijf
en het ander een krancke Vrouw
ende ofmen soodanige die het vervloecte Orgel
inden Godtsdient voostaen ende invoeren
—JAN JANSZ. CALCKMAN

So that one is like a sick wife,
and the other an ill woman:
such are those who are in favor of introducing the damn organ
into the worship service.

CONTENTS

Acknowledgments ix

Prelude 1

Chapter 1: Setting the Stage 9

Chapter 2: The Pipe Organ in the Netherlands 50

Chapter 3: Regional Models of Reform: Theme and Variations 76

Chapter 4: The Curious Case of Dordrecht 120

Chapter 5: Constantijn Huygens: His Friends and Foes 130

Chapter 6: Voetius Outscored 170

Postlude 199

Bibliography 203

Name/Subject Index 231

Scripture Index 236

ACKNOWLEDGMENTS

It is with immense gratitude that I acknowledge the support and friendships of so many that have helped to make this book a reality.

In my earliest years, people like Grampa and Grama Hugen shared a passion for the Genevan Psalms, singing them as I tried desperately to accompany on the organ in their living room on Spruce Street, Pella, Iowa. Later, Gerald van Dusseldorp, church musician and organist, would teach me how to do so more proficiently, even though I did so only with a modicum of skill. My parents Alice Jean (Nikkel) and Verland Dean Engle gave me the gift of Sabbath discipline, and the shalom of genuine biblical piety lived without necessarily having to talk about it. And the gaggle of Nikkel relatives that flocked together each Sunday for coffee after church made the whole of Sunday so much fun that I simply couldn't imagine the Lord's Day being any better. All these folks, with so many more, taught me to value a tradition, to love the church, and to cherish her worship and her ways.

In retrospect, it was little wonder that my career path led me to the church, and service to it as musician, pastor, and student. In those banquet years at Calvin University, Calvin Seminary, and Luther Seminary, mentors like John Hamersma, Anton Armstrong, John Ferguson, Harry Boonstra, uncle Melvin D. Hugen, and Paul Westermeyer came my way—each with a teacher's gift that poured all into a student. Peers like John D. Witvliet and Martin Tel kept vigil to my academic and liturgical rantings and ravings. Colleagues like Brent Assink, and Duane Kelderman, allowed me, with so much grace, to practice ministry with them, and to learn from them and with them.

I thank the H. Meeter Center for Calvin Studies of Calvin College, Grand Rapids, Michigan, for the honor of being a recipient of the Emo Van Halsema Graduate Fellowship Research Award that afforded an indulgent immersion into all things Calvinistic during my time of study and research with them in the summer of 2004—serendipitously, it introduced me to my engaging colleague Dr. John Exalto of Amsterdam's Vrij University, now school inspector for the Netherlands. I was further honored with postdoctoral awards from the Alan Luff Foundation, the American Organ Historical Society, and the Mader Foundation; these awards will further this book's research well beyond these pages.

Special mention must be given to those who assisted me in editing and with translations. First and foremost, Mr. Jan Hofstee, a Dutch linguist *par excellence,* whose working knowledge of the Dutch language of the sixteenth century is unmatched. Our trek into the Dutch world of the sixteenth century ensnared us in linguistic traps of Queen's Dutch, farmer's Dutch, low German, Frisian, and even Gronigers (a regional dialectic of the Frisian language) not to mention the sloppy pen of the beer tax collector Jan Jansz. Calckman. It was John who helped me navigate it all with accuracy and precision. *Hartelijk bedankt van Dominee.*

And there were others. David van Dijk, proofreader and all-around great guy, Latinists Randy Blacketer, Michael Krogh, Todd Rester, Nancy van Baak, and Michael Williams.

During the writing and research process, my mind inevitably wandered back to my own roots in the Netherlands. I could not help wonder if my ancestors—the van Dijks, the Nikkels, the Sjaardemas, the Terpstras—were amongst the Calvinists who "learned the Psalms by heart as a mark of their Protestantism. . . . they were in the villages in the great number where one hears the Psalms sung in the mouths of artisans, and in the fields of the laborers."[1] Privately, I hoped they, my ancestors, numbered among those who argued for the re-inclusion of the arts in their respective Reformed churches of Velsum, Doesburgerbuurt, Oppenhuizen, and Monnikendam.

But it is to the North Hills Christian Reformed Church community that this book and its accompanying *Reader* is dedicated. This incomparable family of faith saw in me more than I saw in myself. In this endeavor they provided the gifts of time and encouragement, and then even sabbaticals and financial support to see to it that I could get it done. They have taught me the greatest life lesson of all, that "from the fullness of His grace we have all received one blessing after another" (John 1:16).

—Randall Dean Engle
October 2022

---

1. Garside Jr., *Calvin's Theology of Music,* 85.

PRELUDE

In 1787 in the city of Wemeldinge, an elderly spinster prepared her last will and testament. Like many other Protestants in the Dutch province of Zeeland, Maria Coomans of Wemeldinge had contempt for the new organ music starting to be used in the Reformed churches; she considered the sounds that belched from organ pipes to be a vainglorious, distasteful remnant of Roman Catholic worship that were best suited for accompanying the kinds of songs sung in alehouses. Consequently, when she bequeathed her entire estate to her church, her gift came with a strict codicil: the church could never purchase a pipe organ. If it did, the value of her estate, which was quite substantial, would be withdrawn from the church and deposited instead into an endowment to support the town's poor.[1]

The condition of Ms. Coomans's put Wemeldinge's church council and city fathers in a bind. Both groups hoped to benefit from the generous bequest, but neither group wanted to submit to her conditions because not all agreed with her distaste for organ music. Their clever solution honored only the letter of the widow's will; they ordered that a mural be painted in the church in the spot where a pipe organ would have been placed had they not inherited the conditions of Coomans's will.[2] As a result, the Reformed congregation in Wemeldinge worshiped without the sound of an organ for over two hundred years.

It was not until 1958 that the church installed a pipe organ, and then a used one from the neighboring city of Kruiningen. To do so, the Wemeldinge church chartered an *ad hoc* "Organ Committee" that purchased

---

1. Lepoeter, *Maria Coomans*.

2. The mural was rediscovered in an 1811 renovation of the church. Kist, "Kerkelijke," 10:299, claims the mural was of a pipe organ!

the instrument (technically not the church), so the conditions of Maria Coomans were honored.

Stories of such organ strife abound during the period of the Protestant Reformation in the Netherlands and across all the countries experiencing reformations. The break with Rome brought about obvious changes in Christian liturgy, but Reformed churches dramatically altered the role of music in public worship, especially the use of the pipe organ. This dramatic difference from Roman Catholic practice can be traced in part to the writings of foundational Reformers; admittedly, instrumental music ranked low on the list of Reformers' concerns—their preferred targets were Catholic indulgences, church administration, and clerical depravity in general. But the subject of organ music was addressed, and then most often unfavorably. In fact, most Protestant churches across Europe initially silenced the pipe organ during worship. Curiously, after most organ proscriptions were officially adopted, in less than one hundred years nearly all Protestant churches heard again the sound of windblown pipes in their sanctuaries—despite the nettlesome protestations of parishioners such as a Maria Coomans. "The situation was unique, without parallel in the history of church music,"[3] wrote Henry Bruinsma, an American scholar of Calvin and music. This book, *Sound Theology*, details this dramatic change in worship practice as well as the accompanying theological debates within the Reformed churches.

Sixteenth- and seventeenth-century clerics and magistrates kept records that documented this "unique situation."[4] According to these records, which will be presented in detail later, Reformed clergy enacted ecclesiastical legislation that prohibited organ use while Dutch magistrates detailed their right to control the instruments regardless of any ecclesiastical ban. Examining these ecclesiastical and secular hierarchical polities are a necessary starting point for this book, as this analysis gives clarity to the origins of the debate. However, Margo Todd, a scholar of the Protestant Reformation in Scotland, notes that such a top-down perspective of scholarship does not always fully account for the full scope of influences at work in any of the national reformations.[5] Thus, in order to understand the Dutch organ controversy clearly, this book will also

3. Bruinsma, "Organ Controversy," 205.

4. See Hooijer, *Oude kerkordeningen*; Rutgers, *Acta van de Nederlandsche synoden*; Reitsma and Veen, *Acta der provinciale en particuliere synoden*; Brandt, *Historie der reformatie*.

5. Todd, *Culture of Protestantism*, 1–8. Also see Benedict, *Christ's Churches*.

read closely the opposing opinions regarding organ music held by the magistrates, clergy, and academics on the one hand, as well as those held by the laity, the people in the pew on the receiving end of the dicta. Their differing opinions fueled the Dutch organ controversy during and after the Reformation, and help explain the marked differences between the theory and practice of this time.

Historical studies on the Dutch organ controversy in the past, limited in number though they are, tend to present the case too simplistically: Calvin called for no instruments in worship, the reforming church obeyed, but the nobleman Constantijn Huygens[6] and the resulting horrendous state of unaccompanied singing reversed Dutch opinion in a generation's time. This caricature stipulates that the nascent Dutch Reformed church did attempt to enact binding, ecclesiastical decisions with regard to the use of instruments in worship. Further, this view assumes that Huygens's work was widely read and obeyed, and that the nobleman had direct influence on the machinations of the newly forming Reformed church. True, in the end, the Dutch Reformed did reintroduce the organ in part to beautify their worship, just as Huygens had pleaded. But the series of events in the controversy is much more nuanced and varied; the pipe organ was reincorporated by the Reformed not just because of the passing of time, nor because of Huygens's arguments, nor only for the poor quality of church music.

Indeed, the Dutch disagreed very vocally on what to do with church organs and held a variety of opinions about the instrument. Some labeled the organ as demonic and sacrilegious, an affront to the gains of the Reformation. Many ministers preached such invectives from their pulpits. Yet across the street, in city council chambers, councilmen declared that organ music was a thing of beauty enjoyed by the town's citizenry, promoted the common good, and therefore should be enjoyed by all. Still further these civic councils blatantly announced that organ use was of no concern of the church or of its ministers. The smoldering power play became increasingly fierce as time went on. For instance, when the provincial synod of Delft in 1638 decided to allow each congregation of its district to decide for itself whether to allow organ music, many laymen were so aggrieved that they appealed to the classis to force their leaders to reverse that decision. In another notable case, the layman and writer Jan Jansz. Calckman published an attack on the organ, Huygens, and the

---

6. Huygens, *Gebruyck of ongebruyck van 't orgel in de kercken der Vereenighde Nederlanden* (hereafter *Orgel Gebruyck*).

synod all at the same time in a reactionary, vituperative publication.[7] In short, there was no one voice that settled the pipe organ issue in Reformed cultures before, during, or after the Reformation.

To further complicate the situation, the Netherlands was at the same time in the political process of becoming a republic marked by tolerance and pluralism. Not by decree nor through the use of government force, Calvinism took root and flourished in the small country largely because of its presbyterian form of government. This structure of church governance placed decision-making largely in the hands of elected local leaders, not unlike the new republican structures of the secular realm. While ecclesiastical power was decentralized in a dramatic change from the days of Spanish occupation, the scattered Reformed churches organized themselves into regional and, later, national synods so that Calvinism ultimately emerged by the end of the century as an influential Protestant movement in the Netherlands.[8] During this process of organization, records from local Dutch church councils and regional synods reveal debates regarding Reformed worship practices, including the proper use of music in worship. Because each congregation's elected leadership had to deliberate and vote on its liturgical policies, musical practices varied widely across this small republic. What can be said for certain is that the Dutch Reformed churches were wracked with confusion and acrimony about what to do with their pipe organs. As a result, a fierce and lengthy controversy erupted in the Netherlands at the convergence of other musical, liturgical, political, and ecclesiastical debates. *Sound Theology* places the Dutch organ controversy in the context of these other debates in order to understand how the organ controversy started, developed, and concluded only after several generations. The analysis shows that the use or nonuse of the organ varied among differing groups that had splintered from the Roman Catholic Church, and was inconsistent among the Reformed inside and outside the Netherlands.

So the story begins. Chapter 1 sets the stage by surveying the use of the organ in Protestant cultures across Europe at this time so that the events in the Dutch Republic can be properly understood in its context. This review shows that the Dutch pipe organ debate is distinct from the debates that took place among the Scots Presbyterians, German Lutherans, Swiss Zwinglians, the Calvinists in Hungary and Poland, and the

---

7. Calckman, *Antidotum*.
8. Israel, *Dutch Republic*, 390–95.

Reformed Church in America. Further, this analysis reveals that no one practice emerged amongst reforming cultures at this time; rather, each group developed indigenous policies in response to its unique circumstances. Consequently, as chapter 1 will review, some Reformed churches outside of the Netherlands during the seventeenth century allowed the organ, while others prohibited it completely.

Chapter 1 also traces how the forceful theology of John Calvin sprouted and took root on Dutch soil during Holland's Golden Age—even despite some homegrown resistance—and how his theology with respect to worship and church music evolved in the Netherlands during the generations after his death. A detailed review of Calvin's Bible commentaries and sermons explain the theological arguments behind his objections to instrumental music in worship in general, and to the pipe organ in specific. This chapter introduces the term "aural iconoclasm" to describe Calvin's staunch insistence that certain sounds, such as florid polyphony, choirs, non-vernacular speech, and instrumental music should not be used in Christian worship. This chapter also analyses whether Calvin's view of instruments in worship unique amongst the Reformers, or if he merely echoed opinions already discussed by others. Also, this chapter examines how Calvin's instruction regarding church music was received as his theology spread and influenced Protestantism throughout Europe.

The next chapter begins with a broad review of the history of the pipe organ in general, and then specifically its use in the Netherlands from its origins in Catholic worship to the scathing judgments of the Reformation. A brief overview of other Christian groups within the Netherlands, such as the German Reformed, Walloon, Anabaptists, Remonstrants, and Moravians, shows that the Calvinists were not alone in their struggles over the use of the organ. A close reading of synodical pronouncements and other church documents from the sixteenth and seventeenth centuries illustrates the frustration of church leaders and laity as they tried to prohibit organ music in their church buildings. Because both the organs and the church buildings in which they were housed were the legal property of each local city council, neither church councils nor ministers had legal authority to enforce the prohibitions, as this chapter will discuss.

Chapter 3 reviews the uneven process of "protestantization" of the Netherlands. Organ dispositions, construction lists of new pipe organs, and a variety of documents from representative locales reveal that organ bans had no effect. The documents examined in this chapter also indicate that the conflict between clergy and magistrates was not limited to control of the church organ. The Reformed notion of the "priesthood of all believers" forced a debate amongst the Dutch as to whether the church or the state had control over ecclesiastical matters.

The situation in Dordrecht is an opportunity to retell a unique and colorful story of the Reformed position toward the pipe organ and organist. Dordrecht hosted the first national synod of the Dutch church, and at that meeting the synod declared a ban on organ use in the worship service. Nevertheless, the city employed an organist, and then signed not one but two contracts for new pipe organ instruments that arrived just in time for the first international synod of Protestants. Evidence suggests that the pipe organ was used during the opening services of this noteworthy meeting, and again at its close. Put all the contradictory events together, and the story deserves an entire chapter of its own.

Chapter 5 examines in detail the rhetoric of leading figures in the pipe organ debate who stood outside of the ecclesiastical assemblies surveyed in chapters 2, 3, and 4. Constantijn Huygens was neither a theologian nor an ordained minister but an aristocrat and a government official, as well as a member of the Dutch Reformed Church. Despite his religious convictions, Huygens argued for a re-inclusion of the organ into Dutch Reformed worship. But Huygens's work was not universally persuasive; his writings provoked lengthy and scathing counter-attacks, notably from layman Jan Jansz. Calckman, which will also be examined in detail.

Chapter 6 contrasts Huygens's pro-organ stance with the anti-organ stance of professor Gisbertus Voetius, one of the most prolific and outspoken opponents of the organ. But even Dr. Foot was not uniformly accepted, as the reactionary work of his student, Martinus Schoock, will show. The chapter ends by making the case that the organ debate concluded not by ecclesiastical decree but through government involvement. In 1773 the Dutch national government commissioned a new edition of the *Psalter* which surely invited and nearly required instrumental accompaniment. As a result, by the late eighteenth century the pipe organ had become firmly incorporated into Dutch Reformed worship, all fervor to the contrary notwithstanding. Whereas some ministers of the sixteenth and seventeenth centuries labeled the organ damned and demonic, some ministers who used the new *Psalter* of the eighteenth century now called the pipe organ a most useful and necessary tool.

In short, the organ controversy in the Golden Age of the Netherlands resulted from the collision in a very small geographic space of unyielding, dogmatic Reformed theology with pluralistic, pragmatic

Dutch republicanism. Reformed theology insisted that proper Christian worship was characterized by supreme reverence for the spoken Word of God, punctuated by solemn silence, and it maintained that all things, especially the liturgy, be done "decently and in good order" (1 Cor 14:40). This stance left no room for any superfluous sound, especially organ music and its supposed association with the Roman Catholic Church. But these ecclesiastical decrees were vapid because these Dutch Reformed congregations did not own the buildings in which they worshiped. Thus any orders by early Reformed synods to silence or remove church organs were not legally enforced. Over time many Dutch Reformed clergy and laymen began to question the one facet of their Calvinist theology that had silenced their beautiful organs; they even debated the biblical exegesis that Calvin used to support his statements on this matter. Finally, the 1773 *Psalter* was a decisive factor that led the Reformed churches to support four-part psalm singing with well-built, well-played pipe organs.

1

SETTING THE STAGE

The Dutch Reformed were not alone in their concern for the theological and musical concerns of the church's liturgy, prayers, and songs during the sixteenth and seventeenth centuries. While all Protestant cultures in Europe debated the use of the organ in worship, and most often heatedly, there was no uniformity of practice or unanimity of opinion. Rather, the specific political climate, the influence of local church leaders, and indigenous customs dictated the fate of the organ. Most Reformed Christians across Europe affirmed John Calvin's liturgical ideals, and his directive that in congregational song "there must always be concern that the song be neither light nor frivolous but have gravity [pois] and majesty [maiesté], as Saint Augustine says."[1] Some Reformed congregations used the organ to enrich the psalmody with such weight and majesty, while others prohibited organ use to keep the psalmody "light." And in between these two extremes, there were all manner of variations—in Zwingli's church the psalms were not even sung but spoken.

Martin Luther in Wittenberg

In Germany, Martin Luther (1483–1546) was the first to make changes to the Catholic liturgies. A miner's son from Saxony, Luther was a musical

---

1. *"Il y a tousiours à regarder, que le chant ne soit pas legier et volage: mais ait pois et majesté, comme dit sainct Augustin."* Ioannis Calvini Opera (hereafter O.C., *Opera Calvin*), 6:169–170. Calvin's reference to Augustine is intriguing, for Augustine's requirement that congregational song have "weight" and "majesty" remains to be found in his writings.

talent who received early classical training in music and was reportedly proficient on the lute and guitar. He loved music and believed that it could be used to honor God,[2] and he often composed or adapted tunes to his own words. Luther drew inspiration from the prophets and kings of the Old Testament who praised God with the singing of hymns and the playing of instruments. Based on those examples, the practice of the earliest Christians and, no doubt, his experience as a Roman Catholic monk, Luther believed that singing the psalms and spiritual songs was a fully proper way of praising God. To that end, Luther actively reevaluated all forms of music and their potential use in the Lutheran liturgy: medieval chant, unison hymns, four-part chorales, and even "secular" folk tunes. Before Luther, the Catholic liturgy was essentially performed in front of the people in Latin; the priest would turn his back towards the congregation during the consecration of the Host, the choir would sing in Latin, and the primary role of the laypeople was to watch and listen. Luther's intent was to adapt and alter the familiar Catholic service to make the liturgy more understandable and participatory. The music ideals of Luther are quite simple: all music is sung prayer (and should be treated as such), and music must never become greater than its message. And so, with Luther's grand theological pronouncement of "every man a monk," hymnody came not from monastic choirs seated in choir stalls but from a full congregation seated in the pews. "Every man" (and woman) of the congregation gave voice to their faith—from the lawyer seated in the expensive forward pews, to the milkmaid from her cheap seat in the back. Next to their Bible, the Lutheran hymnal chock full of chorales became the second most important book of the Lutherans. Thus in both the churches and the schools that Luther established, he allowed no one to teach who could not sing, "nor would I let him preach, either."[3]

Medieval music inherited from the church of Rome had become florid, and its chant melismatic. As the organ previously was not part of the liturgy proper, Luther envisioned a new role for the organ as an aid to congregational singing, and as an active participate during the worship service. Granted, pipe organ use began simply by playing in *alternatum* with some hymn stanzas, but the pipe organ use evolved into

---

2. "*Ich wöllt alle Künste, sonderlich die Musica, gerne sehen im Dienste des, der sie geben und geschaffen hat.*" "I would like to see all arts, but particularly music, in the service of Him who has given and created them." Martin Luther, in the preface of Johann Walter's *Geistliche Gesangbuchlein* (Wittenberg: 1524).

3. Herl, *Worship Wars in Early Lutheranism*, 28–35.

full incorporation so that by the beginning of the seventeenth century it accompanies all the liturgy, including prelude and postlude.

In his thinking on instruments and church music Luther was consistent: all music was to serve the new "choir," the singing congregation now fully engaged in worship. As to the resulting new Lutheran hymnal, tune after tune simply gave one sturdy German (not Latin) syllable of text to every beat—think of the hymn text and tune of *A Mighty Fortress Is Our God*, for example. In some cases, Luther wrote new, sacred texts for well-known secular tunes: the contafactuals. It worked. Adam Contzen, a Roman Catholic, scoffed "Luther has destroyed more souls in the hymns he wrote than in the sermons he preached."[4] The use of the pipe organ ensured this success, and its use became normalized in Lutheran circles, laying the groundwork, of course, for Lutheranism's greatest organist, church musician, composer, and cantor Johann Sebastian Bach (1685–1750).[5]

German Reformed

It was not only Luther discussing new ideals of church music to those in German lands. German Reformed churches beyond the pale also initially wrestled with the propriety of organ music as can be seen by conflicting proclamations regarding the use of the organ in worship in the Church Regulations (*Kirchenordnungen*) of Hessen, Herford (Westphalia), and the Palatinate. On the one hand, early regulations in Hessen stated that organs should not be used in worship because, as they said, using organs was as fruitless as trying to speak an unknown foreign language without the aid of a translator. Furthermore, the Hessians called the organ an Old Testament accoutrement no longer needed for New Testament worship.[6]

---

4. "*Hymni Lutheri animos plures, quam scripta et declamationes occiderunt.*" Contzen, *Politicorum*, 2:19.

5. See Joyce Irwin, "Preaching About Pipes and Praise" for a sampling and exposition of seventeenth-century sermons that extol the use of the pipe organ in Lutheran worship.

6. "*Das Orgelspiel wird abgeschafft, denn wenn vor versammelter Gemeinde der Gebrauch einer fremden Sprache ohne Dolmetscher nicht zulässig ist, so die Orgeln noch weniger, weil sie nur dem Ohr dienen ohne Frucht für den Geist. Überdies gehört das Orgelschlagen zu den Diensten des levitischen Priestertums, die mit dem Priestertum selbst, mit Christi Ankunft, erloschen sind.*" "Playing the organ will be dispensed with because, if the use of a foreign language in front of a gathering is not permitted without a translator, organs are even less so because they only serve the ear without being

Thus a very early prohibition against organ use was adopted by the Synod of Hamburg, which met on October 21–23, 1526. But, on the other hand, this strict decree was just as quickly and decisively overturned when church authorities in neighboring Herford declared that there was no issue with using the organ whatsoever, for the organ was fruitful and

> it is not contrary to scripture to have an organist in each congregation, because the organs, whose sounds excite the people to prayer and to piety, are there. And the people who have worked very hard throughout the week are certainly in need of invigoration.[7]

Zwingli in Zurich

While Luther wrote new German hymns and other German Reformed issued conflicting decrees regarding the pipe organ's legitimacy, in 1521 Huldrych Zwingli[8] preached reform from the pulpit of the Zurich cathedral, the Grossmünster. Considered too "Catholic," within only three years, by 1524, no less than five pipe organs of Zurich's churches were silenced by a city council decree, and in another three years they were destroyed, despite the fact that some had recently been completed with great expense and celebration.[9] Heinrich Bullinger (1504–1575), Zwingli's successor as leader of the Swiss Reformation after Zwingli's death on the battlefield in 1531, later reported:

> The organs were not particularly old, especially in this country. And since they do not agree with the apostolic teaching of I Corinthians 14, they were, in Zurich and in the Grossmünster, broken up on 9 December in the year 1527. From then on, no

---

fruitful for the spirit. Moreover, playing the organ is the job of the Levitical priesthood which disappeared along with the priesthood itself at the arrival of Christ." Goeman, "Emder," 174.

7. "Auch ist es nicht gegen die Schrift, einen Organisten zu haben in einem jeden Kirchspiel, weil die Orgeln, deren Klang die Leute zum Gebet und zur Innigkeit anregt, nun mal vorhanden sind. Und die Leute, die die Woche hindurch viel Mühe auf die Arbeit verwendet haben, bedürfen dann wohl der Erquickung." Dreier, *Reformatorische Frömmigkeit*, 38.

8. Gordon, *God's Armed Prophet, Zwingli*.

9. These events are documented and discussed fully in Jakob, *Orgelbau*.

one wanted to continue having either singing or organs in the church.[10]

Bullinger's matter-of-fact argument would have pleased Zwingli, but contemporary musicians were not so detached about these events. When the organ in Zurich was dismantled, Pelagius Kaltschmid, the Cathedral's organist, "stood by, helpless and weeping."[11] Friedrich Blume cast a sinister light upon Zwingli by reporting that the cathedral organ "was pulled down . . . while Zwingli stood by."[12]

How could Zwingli, himself a prodigious organist,[13] not only condone but also witness the destruction of such magnificent instruments? First, for Zwingli the organ was a "useless popish thing" (*unnütz papistisch ding*), one of many "superfluous papist" items filling the Swiss churches.[14] He minced no words in this typical condemnation of Catholicism and its liturgical music:

> Crusades, indulgences, prayer for reward, *singing*, crosses and the like, numerous, human money-making schemes that have not come from the Lord, are nothing but utter deceits; and it is no wonder that they have decreased for where the light penetrates, darkness flees.[15]

In order to remove any vestiges of the Roman church, he preached, the organs must be removed.

Zwingli knew firsthand about Roman Catholic church music because he served as a monk before converting to the Reformed cause. Perhaps he knew from chanting prayers in the cloister that the ability of music to stir the soul and charm the listener was inconsistent with the main goal of his anti-Catholic liturgy: the clear, pure reading and explanation of the word of God. Since the organ, like polyphonic choral

---

10. "*Die orgelen in den kylchen* [kyrchen] *sind nitt ein bsonders allts werck, in sonders in disen landen. Diewyl sy dann ouch nitt wol stimmend mitt der apostolischen leer 1. Corinther 14 ward Zürych die orgelen in dem großen münster, des 9. decembris, in disem 1527. jar abgebrochen. Dann man fürohin weder des gesangs noch orgelens in der kylchen* [kyrchen] *wolt.*" Jakob, *Orgelbau*, 2:27.

11. Nettl, *Luther and Music*, 5.

12. Blume, *Geschichte der evangelischen Kirchenmusik*, 107.

13. "*Hat also der Zwingli al musicos, organisten, hocber, pfifer, senger, zsamen . . . .*" Sicher and Götzinger, *Mitteilungen*, 164.

14. ". . . *nicht nur die orglen, sonder auch bilder, altär, kertzen, chorhembder unnd anderen uberleibeten deß bapstumbs noch breuchig.*" Jakob, *Orgelbau*, 1:128–29.

15. Nüscheler, *Magister Ulrich Zwingli*, 75, emphasis mine.

singing and clerical chanting, could not proclaim the word clearly and actually called attention to itself at the expense of the word, its very presence was a "foul distraction."

But Zwingli did more than ban organ playing in the church: he banned all music including unaccompanied psalm singing. In his 1523 publication *Auslegen und Gründe der Schlußreden* ("Conclusions"), he wrote that true worship is "in spirit and in truth without clamor before men."[16] With this terse statement, Zwingli identified two sources or locations of worship: one is the external form ("clamor before men"), while the other is internal ("in spirit and in truth"). For Zwingli true worship was the latter; conversely, true worship could not to be found in outward forms that were devoid of sincere inner content. Therefore no music at all, even unaccompanied singing, was permitted in worship since it was an outward form susceptible to misuse and hypocrisy. In articles 44–46 of *Conclusions* he fortified this point by declaring that proper prayer ought to be silent according to the teaching of Matt 6:6.[17] Echoing the apostle Paul's exhortation to the Colossians (3:16) to sing "from the heart" as well, Zwingli taught that true prayer came "from the heart, not with the voice."[18]

Zwingli's understanding of prayer directly reflected his understanding of true Christian faith. For Zwingli, faith takes place in the believer's heart through the action of the Holy Spirit; by definition then the action of the Holy Spirit cannot be perceived by human senses.[19] Indeed, said Zwingli quoting the apostle Paul, it is impossible to make faith dependent on worshipers' sight or hearing, for "who hopes for what he sees?"[20] This former Catholic monk concluded that all forms of instrumental music in worship were contrary to both Scripture and the practice of the apostles, and that all sensate art must therefore be prohibited from worship in the true Church, which Zwingli believed he was bringing about.

Consequently, Zwingli went to the city officials in 1524 to demand the removal of the noisy, pestilential organs from Zurich's churches. In

---

16. Zwingli, *Zwinglis Sämtliche Werke*, 1:463.

17. "And when you pray, go into your room, close the door and pray to your Father, who is unseen. Then your Father, who sees what is done in secret, will reward you." This Scripture quote, and all others, is from the New International Version of the Bible.

18. . . . *in cordibus enim inquit, non vocibus*. Zwingli, *Zwinglis Sämtliche Werke*, 1:463.

19. Zwingli, *Zwinglis Sämtliche Werke*, 2:786.

20. Rom 8:24.

an ironic flourish (which admittedly could be an apocryphal story), Zwingli sang his plea before the city leaders.[21] When the puzzled magistrates asked him to explain his strange presentation, Zwingli answered that it was a lesson: it was just as inappropriate for him to address the magistrates in song as it was for Christians to bring their prayers before God accompanied by song and organ music. Even though the Swiss cherished their beautiful, expensive church organs, by this time Zwingli had amassed such influence in that part of the country that there was little resistance. The organs were shuttered.

Other writings of the Swiss Reformed "enemies of the organ" (*Orgelfeinde*) provide three arguments against organ use that will prove valuable for understanding the complex theology that was used to silence the Swiss and most other Protestant pipe organs. The first such argument was that the organ was a "sounding instrument," a noise machine. As a sounding object, the pipe organ was contrary to Zwingli's notions of *innig[es] Gebet*, praise and prayer emanating from the heart, based on 1 Cor 14:7.[22] Therefore the organ had no place in worship. Further, as a sounding instrument, the organ was an aural reminder of the former and heretical pagan ceremonies when, according to Swiss theologian Rodolphus Hospinianus (= Rudolf Wirth, 1547–1626), it provided "amorous and scandalous songs to which the whores and clowns danced."[23] Finally, as a "sound producer" without words, the organ could not be "understood," against Paul's exhortation to the Corinthians, and thus was therefore unenlightening (*unerbawliche*).

Besides being an aural disruption to pure Reformed worship, the second argument put forward by the Swiss *Orgelfeinde* and others was that the organ was a visual object (*Bild*) that could too easily tempt Christians to distraction or even idolatry. As a visual, tangible object, the organ was in the same category as all other "superstitious" items that had, according to Reformed theology, tainted the church; therefore, the church was cleansed of anything with such power. A June 1524 editorial confirmed that "no one in the city [of Zurich] and in the church buildings was [allowed] to play the organ . . . . But instead all such superstitions

---

21. Kist, "Kerkelijke," 234.

22. "Even in the case of lifeless things that make sounds, such as the flute or harp, how will anyone know what tune is being played unless there is a distinction in the notes?"

23. "*Audiuntur amotoriæ fœdæó cantilenæ, ad quas scorta mimic saltitant.*" Hospinianus, *Templis*, 3:23, 310.

must be refrained from altogether as they all stand against God's definite word."[24] As the organ was "showy" (*brachtig*) it could too easily lead to vanity (*Hochmut*) of a congregation, not keeping with the modest and simple ideals of the early church to which the Swiss Reformed aspired.

Third, the organ was simply an unnecessary and luxurious expense (*unnütz, unnöthig, unbrauchlich*), and not an essential (*nothwendig*) object for worship. Accordingly, many pipe organs were carefully and intentionally repurposed for another use that benefited the poor. For example, in Winterthur metal organ pipes were melted down and recast as a roof for the prison tower there. In Geneva the metal pipes were refashioned into dinnerware for use in the city's hospital.[25]

The depth and strength of anti-organ sentiments amongst the German-speaking Swiss can be shown by the events that took place in Schaffhausen where the cathedral organ was destroyed in 1529. About seventy years later, in 1597, the town council had second thoughts and ordered the cathedral organ restored. The very next day indignant ministers issued a vehement four-point document against the restoration of the cathedral's instrument and demanded the council rethink its intention. The town council immediately conceded and attempts to restore the organ were stopped.[26]

Oecolampadius in Basel

Despite the fact that organs all across northern Switzerland were defaced, silenced, dismantled, or recycled, the central city of Basel, which

---

24. "*Vil supersition abgethan. Diser zyt gebod ouch die oberkeit Zürych, das man in der statt und in den kylchen [kyrchen] nitt me orgelen, noch den todten, oder über und wider das wäther [wätter] lüthen [lüten], desglichen keine palmen, saltz, wasser, noch kertzen me sägnen, und niemann me den jungsten touff oder letste ölung bringen solle, sunder aller der glychen superstitionen mussig gan [ganz] und gar abstan, alls die alle wider das klar wort Gottes strytind.*" "Petition to abolish superstition. The authority of Zurich demanded at that time that nobody in the city and in the church buildings was [allowed] to play the organ or ring the bells for the dead or about and against the weather, or consecrate palms, salt, water, or candles and that there should be no more baptisms or administrations of the last rites. But instead all such superstitions must be refrained from altogether as they all stand against God's definite word." Jakob, *Orgelbau*, 2:27.

25. Jakob, *Orgelbau*, 1:88–91.

26. Zurich: Zentralbibliothek, Ms. A 134, Folio 424r–v, reprinted in Ex. 2 of Davies, *Destroying the Devil's Bagpipe*.

is located only eighty-three kilometers to the west of Zurich, established quite a contrary practice. On the one hand, Basel did succumb to iconoclastic riots such that Erasmus of Rotterdam (1457–1536), before leaving Basel, his "adopted city," testified that "neither costliness nor artistic worth availed to save anything at all" as he lamented that "the arts in Basel are dead."[27] Johannes Oecolampadius (= Johann Husschin, 1482–1531), the city's main reformer, confirmed this observation when he noted that "the idols had become ashes" and that Roman Catholics were "weeping blood."[28]

However and importantly, Oecolampadius was an unapologetic critic of Zwingli's musical policies, and he protected the Basel pipe organs from the iconoclasts. What is more, in one of the few differences in church reform between Basel and Zwingli, Basel worshipers sang the psalms despite the 1529 ban on music. One observer in 1528 commented deftly on this crucial difference: "Husschin [Oecolampadius] upholds the singing of psalms, but Zwingli . . . cannot tolerate psalms."[29] Basel's musical bent, partly due to Lutheran influence,[30] became fully pro-organ with the 1553 appointment of Simon Sulzer as the cathedral's superintendent (*Antistes*) who officially re-established organ use in worship. Astonishingly, Sulzer in turn appointed Gregor Meyer from Solothurn as organist, *ein gar bäpstischer mann* (a Roman Catholic). Such a bold move caused the rector of the university, Christian Wurstisen (1544–1588), to lament the use of the "Pope's Hurdy-Gurdy" that had "wormed" its way back into the well-Reformed church.[31] Wurstisen's protestations had no effect; in Basel organ music in Reformed worship continued despite the practices of other communities of the Swiss confederacy. In fact, Basel would be the sole exception with regard to organ use; for one hundred and seventy

---

27. Davies, *Destroying the Devil's Bagpipe*, 12.

28. Eire, *War Against*, 106–7.

29. "Husßchin haltet das gesang der psalmen; aber Zwinglein . . . mag keine psalmen erleyden." Staehelin, *Breife und Akten*, in Jakob, *Orgelbau*, 1:173–74.

30. Brady, *Turning Swiss*.

31. "Dise achtet man nach der reformation als ein unnütz papistisch ding in der kirchen, so nur zum eusserlichen gepreng angesehen were etc., deßhald auch vil pfeiffen davon khamen . . . . Summa, der oberkeit ward von gedachtem S. Sulcero eingebildet, es were zu thun, das man die orglen widerumb zurichten unnd solte schlagen lassen, das junge volck in der kirchen zu behalten. Erhielts also, das man es erstlich nach den mittagpredigen für die hand name, bald nach der abentpredig, letstlich auch am morgen. Dergestalt ist dise unerbawliche bapstleir in ein wolreformierte kirchen eingeschlichen." *Basler Beiträge*, 1:128–29.

years, Basel was the single Protestant city in the Swiss Confederation where an organ could be heard in worship. Only in 1735 did Bern become the second.[32]

Menno Simons in the Old and New World

Other Reformed associations, such as the Swiss Brethren, confirmed the organ's ignominy throughout the sixteenth century. In 1683 the Swiss Brethren, who broke with Zwingli as early as 1525 in order to follow Menno Simons (1496–1561), and then resettled in the New World. Like their Anabaptist forebears and Reformed countrymen of Switzerland, the Swiss Brethren worshiped by singing with "their hearts alone," and shunned instruments both in worship and for private devotional use at home. In America and as late as 1875 the Swiss Brethren, now known as the Mennonite Church in America, agreed that instruments did not "lead to humility, but rather to pride and display"[33] and upheld instrumental proscriptions during worship; in fact, instrumental use at home was likewise discouraged lest "Cain's posterity" intrude into the church "little by little."[34] One historian of Mennonite church music recorded that when a harmonium (a portable reed organ) was brought into worship on a trial basis, one Mennonite "cried through the entire service" while another walked out, reportedly refusing "to have anything to do with such works of the devil."[35]

Bucer in Strasbourg

At the same time as the Swiss were silencing and melting down their church organs, in Strasbourg, France, Zwingli's colleague Martin Bucer also pastored a Reformed church. While these two Reformed ministers were kindred spirits in most respects, Bucer rejected Zwingli's teaching on church music. Bucer's congregation sang in worship regularly; what is more, they sang not only the Psalms, but also hymns, antiphons, and responses.[36] Bucer's principal treatise on the liturgy appeared exactly one

32. Jakob, *Orgelbau*, 2:403–8.
33. *Minutes of the Indiana-Michigan Mennonite Conference*, 23.
34. *Minutes of the Indiana-Michigan Mennonite Conference*, 38.
35. Sprunger, *First Hundred Years*, 115–16, 155, 309–10.
36. Initially a choir was even used to sing the responses; however, gradually a

year after Zwingli's *Conclusions*, in 1524. In the final chapter of his book, Bucer emphatically disagreed with Zwingli's doctrine that Christians should keep silent in church and pray to God "in their hearts," since

> With all our might we are to love God. Why, then, should we not also sing to Him as all the saints of the Old and New Testament have done, provided that such song take place in the heart and not with the mouth only; but rather that it arise and come forth from the heart. This is what the Apostle means when he says: "and sing to the Lord in your hearts," for his meaning is not that we sing without voice, for how could the others be admonished and edified, or how could we discuss with each other what he writes to the Ephesians?[37]

In other words, although Bucer read the same New Testament that Zwingli used to ban singing ("sing to the Lord in your hearts") and require silent prayer, Bucer found, as did Oecolampadius in Basel, that Zwingli's conclusion was simply illogical and unnatural; rather, the apostolic injunction to "sing to the Lord" meant to do just that, to sing with heart *and* mouth.

As the waves of the Reformation rolled throughout the more northerly German lands, church music was largely dependent on the views of the principal Reformers. In Zurich and environs where Zwingli had the strongest hold, organ use was not permitted; indeed, organs were physically destroyed and no music whatsoever was used. Even though psalms were used during worship in Zwingli's churches, the psalms were spoken and not sung. But in other centers such as Basel or Strasbourg, under the influence of Reformers Oecolampadius and Bucer, the situation was different. Those cities promoted unison singing of the psalms and even employed instrumental accompaniment. In other words, while the ideal of psalmody as the canon of repertoire seems to be largely held amongst the Reformers, the manner in which these psalms were sung was an issue of local interpretation and leadership.

---

precentor taught the congregation to sing. O.C., 16:29. Poll, *Martin Bucer's Liturgical Ideas*; Wackernagel, *Bibliographie zur Geschichte*.

37. "*Von allen krefften sollen wir je gott lieben, warumb solten wir im dann nit auch singen, wie alle heyligen des alten und newen testaments thon haben, allein das solich gesang im hertzen gescheh nit allein mit dem mund, sonder das es auß dem hertzen quelle und herkome. Das der Apostel damit meinet, da er spricht: und singet dem herrn in ewern hertzen, dann sein meinung nit ist, on stym zů singen, wie künten sust die andern ermanet und bessert werden oder wir mit einander reden, das er zun Ephesiern schreibt?*" Bucer, *Deutsche Schriften*, 275–76.

John Calvin in Geneva

Recognizing the variety of music use in early Reformed liturgy is crucial to understanding Reformed church music practice in the Netherlands because it was in Bucer's Strasbourg church that John Calvin found refuge when he was exiled from Geneva in 1538. There Calvin witnessed firsthand the careful, reverent, and very restricted way that Bucer permitted music to be used in Reformed worship. Consequently, it was not Zwingli's strict approach but rather Bucer's use of music in worship that formed Calvin's own views on church music.

From his humble beginnings no one could have guessed that Jean Cauvin (= John Calvin, 1509–1564) would become a prominent figure of the Reformation. He was born in the French town of Noyon in Picardy on July 10, 1509 to Catholic, middle-class parents and went to Paris at the age of twelve to study at Collège de la Marche. Later he transferred to the Collège de Montaigu and, after he had completed his basic studies there, matriculated at l'Université d' Orléans where he was granted his law degree in 1531. Calvin was a brilliant student of the law, and the skills he developed in carefully analyzing and clearly explaining the minutiae of complex texts is evident in his later theological writings and Bible commentaries.

As a student in Paris, Calvin was influenced by Lutheranism. The Sorbonne, prized keeper of Catholic orthodoxy in Paris, reprimanded Calvin for his suspected Lutheran sympathies but could not prevent him from giving theological direction to the factions of the Reformation. However, rather than merely lending his support to existing movements inside and outside of the Catholic church, Calvin reformulated doctrine, scriptural exegesis, and church polity with such clarity and force that, in a sense, he established his own faction.

Calvin went quite by accident to Geneva for what was supposed to be a one-night stay. However, at the age of thirty-two, he stayed in Geneva and worked alongside Guillaume Farel (1489–1565), a reformer whose work had laid the groundwork for the Reformation in Geneva years earlier. Even though the duo were exiled for a time in 1538 by the Genevan civil leaders for alleged insubordination, upon Calvin's return by invitation in 1541, Geneva's influence over the Reformation grew so powerful that it became known as "a second Wittenberg." Calvin's *Institutes of the Christian Religion* (written and then expanded between 1536 and 1559), his Christian academy, his Bible commentaries, and his voluminous correspondence molded Protestantism in France, the Netherlands, Scotland, the Swiss Confederation, and England. His influence penetrated Poland and Hungary, and before his death Calvinism was taking root in southwestern Germany. This far-reaching influence was not due to any clerical credentials or physical strength; in fact, Calvin was never ordained and was generally in poor health. Yet he was indefatigable; he worked with extraordinary breadth, precision, and stamina to explain his views on every aspect of Christian doctrine and practice, including instrumental music in worship.

Indeed, his influence over the Reformation was and remains so powerful that, besides Lutheranism, only one other Protestant movement, Calvinism, is named after the leader whose ideas still guide its members.

Calvin taught that of all the arts music is the least to be condemned (*minime contemnenda*). In his commentary on Gen 4:21, where Jubal is identified as "the father of all who play flute and harp," Calvin praised music wholeheartedly: "For the invention of arts, and of other things which serve to the common usage and convenience of life, is a gift of God by no means to be despised, and a faculty worthy of commendation."[38]

Yet, Calvin was extremely cautious about the use of this art form. He was convinced, based on his study of the Greek philosopher Plato, that music could be either uplifting and spiritual or destructive and pernicious; in other words, just because God was the Creator of everything including music, listening to music did not automatically lead to godliness:

> Finally, we all experience how great the power of music to move men's feelings is: as Plato reports that not from mere chance is music very powerful to turn the morals of the state hither and thither.[39]

Thus it is clear that Calvin respected music, but he, like Plato, was aware of its great potential for both good and evil upon a society.

Calvin based his conclusions not just on Plato but also on Holy Scripture. In his commentary on Isaiah 5, where the prophet proclaims the Lord's judgment against those who played "harps and lyres . . .

---

38. "*Artium enim et aliarum rerum inventio quae ad communem vitae usum et commoditatem valent, donum est Dei minime spernendum, et virtus laude digna.*" O.C., 23:99.

39. "*Denique omnes experimur quanta sit vis musicae ad sensus hominum movendos: ut Plato non abs re musicam ad mores civitatis huc illuc flectendos plurimum valere tradat. In aerem loqui est aerem frustra verberare ac si diceret: Vox tua neque ad Deum pertinget, neque homines, sed evanescet in aere.*" O.C., 49:520.

tambourines and flutes,"⁴⁰ Calvin explains that musical instruments are not sinful per se but condemnable when they incite the lewd, indulgent passions of men at the expense of their conscience:

> He [Isaiah] adds the instruments of pleasures by which men addicted to intemperance provoke their appetite. These might be different from ours, but they belonged to music. Now, Isaiah does not blame music, for it is a science which ought not to be despised; but he describes a nation swimming in every kind of luxury, and too much disposed to indulge in pleasures.⁴¹

Calvin was a scholar and theologian with the mind of a lawyer, and he used intricate, painstaking arguments from the Bible to support his theology, church polity, and liturgy. Therefore, since the Old Testament is replete with examples of the Israelites using music to praise God, one might expect Calvin to require the use of instrumental use in worship, but after a lengthy, judicious argument, Calvin reached a different conclusion. For instance, in his commentary on Ps 71:23, Calvin admitted that the Old Testament practice of using instruments glorified God:

> In the terms "Nebel" and "Cithara" he [David] alludes to a custom then in vogue, for it is not doubtful that part belonged to lawful instruction, and that it was the learned manner to sing God's praises to the cithara and the nablum.⁴²

He even allowed that musical instruments incited the Israelites to a more zealous praise of God in his commentary on Psalm 33:

> It is not doubtful that he [the Psalmist] expresses by the verse [2] the fervency and the ardor of love in praising God when he bids us to apply musical instruments for this use, for he wishes nothing to be omitted by the faithful which can fire men's minds and senses to singing God's praises. . . . [Instruments] are the

---

40. Isa 5:12.

41. "*Addit instrumenta voluptatum, quibus suam ingluviem irritant hominess crapulae dediti. Haec poterant diversa esse a nostris: ad musicam tamen pertinebant. Musicam certe non improbat Isaia: est enim scientia minime contemnenda: sed depingit populum omni genere luxuriae diffluentem, sibique nimis indulgentem in captandis voluptatibus.*" O.C., 36:110.

42. "*In nominibus Nebel et Citharae alludit ad morem tunc receptum, nec enim dubium est quin pars illa fuerit legalis paedagogiae, et umbratilis cultus, ad citharam et nablum canere Dei laudes.*" O.C., 31:662.

auxiliaries by which the faithful are wont to inspire themselves the more.[43]

Calvin stressed in his sermon on 1 Samuel that it is not the instrument or the musician himself who drew the listener closer to God through music but rather the power of God working through the music: "Saul had indeed been refreshed by David's harp, but it was really by the Lord's doing and inspiring that power within [David]."[44]

However, the Israelites needed music to help them worship Yahweh, Calvin claimed, because their relationship with God was immature and incomplete, as he analyzed in a sermon on 1 Samuel 18:

> And so let us believe that instrumental music then had been tolerated by reason of that period and of that people, because they were as children, just as Sacred Scripture says, who were in need of those childish instructions, which today ought not to be recalled voluntarily: unless we wish to obliterate evangelical perfection and to dim the full light which in Jesus Christ our Lord we have attained.[45]

Calvin concluded that the presence of Jesus Christ in the Church by means of the Holy Spirit nullified the puerile epoch of redemptive history of the Old Testament church and its forms of worship: animal sacrifices, blood offerings, annual rituals, and musical instruments, even when and if they are used to excite holy fervor. He illustrates this view in his commentary on Exod 15:20, which described how "Miriam the Prophetess, the sister of Aaron, took a tambourine in her hand . . .":

> . . . it must be noted that musical instruments have been used amid lawful ceremonies, which Christ has abolished by his

---

43. "*Non dubium est quin vehementiam et ardorem affectus in Deo laudando hoc versu exprimat, ubi in hunc usum instrumenta musica applicari iubet, nihil enim vult a fidelibus omitti quod mentes sensusque hominum ad canendas Dei laudes accendat. Etsi enim nonnisi articulata voce proprie celebratur Dei nomen, haec tamen adminicula quibus se magis incitare fideles solent. . . .*" O.C., 31:324.

44. "*. . . Davidis cithara quidem fuisse Saulem recreatum, sed Domino faciente et vim illam intus inspirante.*" O.C., 30:183.

45. "*Musicuam itaque illam instrumentalem teneamus tunc ratione temporis illius et populi fuisse toleratam quod essent ut pueri, quemadmodum sacra scriptura loquitur, qui puerilibus istis rudimentis indigerent quae hodie non sunt ultro revocanda: nisi perfectionem evangelicam velimus abolere, et plenum lucem quam in Christo Domino nostro consequuti sumus obscurare.*" O.C., 30:259-60.

advent and therefore a different simplicity must be observed by us under the Gospel.⁴⁶

What was the "simplicity" Calvin sought for Christ's Body, the Church? No doubt to the surprise of Zwinglians it was music. In his commentary on Heb 2:12 he wrote, "Christ urges us to sing [God's praises] publicly in such a way that they may be heard by as many as possible."⁴⁷ Also, commenting on Isa 42:10 he wrote, "Therefore, with the Spirit as leader and urger, it is necessary that we truly sing those praises."⁴⁸ After asking rhetorically, "What is spiritual joy?" in his commentary on Eph 5:18, Calvin answered, "Hymns, psalms, God's praises, thanksgiving. These are truly the pleasant and delightful fruits of the Spirit; this signifies the joy in the Holy Spirit."⁴⁹

Indeed, Calvin argued, God intended that his praise be sung by the most beautiful of all created instruments, the human voice: "Surely man's voice, although it is not commonly so understood, surpasses all dead organs [i.e., musical instruments]."⁵⁰ He was convinced that unison singing was best suited for worship because it guaranteed that the congregation could proclaim the texts clearly and that the singers would not be tempted to commit unnecessary elaboration or ornamentation. Rather, the whole congregation (not the trained choir or the priest) would produce a "perfect melody" marked by simple majesty and driven by sincere faith. Said Calvin:

> They [the people] do not at all understand the word of Faith and the word of Belief. And in order to understand well, it is necessary to make a connection between Faith and the Promise. For one can indeed sing well with one voice; but we do not have a perfect melody unless there are several voices and good

---

46. "*Quanquam simul notandum est, musica instrumenta inter legales caeremonias fuisse, quas abolevit Christus suo adventu, ideoque alia nobis sub evangelio simplicitas tenenda est.*" O.C., 24:162.

47. "*Ac interea suo exemplo nos hortatur Christus ad eas publice canendas, ita ut a quamplurimis exaudiantur.*" O.C., 55:29.

48. "*Spiritu ergo duce atque impulsore opus est ut laudes istas vere cantemus.*" O.C., 37:68.

49. "*. . . hymnos, psalmos, laudes Dei, gratiarum actiones. Hi sunt vere iucundi fructus et delectabiles. Spiritus hic significat gaudium in spirito sancto.*" O.C., 51:221.

50. "*Certe vox hominis, quamvis non vulgo intelligatur, mortuis omnibus organis praestat.*" O.C., 31:325.

correspondence. So is it with Faith: for if the word of God proceeds and the Faith is not in accord with it, there is no melody.[51]

Against Rome

Scholars disagree on exactly how much organ music was used by the Roman Catholic Church of Calvin's day, but it was widespread and elaborate, even though the *a cappella* music of Palestrina was also used at this time.[52] Luther complained "now the whole world is full of church service and singing and praise, preaching, organ playing, and piping, and the *Magnificat* is beautifully sung—but it is lamentable how little the deeper meaning of the hymn is grasped."[53] Luther's student Justus Jonas went further when he wrote: "in the manner of the priests of Baal, the chorale is roared, not sung."[54] Erasmus of Rotterdam accused the Roman Catholic Church of introducing

> an artificial and theatrical music into the church, a bawling and an agitation of various voices, such as I believe had never been heard in the theatres of the Greeks and Romans. Horns, trumpets, pipes vie and sound along constantly with the voices. Amorous and lascivious melodies are heard such as elsewhere accompany only the dances of courtesans and clowns. The people run into the churches as if they were theaters, for the sake of the sensuous charm of the ear.[55]

Thus, it is no surprise that Calvin condemned the Roman Catholic practice of using instruments in worship. He observed that priests in his day did not even understand the words of the Latin liturgical chants, and he found the Catholic Church's misuse of pipe organs especially worthy of complaint—for instance in his commentary on 1 Samuel 1 and in the *Institutes* he wrote:

---

51. "*C'est qu'ils n'entendent point ce mot de Foy, ou ce mot de Croire. Et pour le bien entendre il nous faut metre une conionction entre la Foy et la Promesse. Car on pourra bien chanter à une voix: mais nous n'aurons point une melodie parfaite, sinon qu'il y ait plusieurs voix et bonne correspondance. Ainsi est-il de la foy: car si la parole de Dieu ne precede et que la foy ne s'accorde avec icelle, il n'y aura nulle melodie.*" O.C., 33:689.

52. Arnold Schering argued that even then many vocal masses were really rendered as solo pieces played by the organ. Schering, *Niederländische Orgelmesse*, 55.

53. Nettl, *Luther and Music*, 99.

54. Nettl, *Luther and Music*, 41.

55. Leichtentritt, "Reform of Trent and its Effect in Music," 319.

> Thus in the papacy has been a too ridiculous and inept imitation, when they started to embellish the churches and to make God's worship more ornate, if they had added organs and many other theatrical devices of that kind.[56]
>
> The songs and melodies which are composed to please the ear only, as are all the quaverings and trills of Papistry and all that they call broken-music and composition and four-part songs, in no wise accords with the majesty of the Church, and cannot be other than gravely displeasing to God.[57]

In response to the spiritual ruin brought about in the church by Catholic overreliance on elaborate music and ritual, Calvin looked to the worship patterns of the earliest apostolic church. There he claimed to find authority for his orders that the Reformed church must use psalmody in worship. In the 1542 *Genevan Psalter* preface Calvin wrote:

> As for public prayers there are two kinds. The ones with the word alone: the others with singing. And this is not something invented a little time ago. For from the first origins of the Church, this has been so, as appears from the histories. And even St. Paul speaks not only of praying by mouth but also of singing. And in truth we know by experience that singing has great force and vigor to move and inflame the hearts of men to invoke and praise God with a more vehement and ardent zeal. Care must always be taken that the song be neither light nor frivolous but that it have weight and majesty (as St. Augustine says), and also, there is a great difference between the music which one makes to entertain men at table and in their houses, and the psalms which are sung in the Church in the presence of God and his angels.[58]

---

56. "*Quare fuit in papatu ridicula nimis et inepta imitatio quum templa exornare, Deique cultum reddere celebriorem existimarunt si organa et alia istiusmodi multa ludicra adhiberent.*" O.C., 30:259.

57. "*. . . les chants et melodies qui sont composées au plaisir des aureilles seulement, comme sont tous les fringots et fredons de la Pápisterie, et tout ce qu'ils appellent musique rompue et chose faite et chants à quatre parties, ne conviennent nullement à la maiesté de l'Eglise, et ne se peut faire qu'ils ne deplaisent grandement à Dieu.*" O.C., 4:420. It should be noted here that the clause *fringots et fredons de la pápisterie* is only in the 1559 edition of the *Institutes*. This leads some scholars, chiefly Doumerge, to hypothesize that the phrase is not of Calvin but a later insertion of an editor.

58. "*Quant est des prieres publiques, il y en a deux espèces. Les unes se font par simple parolle: les aultres avecque chant. Et n'est pas chose inventée depuis peu de temps. Car dés la première origine de l'Eglise, cela a esté, comme il appert par les histoires. Et mesme Sainct Paul ne parle pas seulement de priere de bouche, mais aussi de chanter.*

Aural Iconoclasm

This instruction for the singing of psalms to music of weight and majesty resulted in what I call Calvin's "aural iconoclasm." Calvin's visual iconoclasm is well understood and studied, a reference to his purging of icons, statues, and all other plastic arts from Reformed worship. He taught that visual images could confuse the eye and distract a worshiper; consequently, all representative art such as paintings and crucifixes were to be removed from the church. Likewise Calvin also taught that elaborate sound could confuse the ear and distract a worshiper; thus, he objected to all foreign verbiage, florid music, and unintelligible speech in worship. The purpose of these sweeping changes was to focus worshipers more clearly on the teaching of the Gospel rather than on the medium used to transmit it. In other words, Calvin simplified worship from its existing Catholic and Lutheran forms, made worship didactic, and emphasized the spoken word of the minister.

Calvin replaced the Catholic priest, who turned his back on the congregation while consecrating the eucharistic host, with a minister who stood in a central pulpit and faced the congregation at all times; in fact, "sound boards" were placed above pulpits to insure the minister's words would project distinctly to the farthest corners of the church. The priest's homily became a preacher's sermon, and the sermon replaced the Mass as the central act of worship. A choir of monks either chanting plainsong or singing complex polyphonic motets behind a gated rood was replaced with an entire congregation singing a psalm in one unaccompanied, unison voice. Liturgical Latin was replaced with vernacular French, and from the pulpits preachers read no missal but only the Bible. Instead of the Catholic practice of chanting prayers, the Gospel, and other parts of the Mass, Calvinist pastors simply spoke their prayers, the Scripture lesson, and their sermon lest any musical decoration distract the congregation from Almighty God, the author of the Bible and the recipient of the worshipers' prayers. To encourage congregational participation, the texts of the psalms were set to music and sung as a prayer; in this way,

---

Et à la verité, nous congnoissons par experience, que le chant a grande force & vigueuer d'esmouvoir & enflamber le coeur des hommes, pour invoquer & louer Dieu d'un zèle plus vehement & ardent. Il y a tousjours à regarder, que le chant ne soit pas legier & volage: mais ait poids & majesté, comme dit sainct Augustin, & ainsi qu'il y ait grande différence entre la musicque qu'on faict pour resjouyr les hommes à table & en leur maison: & entre les psalmes, qui se chantent en l'Eglise, en la presence de Dieu & de ses anges." Pidoux, *Psautier,* 2:17.

the psalms were made an essential, musical element of Calvinist public worship.

John Calvin's teachings about church music spread throughout Europe and beyond all the more when he founded the Genevan Academy, a school to train ministers (later it became the city university). The opening of this academy, already envisioned in Calvin's "The Ecclesiastical Ordinances for the Church of Geneva"[59] of 1541, was delayed until 1559 for of lack of funding, but when its doors did finally open students were taught courses in language and theology from a Calvinist perspective. While such a parochial program might seem very narrow, within a mere five years the academy grew to three hundred pupils and graduated such notable alumni as Philip Marnix van Sint-Aldegonde, a councilor of Willem van Oranje; Jacob Hermansz. Arminius, whose theological writing ignited the Reformed tradition's great doctrinal battle that culminated at the 1618–1619 Synod of Dordrecht; and John Knox, who would return to his native Scotland and plant Calvinism there.

John Knox in Scotland

Before John Knox (1505–1572) brought Calvinism to Scotland, the Catholic Church owned one-third of the land in that country and generated half of the wealth. In turn, the bishops used this wealth to appoint the interior of their churches with the best of liturgical furnishings, the organ chief among them. Fifteenth-century records document the existence of at least ten pipe organs in cathedrals, monasteries, and the royal court and chapel in Scotland.[60] Though the early growth of Protestantism sentiments is elusive, what is known is that by the 1530s there was sympathy for the Protestant cause, several cases of iconoclasm resulted,[61] and small groups of militant converts drove the Scottish Reformation in concentrated bursts of evangelization. Protestors of Rome preached openly across the countryside, winning many to their views including the young John Knox. When Knox lived as a Scottish refugee for a time in Calvin's Geneva, he became convinced that his countrymen could not realize the fullest reformation of the church because of their Scottish sovereign. Knox queried Calvin about these concerns, and Calvin was very

---

59. *Les Ordonnances ecclésiastiques de l'église de Geneve*.
60. Inglis, *Organ in Scotland*, 10.
61. Benedict, *Christ's Churches*, 153.

clear in his reply that monarchs had the divine right to rule, and under no circumstances was it lawful for insubordination, even to rid a country of "idolatry."[62]

Nevertheless Knox returned to Scotland from Geneva in 1562 and directed his own war against idolatry. Knox regarded the organ as "the devil's whistling chair,"[63] a "trapping of ecclesiastical wealth," and a symbol of "elaborate worship" he detested.[64] The organ and all other musical instruments quickly fell out of favor in the Kirk. In place of organ music, the *Psalter* was sung "in plain tune" and, in the words of John Fergushill (1564–1633), minister of Ayr, "without dead instruments."[65] Fergushill also worried that if the organ were used, next would be "bagpipes for every congregation."[66] These attitudes might explain the sale of three "bellices [bellows] of the organ" in Edinburgh,[67] and the 1574 order of the Session of Aberdeen that the "organs with all expedition be removed out of the Kirk, and made profit of to the use and support of the poor"[68] even as the Session demanded that the Aberdeen city fathers put a stop to other such "abuses" as idolatry, observance of festival days, and Sunday markets.[69] Throughout the country, Presbyterian pipe organs virtually disappeared as they were destroyed in the "casting down" and refurbishing of worship spaces. In the farthest northeast corner of Scotland, the last part of the country to be touched by the Reformation, some organs survived.[70]

The Psalms then were led by cantors in most every parish of the Kirk. But according to William Maxwell, many Scottish precentors were more remarkable for their idiosyncrasies than for their musical skill.[71] It

62. Laing, *Works of John Knox*, 4:240.

63. Fock, *Hamburg's Role in Northern European Organ Building*, 7.

64. Inglis, *Organ in Scotland*, 33.

65. National Library of Scotland, Wodrow MS 84, 17v–18, as cited by Todd, *Culture of Protestantism*, 71.

66. National Library of Scotland, Wodrow MS 84, 17v–18, as cited by Todd, *Culture of Protestantism*, 71.

67. *Dean of Guild Accounts (1552–1567)*, 117, as cited by McMillan, *Worship of the Scottish Reformed Church*, 95.

68. *Selections from Ecclesiastical Records of Aberdeen* (Aberdeen, 1846), 19, as cited by McMillan, *Worship of the Scottish Reformed Church*, 95.

69. National Archives of Scotland, Edinburgh MS 448, 458–459, as cited by Todd, *Worship of the Scottish Reformed Church*, 196.

70. Inglis, *Organ in Scotland*, 34.

71. Maxwell, *History of Worship in the Church of Scotland*.

appears that some precentors embellished the tunes with grace notes or melismas (whether intentionally or out of poor skill it is not known) such that the congregation's attempts to copy the precentor's example were disastrous if not comical. Such a situation prompted a late arriving worshiper in Berwickshire to ask the question "What tune are they at?" He received the reply "I no ken tell, I'm at the Auld Hundert."[72] Later, some churches attempted to resolve the confusion by displaying the name of the tune on a chalkboard or printed card that was set in clear view of the congregation upon the cantor's desk.[73]

Some Presbyterians kept the memory of the organ and other instruments alive, however. Though the majority of churches silenced their organs, the Scottish Metrical Psalter Part Books compiled by Thomas Wode (= Thomas Wood, 1445?–1502) included two plates that depicted musicians, and the page border's illuminations were of musical instruments such as organs, trumpets, harps and viols. Apparently, even as the Scots sang their Psalms unaccompanied, "graven images" of instruments reminded them of former days when instrumental accompaniment was sanctioned. Or, perhaps more likely, such evidence underscores the fact that in reality, some instrumental music continued unofficially in some churches, or in private homes.

Meanwhile, musical instruments enjoyed royal favor in Scotland. When Queen Mary I, England's first queen and last Roman Catholic sovereign, came to her kingdom from France in 1561, just one year before John Knox's return, she entered a country where the Reformers had gained much influence. Nevertheless she came with her own Catholic clergy and Mass was celebrated in her chapel at Holyroodhouse. In fact, the queen was so bold as to reinstall an organ that had been earlier removed from the royal chapel.[74]

Mary's organ music was short-lived; after her deposition, an act of Parliament in 1571 ordered the "purging" of the Chapel Royal which included the removal of all monuments, vessels, "apparelling," items "dedicated to superstition" and the organ.[75] But when King James VI later rebuilt the royal chapel a large organ was integral to the plan such that from May 1617 forward royal worship was complete with choristers,

72. Millar, *Four Centuries of Scottish Psalmody*, 136–37.

73. Maxwell, *History of Worship in the Church of Scotland*, 165.

74. Inglis, *Organ in Scotland*, 35.

75. Rogers, *History of the Chapel Royal of Scotland*, 76; Le Huray, *Music and the Reformation in England*, 83.

surplices, and organ music.[76] Yet when Charles came to Scotland in 1641 and worshiped at the Chapel Royal, it is recorded that this service was conducted in the "Scottish fashion, without organes" as he was accustomed to in England.[77]

The royal vacillations between organ use and nonuse ended two years later, in 1643, when the Kirk of Holyroodhouse agreed to sell the chapel organ and use the proceeds to aid the poor. In 1649 following King Charles I's execution, and at the height of the Presbyterian-Puritan ascendancy, the Scottish Parliament ordered the removal of whatever remained of the organs from the royal chapel, and diverted certain small land revenues which had been dedicated to fund the maintenance of organs to support the minister of Glencorse instead.[78]

Outside of the Holyroodhouse Palace, and by the time of the National Covenant and Solemn League and Covenant of 1644, Scottish worship had been organless for three quarters of a century. The National Covenant went so far as to congratulate officially their English compatriots on "the great good things the Lord hath wrought among you," meaning that they were "greatly refreshed" to learn that in London the "great Organ of Paul's and Peter's[79] were taken down."[80] Such an anti-organ bias was also reinforced outside of the Kirk by some in the Scottish academy,[81] and by ministerial influence such as David Calderwood (1575–1650) who taught that a pastor should "loveth no music in the House of God

---

76. Maxwell, *History of Worship in the Church of Scotland*, 74.

77. "*Well, vpone the morne, being Sondag the 15th of August, his Majestie went to the abbay kirk, and hard one of our sermonis efter the Scottis fashion, befoir and efternone, without organes or prayeris, as he wes usit with at home.*" Inglis, *Organ in Scotland*, 79, quoting John Spalding, *Memorialls of the Trubles in Scotland and England, A.D. 1624–1645* (Aberdeen, 1850), 2:62.

78. *Acts of Parliament of Scotland* (1649), 4:482.

79. That is, Westminster Abbey, the official name being St. Peter's, Westminster.

80. *Principall acts of the Generall Assembly*, 1644, 29.

81. In 1640, for example, when Dr. William Guild (or Goold) became principal of King's College, Aberdeen, he ordered the organ in the college chapel removed for not only was it an organ, but on its case was painted an image of the virgin Mary. James Gordon recorded: "*In the University of Old Aberdeen ther stood the remainder of ane old organ, upon which was painted in a coarse draught the pourtaicte of some woman, nobody could tell who, and had hunge ther half borkne and wholly neglected for many yeares' this was borkne down, and complained of as a thing very intollerable in the churche of a colledge.*" *History of Scots Affairs*, 3:218. In 1657 professor William Douglas of Aberdeen dedicated a chapter of a book to prove that organs had no place in Christian worship: *Vindiciæ Psalmodiæ*, 31–33.

... and stoppeth his ear at instrumental music ... and would have antiphony and organs in the Cathedral kirks upon no greater reason than other shadows of the law of Moses, or lesser instruments as lutes, citherus or pipes might be used in other kirks."[82] Likewise, Samuel Rutherford (1600–1661) included organs in his list of "badges of Jewish and popish religion"[83] and asked "Who can say that the grace of Joy in the Holy Ghost wrought by the droning of organs ... is a work of the Spirit merited by Christ?"[84]

However, and like so many noninstrumental ecclesiastical cultures elsewhere, outside the control of the church and beyond earshot of the ministers, instrumental music was enjoyed in nonecclesiastical venues. Public concerts of music in the 1690s heralded a renaissance of secular music in Scotland, and instrumental music at home was common. Thus, while on Sunday at service Scottish Presbyterians sang their Psalms without the organ, throughout the week instrumental music could be enjoyed at home or at concerts. Gradually—and for the Scottish Presbyterian it must be emphasized, very late—the Reformation heritage with its bias toward unaccompanied singing in the Kirk was lessened by successive generations of Presbyterians, until it fully eroded and gave way to the reinclusion of the organ.

Nevertheless, as stated earlier, official sanctions for organ use came comparatively late to Scottish Presbyterians, no doubt an outcome of the most solid anti-idolatrous and anti-instrumental sentiments established by Knox and others. In the early nineteenth century attempts to reinstate the use of an organ at St. Andrew's Church in Glasgow and at Roxburgh Place Relief Church in Edinburgh failed. Further attempts to restore organs and organ accompaniment ignited debate, but the protests against the church organ did gradually die out, and with a small concession to organ use the "Pirie Act" of 1865 allowed churches to be "licensed" to use the organ, but then only under the supervision of the local presbytery.[85] By 1868 Boyd recounted that seven or eight congregations in the Presbytery of Glasgow were using the organ, and organ use in the entire United Presbyterian Church was finally sanctioned in 1872.[86] Even then, some

---

82. Calderwood, *Pastor and the Prelate*, 1.

83. Rutherford, *Divine Right of Church-Government and Excommunication*, 43.

84. Rutherford, *Divine Right of Church-Government and Excommunication*, 136.

85. Forrester and Murray, *Studies in the History of Worship in Scotland*, 90.

86. And then only narrowly: the vote taken after a lengthy debate carried by 390 votes to 259. Forrester and Murray, *Studies in the History of Worship in Scotland*, 90.

factions such as the Free Church held reservations about the organ's use and continued the restriction, warning that the pipe organ was a "Dagon in the sanctuary,"[87] an object whose only purpose would be to encourage false worship.[88]

Scottish Reformers silenced nearly every pipe organ in the country, and the ban held longer in Scotland than in any other Calvinist group. And, just as was the case elsewhere, the "Calvinist" manner of singing the Psalms, theologically and musically ideal as they were, was simply a musical failure without the aid of the organ or other instruments. The use of precentors led to frustration and ultimately robbed the Kirk of the simple beauty in worship she desired. The Scots looked to their organs for assistance; the fact that the organ continued to be used, albeit sporadically, in the royal chapel, ensured the presence of the instrument in Scottish culture. Gradually, laboriously so, almost all factions of the Presbyterian churches conceded the point and joined the ranks of Calvinists elsewhere who sang their Psalms with the "kist o' whistles."

Church of England

In England and Wales the Reformation began as a political maneuver in the 1530s, and until the death of Henry VIII in 1547 its impact on the liturgy was very limited. With the accession of Edward VI (1547–1553) the Protestant party in the Church of England was dominant, and the first complete liturgy in English was published in 1549. This was, however, a fairly conservative liturgy, modelled on existing Lutheran patterns rather than Calvinist ones, and it retained a considerable element of singing in the services. Provision for this was made in John Marbeck's *Booke of Common Praier Noted* published in 1550. The extreme Protestant party in the English church, however, was not satisfied with these reforms and pressed for the adoption of a liturgy along more Calvinist lines. The 1549 liturgy was replaced by a new prayer book in 1552, which made far less provision for music in the services.

However, this new, musically spare liturgy was short-lived. During the reign of Mary I (1553–1558), when England and Wales returned to Roman allegiance, Catholic liturgies were celebrated again, and

---

87. Wotherspoon, "Present State of Church Music in Scotland," 38.

88. The Reformed Presbyterian Church of the United States, to this day, does not use instrumental accompaniment, and sings only the Psalms.

Protestants who refused to recant either went into exile or were executed. When Elizabeth I succeeded to the throne in 1558 all the evidence, including the furnishings of her private chapel, suggested that she would have preferred to return to the religious situation at the beginning of Edward VI's reign, namely a vernacular liturgy that retained considerable ceremony. Because all but one of the existing bishops refused to support these changes, and because she was forced to rely on returning Protestant exiles to provide an alternative religious leadership, Queen Elizabeth I had to settle for a more Protestant-oriented church than she would have liked. The English liturgy of 1559 was basically that of 1552 with a few modifications in a more Catholic direction. The evidence is that choirs and organs continued in use in some parishes as well as in cathedrals and collegiate churches.

As the extreme Protestant party in the English church, the Puritans, gained influence by the last quarter of the sixteenth century, they challenged the quasi-Catholic liturgical practices of the Church of England. Since the Puritans considered the pipe organs that were left in English churches to be vestiges of Roman apostasy, an increasing number of parish churches abandoned the use of choirs and organs and substituted the congregational singing of metrical psalms led by the parish clerk.[89] While to the north Knox was prohibiting the use of the organ in Scotland, in England many pipe organs were also destroyed; those that were not destroyed were neglected. In 1572 an anonymous pamphlet appeared entitled *Admonition to the Parliament: A View of Popish Abuses*. The pamphlet solidified Puritan ideals and argued for a return to the "primitive church" stripped of all accoutrements of the Roman Catholic Church, including copes, surplices, and organs. McGinn argued that the publication of *Admonition* "marks the point at which Puritanism began to be a hostile force, determined to do away with the existing system of polity and worship in the English Church."[90]

The tension between Anglicanism and Puritanism was not resolved during Elizabeth's lifetime. Instead the two sides seemed to live in a tense truce: "As far as music was concerned, the Anglican ideal prevailed in cathedrals, while in parish churches the Puritan pattern of congregational metrical psalm singing was allowed to establish itself."[91] This might ex-

---

89. Temperley, *Music of the English Parish Church*, 43–44.

90. The editors are believed to be John Field and Thomas Wilcox, ministers in London. McGinn, *Admonition Controversy*, 25.

91. Temperley, *Music of the English Parish Church*, 42.

plain the Canons of 1604 that directed worshipers to show reverence to the altar, even as seventeenth-century Puritans vigorously opposed this and other practices. Richard Culmer, a Puritan minister in Canterbury, was appalled by the shadow of Roman Catholic worship at the cathedral there:

> The Pettie Canons, and Singing Men there, sing their Cathedral Service in Prick-Song after the Romish fashion, chanting the Lord's Prayer, and other prayers in an unfit manner, in the chancel, or Quire of that Cathedral; at the East end wereof they have placed an Altar (as they call it) dressed after the Romish fashion, with candlesticks, and tapers . . . towards which Altar they crouch, and duck three times at their going up to it.[92]

Given time, these "Romish" innovations were swept away, and the Anglican prayer book was replaced by the *Puritan Directory for the Publique Worship of God*. Then again, in due course, Anglicanism was restored in 1662 with a new, slightly altered version of the 1559 prayer book. Anglican high churchmanship was once again triumphant and music was gradually restored as an important component of its worship.

Catholicism and Rome

Because Calvin's liturgical practices would be seen as conspicuously anti-Catholic by anyone who attended a Reformed Sunday service, they were among the first to be clarified in the Counter-Reformation, which began with Council of Trent (= Concilium Tridentinum). This council was convened on December 13, 1545 by Pope Paul III to address the political, religious, and social upheaval that boiled throughout Europe, as well as the fact that "the unity of the Christian name was rent and well-nigh torn asunder by schisms, dissensions, heresies"—in other words, by Protestantism.

The council's task was a mighty one, and its work proceeded slowly. In fact, when Paul III died in 1549, the council fell under the successive supervision of Julius III (1550–1555), Marcellus II (1555), Paul IV (1555–1559), and Pius IV (1559–1565). On September 17, 1562, in the twenty-second sitting, the council formulated a "Decree Concerning the Things to be Observed and to be Avoided in the Celebration of Mass." Particular consideration was given to the expectation of proper

---

92. Culmer, *Cathedrall Newes*, 2.

and dignified music during the mass. The council gave this directive for bishops:

> Let them exclude from the churches those pieces of music, whether sung or played, which are tainted with anything frivolous or shameful, and all things secular, and vain or even blasphemous utterances, so that the House of God may both seem and be called a house of prayer.[93]

It might be easy to infer that "blasphemous utterances" might be the roar of the organ or other instruments. But not necessarily so. In the preparatory canon, number eight, of September 10, 1562, which referred to the celebration of Mass in general, and from which the material of canon nine was eventually derived, we find this pronouncement not for the musicians but for celebrants:

> When priests offer the Sacrifice of the Mass . . . let them also take care that they do not pronounce the words with so low a voice that they may not be easily understood by others, nor, on the other hand, in such fashion that they destroy the fervor of those who listen by the noisy rumbling of their voices.[94]

In this context, what is important for this study is the Catholic Church's statement on the role and use of the pipe organ: so long as it remained pure and added to the solemnity of worship, the pipe organ was permitted to retain its position. Since the organ's use was prominent at this point in history, the silence of the council seems to support the organ's acceptance and use.

Lasco in Poland

Meanwhile, across the English Channel, the first Reformed church service in Poland was held in 1550 in Pińczów, a small town outside Kraków.[95] Here the local nobles, several of whom entered into correspondence with

---

93. "*Ab ecclesiis vero musicas eas, ubi sive organo sive cantu lascivum aut impurum aliquid miscetur, item saeculares omnes actiones, vana atque adeo profana colloquia, deambulationes, strepitus, clamores arceant, ut Domus Dei vere domus orationis esse videatur ac dici posit.*" Concilii Tridentini Acta, 5:963.

94. "*Sacerdotes, dum missarum sollemnia agunt . . . caveant etiam, ne ita submissa voce verba proferant, ut non commode ab aliis intelligantur, sic tamen, ne clamoroso vocis strepitu audientium fervorem frangant.*" Concilii Tridentini Acta, 5:927.

95. Lubieniecki, *History of the Polish Reformation*.

Calvin, converted to the Reformed faith, expelled the monks, and purged the city church of Catholic elements. The movement gathered strength, and non-Lutheran Protestant groups met in the region of Słomniki, near Kraków, in 1554 in what later synodical minutes would record as the first synod of a Reformed church.⁹⁶ But these synodical minutes document that the desire to instill Protestant worship began before the 1554 meeting: as early as 1540 Polish Catholic churches were purged of all papist elements, most strongly in the region between Kraków and Lublin, which would become the heartland of Polish Protestantism.⁹⁷ Further, this still largely inchoate church resolved to reform their rites of "papal superstition"⁹⁸ and declared John Calvin, Jan á Lasco, and Phillip Melanchton to be authorities of the true Christian faith.⁹⁹

In 1556 the Polish native John á Lasco (=Jan Łaski, 1499–1560), responding to a specific invitation from the king, returned from Germany to organize emerging Reformed movements in Poland.¹⁰⁰ Knowing that the new king Sigismond II Augustus was sympathetic to the Reformed cause,¹⁰¹ Lasco proposed a unifying confession that would preserve the assorted Protestant currents within the Polish commonwealth. By the late 1550s it appeared as though the Reformed cause was gaining ground rapidly, but the momentum of its growth was disrupted by schism and the 1560 death of Lasco.

Any further gains the Reformed movement made were quickly undone by an equally strong Catholic Counter-Reformation. Jesuits were invited to Poland by Catholic clergy in 1565, and they advocated stringent methods of combating "Reformed heresy." Religious riots followed, and Protestants were expelled from important cities of Poland. By 1595 fledgling Protestant unions disorganized just as a new Catholic king Sigismond III took the throne. Nearly all of Poland's aristocrats converted back to Catholicism and by the beginning of the seventeenth century a very small percentage of the population remained Protestant. Such a lack

96. Davies, *God's Playground*, 167–83.
97. Benedict, *Christ's Churches*, 262.
98. Conradt, "John Calvin," 6.
99. Conradt, "John Calvin," 7.
100. MacCulloch, *Reformation*, 257.
101. Ungvary, *Lutheran and Calvinist Influences upon the Hungarian Reformed*, 13. The king was known to have read Protestant literature at court, including Calvin's *Institutes*. Benedict, *Christ's Churches*, 265.

of social depth made the Reformed cause even more vulnerable to erosion in succeeding generations.

Previously, John Calvin was in direct correspondence with King Sigismond I on several occasions. In a letter[102] dated December 24, 1555, Calvin urged the king to "wipe out all idolatry," and warned the Polish king that unless he called his subjects away from the "filthy dissipation of Popery to the obedience of Christ," Poland would incur the wrath of God.[103] Calvin decried Polish worship as "befouled and polluted by the corruptions of the papacy," and lamented that the people "went after the inventions of men."[104]

With these "inventions of men" we do not know if Calvin specifically meant the pipe organ, but the pipe organ in Poland was just as predominant in Polish culture as it was in lands already discussed. In fact, the Poles had specifically adapted the pipe organ in two important ways in order to accommodate their liturgy. First, in addition to building large instruments inside the church buildings, the Polish made extensive use of the portable (*portative*) organ.[105] These portable "box" or "chamber" organs became necessary instruments used in liturgical processionals outside of the church building proper.[106] The entire instrument could be carried or moved about on a cart. Sometimes these portatives were even used inside the churches, since its smaller bellows were more easily pumped than those of a large organ.[107]

Another feature in use in many Polish pipe organs was the mysterious *Tympani* organ stop. Found in almost all Polish organs from this time, even on the smallest of country church instruments,[108] the *Tympani* stop was called for specifically in Catholic ritual. When the tympani stop was drawn, two bass pipes spoke together though not at the same pitch. The resulting rumble, or "tympani," was used at the moment of elevation

---

102. Lubieniecki reprinted these letters.

103. "*Nam quum gregarios quoque discipulos lucernis similis esse velit Christus, quae in sublimi positae fulgorem suum longe emittunt: quid a rege exiget quem in summo dignitatis fastigio locavit ut aliis omnibus praeluceat?*" O.C., 15:330.

104. Lubieniecki, *History of the Polish Reformation*, 118.

105. From these "portable" organs would emerge the modern accordion so often associated with Polish music.

106. Gołos, *Polish Organ*, 35.

107. Gołos, *Polish Organ*, 62.

108. Gołos, *Polish Organ*, 64. This organ stop was variously labeled: sometimes even *kotły* or *bęben*, kettle drums or drums, respectively.

of the host and the chalice during celebration of the Mass.[109] In some rare cases where the stop was not available, the organist was instructed to simultaneously depress two or three of the lowest pedal notes to achieve a similar thunderous effect.

The origin of this custom is found not so much in the need for a theatrical gesture at this climactic moment in the liturgy, or even as an indication that the host was undergoing transubstantiation—hand bells were used for that purpose. Rather it seems that tympani practice evolved from secular use, borrowed from pagan ceremony.[110] Creating such a noise had originally had the meaning of warding off evil spirits, and as such it was incorporated early on into their liturgy. Thus in certain parts of Poland when the Mass was celebrated out of doors without an organ, the acolyte beat on a kettledrum.[111] Ultimately, such practice was banned by continuing Catholic reforms, and as late as the nineteenth century the Italian bishop Giuseppe Callegari decreed:

> We command that bells, [organ] stops imitating birds, drums, and all those kinds of instruments be taken out of organs— where this cannot be implemented, it is forbidden henceforth to use them.[112]

The bishop might have been too late in his pronouncement: according to Antoni Sapalski

> ... the drums which our village folks still cannot part with to this day, and sometimes base the whole worth of the organ on them ... already abandoned everywhere on account of their harmful effect on nervous women.[113]

Polish Catholics were not the only ones using the pipe organ in worship; there was some use of the organ were Reformed congregations survived. The Reformed presence in Danzig (now Gdańsk) was influenced by Lutheran territories. Like their Lutheran neighbors, Reformed congregations here continued to use the organ in worship.[114] According to Christoph Hartknoch's *Preussische Kirchen-historia*, when a *Preussische*

---

109. Gołos, *Polish Organ*, 64–65.
110. Gołos, *Polish Organ*, 69.
111. Gołos, *Polish Organ*, 76–77.
112. As cited by Callegari, "Okólnik."
113. Sapalski, *Przewodnik dia organistów*, 131.
114. Herl, *Worship Wars in Early Lutheranism*, 131–32.

(Reformed) faction gained control of several churches in Danzig in 1589, they eliminated paintings, private confession, the reading of the Latin epistles and Gospels, Latin singing, candles on the altar, the host (replacing it with bread), the chanting of the Words of Institution, and the fraction.[115] In 1591 the pastor of Danzig's Holy Trinity Church abolished the five- to eight-part Latin motets sung in the church and replaced them with the metrical psalms typical of Reformed worship. Nevertheless, despite this purging of all things Catholic, the organ remained. It may even have been used to accompany the singing. As Hartknoch notes, "these psalms were sung in four parts in the choir, and the organ was played with them."[116] A similar citation occurs in a 1601 "Order for Singing in the Choir and in the Church" for Danzig's St. Katharine's Church:

> Since during the distribution of the Lord's Supper or during the Communion on holy days and Sundays after the sermon the German psalms of praise on the Lord's Supper have previously been sung, as desired by the council, the same shall henceforth once again be sung during the communion in the choir; on the first Sunday the first psalm, *Gott sei gelobet und gebenedeiet*, and on the following Sunday the second, *Jesus Christus, unser Heiland*, in their entirety shall be sung and simultaneously played on the organ so that the common man who is inexperienced in reading, shall be awakened to thanksgiving.[117]

The singing of psalms during the Communion was nothing new for the Reformed. What is unusual here is the incorporation of both psalm and hymn, as is the directive that the singing be accompanied by the organ.

---

115. Hartknoch, *Preussische Kirchen-historia*.

116. ". . . so sind diese Psalmen in vier Stimmen auff dem Chor gesungen, und dabey die Orgel geschlagen worden." Hartknoch, *Preussische Kirchen-historia*, 760, citing Schmidt, *Verantwortung*, 60.

117. "Weill bey der Ausspendung des Herren Abendtmahles oder vnter der Communion, des Fest undt Sontages nach der Predigt die deutschen Lobe-Psalme vom Abendtmahl des Herren vormals gesungen, alß weil Ein Erb. Rahtt, das dieselben hinführo wiederumb vnter der Communion zu Chore, des einen Sontages der eine Psalm, nemblich Gott sey gelobet vndt gebenedeyet. Des anderen Sontags aber, der Andere nemblich, Jesus Christus, vnser Heillandt gantz sollen gesungen vndt zugleich auff der Orgel gespielet vnndt geschlagen werden. Damit der gemeine Man so im lesen vnerfahren, zuer Dancksagung erwecket werde." Staatsarchiv Danzig 300, 35 (37B) as cited by Rauschning, *Geschichte der Musik*, 79. The reference to "the choir" (*zu Chore*) is a reference to the place where the singing was done in the sanctuary.

That some Polish Reformed zealously enjoyed, even demanded, the use of the organ at this time is shown again in later records from Danzig dating from 1614 and 1633. According to the minutes of St. Bartholomew's Church, the organist was dismissed because "hardly any psalm . . . is played by him in such a way that the congregation can thus sing along."[118] And at St. Mary's Church, the famed organist Paul Siefert remarked that his increased workload included playing "spiritual songs before and after the sermon on the organ, joining in with the congregation."[119]

However, this zealous, forward-looking directive appears to have been the case primarily in this region of Poland. The exhaustive organ building records from Poland provided by Jerzy Gołos[120] reveal a different story for the Reformed living in the central regions of the country. Of the sixteen hundred purchasers of organs at this time, nearly all were Catholic, only a handful Protestant, but even then, these instruments were not constructed until the eighteenth century. Thus, it is assumed that the small Reformed faction in central Poland did not even have pipe organs at their disposal, much less use them like their fellow congregants nearer the border.[121]

The evidence from Poland suggests that although John Calvin had direct contact with King Sigismund I and urged reform, and though the earliest synods endorsed Calvin, nevertheless organ use continued *contra* his ideals. Although synods convened to discuss Reformed movements in Poland, unification of emerging movements in the face of political and ecclesiastical opposition took precedence over musical reforms. Thus the few Polish Calvinists who remained after the Counter-Reformation did not develop as strong an anti-organ stance as did other Reformed groups

---

118. Staatsarchiv Danzig 300, 37B, 18, cited by Rauschning, *Geschichte der Musik*, 57.

119. Staatsarchiv Danzig 300, 42, 151, cited by Rauschning, *Geschichte der Musik*, 151.

120. Gołos, *Polish Organ*, 238–451.

121. This may well explain seemingly contradictory statements about organ use in Poland. For example, Junior stated: "There are many of the Reformed Churches, and some of 'em, the best in the World, that never us'd Organs, or any other musical instruments in their Sacred Assemblies and Worship. As the Reformed Churches . . . in Poland. . . . On the other Hand, Organs are us'd in some of the Churches . . . in Poland." Junior, *Church-Pageantry*, 10. But Gisbertus Voetius wrote that Polish churches did not use organ music: ". . . in Ecclesiis . . . Polonicis . . . cultu publico abest Musica Organica." Voetius, *Politicae Ecclesticae* (hereafter PE), 1:561, as did Eubulus, *Pointen*, 186.

in Europe. In Polish areas where the Reformation did take hold, organ use continued unabated because of neighboring Lutheran influences.

Hungary

The middle of the sixteenth century saw the establishment of Calvinism in Hungary in the midst of political conflict, surviving on narrow ground between Habsburg rule and growing Ottoman influence largely thanks to the patronage of Transylvania's princes.[122] The royal court of Lajos II had embraced Lutheran teachings before 1526, but that year the country endured a crushing defeat by Ottoman Turks under Sultan Suleiman I. Heavy casualties resulted in a subsequent weakness of the old hierarchy, and coupled with a new division of jurisdictions, the Pope's hold over the country loosened and allowed religious diversity to thrive. After an initial acceptance of Lutheranism, the Hungarians changed direction to finally accept Helvetic tendencies.[123] In 1557, a Reformed synod representing both Calvinist and Lutheran beliefs published a *Confessio Hungarica*, or *Czengerina*. By 1564, however, differences concerning the meaning of the Lord's Supper caused a formal separation between the Lutherans, who were ethnically Saxon (thus German), and Hungarian Calvinists. In 1567, the Calvinists chose to append the *Confessio Hungarica* with the *Second Helvetic Confession* and the *Heidelberg Catechism*, creating an official confessional standard for the Reformed Church of Hungary.

Under Transylvania's constitution, the Reformed church (*Kolozsvár*) had become one of four tolerated religions under a royal edict of 1568 that extended religious toleration also to Catholics, Lutherans (*Szeben*), and the Creed of Francis Dávid (anti-Trinitarianism). By the early seventeenth century a series of Reformed princes worked with the church hierarchy in Transylvania and Hungary to develop local academies and schools, and to increase contact with Dutch and English co-religionists. These contacts urged further reforms to styles of worship, standards of moral discipline, and forms of church government.

Yet this is not to suggest that the Hungarian and Transylvanian Reformed merely mirrored their Reformed counterparts to the west. One unique feature was the Hungarian Reformed use of vivid color, and even figure decorations, within their church buildings, a custom that would

---

122. Benedict, *Christ's Churches*, 271–80; MacCulloch, *Reformation*, 442–49.
123. Ungvary, *Lutheran and Calvinist Influences*, 143.

surely have alarmed censorious western European Calvinists.[124] But perhaps the most striking characteristic of the Reformed church in Hungary and Transylvania was their choice of governance: the church appointed superintendents, referred to as bishops, who were assisted by archdeacons in localized districts[125] rather than the presbyterian form used in Geneva, the Netherlands, and Scotland that was based on the equality of ministers and laity.

This hierarchical system of governance was met with criticism, especially from Hungarian students who studied abroad and returned home wanting to introduce a presbyterian system.[126] These student protestations were not alone. Soon the writings of English Puritans such as Ames and Perkins were translated into Hungarian, and the 1636 Pál Medgyesi translation of *The Practice of Piety* of Bayly received wide commercial success. This growing Puritan faction then expressed grave concern with the church's coexistence with anti-Trinitarians, and objected to the church's observance of the Christmas and Easter festivals. They even suggested that the psalms, though cast in vernacular Hungarian, still ought to be sung to the exact tunes used in Geneva. Thus the emerging Reformed movement in Hungary and Transylvania met another strand of Reformed Protestantism. The result was the same as was experienced by Reformed groups in other countries: nonconformity of liturgical practice. For example the Transtibiscan district used Ludwig Lavater's *Rites and Institution of the Zurich Church* (1559)[127] to form its liturgy along strictly Genevan lines: churches were stripped of images and altars, and clerical vestments were burned.[128]

But the churches of the western districts retained more Catholic elements;[129] for example, Catholic antiphons and Latin hymns were used, albeit after being carefully filtered of all Catholic content.[130] Moreover,

---

124. See MacCulloch, *Reformation*, plate 19a for a splendid example; Starr, "Art and Architecture and the Hungarian Reformed Church," 301–40; Murdock, *Calvinism on the Frontier*, 153–54.

125. MacCulloch, *Reformation*, 250, 445–46.

126. MacCulloch, *Reformation*, 46.

127. Lavater, *Ritibus et Institutis ecclesiae Tigurinae opusculum*.

128. Benedict, *Christ's Churches*, 280.

129. Bucsay, *Geschichte des Protestantismus in Ungarn*, 120–23.

130. Kovács, *Keresztyéni énekek*. This hymnal was reprinted no less than eleven times before 1655.

their *Book of Order* contained a liturgy for the casting out of demons,[131] and retained the use of the word "altar" and "wafer"[132] when discussing issues pertaining to Communion. Further, the Debrecen Articles of 1562 suggested that a lectionary should be followed, a Catholic practice that John Calvin and John Knox had dispensed with in their areas of influence. Thus in Hungary it was largely impossible to codify Reformed Christianity by external liturgical formulae alone. Liturgical practice varied from fully Genevan to quasi-Catholic.

The city of Debrecen became a leading center of Calvinism and was later even dubbed the "Hungarian Geneva," and here an extremely valuable proclamation was made regarding instruments in worship. In 1562 Péter Méliusz Juhász, a leading defender of Reformed views, held a district synod and the resultant "Confession of the Church of Debrecen, concerning the main articles, and concerning some questions which are necessary to give counsel to disturbed consciences: It is made public to be a testimony of doctrine and faith, against those who denigrate sound doctrine"[133] was adopted as an initial constitution for governance of the Hungarian Reformed Church. This thoroughly Calvinist document insisted that congregations sing in the vernacular, do away with "Papist howling"[134] and prohibit unequivocally musical instruments in worship. Because this article is one of the earliest statements about the organ in specific, it merits citation in full:

> On musical instruments [*organa*]
>
> It is an established fact that the use of musical instruments [*instrumenta*] in the Church of old, in the temple of Solomon, was accepted. Now, together with the ancient priesthood and sacrifice, as well as other shadows of the Law, the use of instruments [*organa*] in churches has ceased like a shadow through the coming of Christ. For instruments [*organa*] of every kind signified the parts of the elect; they are to worship the Lord with their voice and by any means. Thus David mentions every kind

---

131. Revesz, translated by Knight, *History of the Hungarian Reformed Church*, 82.

132. Revesz, translated by Knight, *History of the Hungarian Reformed Church*, 82.

133. "*Confessio Ecclesiae Debreciensis de praecipuis articulis, et quaestionibus quibusdam, necessariis ad consulendum turbatis conscientiis, exhibita ut sit testimonium doctrinae et fidei contra calumniatores sanae doctrinae.*" I am deeply indebted to Dr. Csaba Fekete, Librarian of the College Library of the Transtibiscan Reformed Church District (Debrecen, Hungary) for the retrieval and transcription of this document.

134. Murdock, *Calvinism on the Frontier*, 166.

of musical instruments [*instrumenta*], in order that man might worship God with all his strength, mind, and members. In the congregation one is to speak or sing in spirit, with grace. Paul is so far from approving the sound[135] of voiceless instruments [*organa*] that not even human voices, or sounds that are not understood, or that do not edify, are permitted in the Church. In fact, he teaches that those who teach or sing in the congregation, in something like a foreign and unintelligible tongue, are insane (1 Cor 14). The Fathers also teach the same thing. Nor is there mention of instruments [*organa*] in the New Testament, or that the pristine early Church accepted their use, except that the popes in their pleasure-loving way established theatrical Masses so that actors could jump about as in obscene plays. And the papist *Chronicle* attributes the institution of the organ [*organum*] to Pope Vitalianus. And decrees condemn, with Jerome,[136] the stentorian bawling in churches, in the manner of loudly declaiming tragic actors. In the prophets the Lord rejects the songs of the lyre, and instruments [*organa*], and the Lord commanded the human voice, not with shadows or voiceless teachers. They are wrong, therefore, who mindlessly mutter the canonical hours like so much superstitious gibberish, pleasing to God on the basis of just doing it [*ex opere operato*], or who retain instruments [*organa*] in the assembly of the saints, as the Papists and other do. Mt 15[:13]: "That which the Lord has not planted will be uprooted." Now to praise God seven times means to worship and extol him always, in spirit and in truth, for "seven" means "multiple times," "ceaselessly" (Mt 18; Lk 18). Augustus Hilla on the passages noted.[137]

---

135. Reading: *sonum* for *sensum*.

136. Jerome records that once an organ was produced using two elephant skins over an empty vessel. This "bellow" produced such a loud sound from its fifteen pipes that the noise resounded like "thunder from Jerusalem to the Mount of Olives." Jerome, *Epistola ad Dardanum*, 213.

137. "*De organis musicis. Usum instrumentorum musicorum in veteri Ecclesia in templo Salomonis receptum fuisse constat. Nunc cum sacerdotio et sacrificio veteri, ceterisque umbris legalibus per Christi adventum, organorum usus in templis cessavit tanquam, umbra: Organa enim omnis generis significarunt electorum partes, voci et omnibus modis celebrare debeant Dominum. Ita David omnis generis musicorum instrumentorum meminit, ut homo totis viribus, mente, membris Deum celebret. In spiritu cum gratia loquendum, canendum est in coetu. Tantum abest enim ut sensum mutorum organorum Paulus approbet, ut nequidem humanas voces, sonos non intellectos, non aedificantes permitti in Ecclesia: Imo insanire docet eos qui tanquam barbari lingua peregrina, et non intellecta docent, canunt in coetu. 1 Cor: 14. Idem et patres docent. Neque Organorum fit mentio in novo testamento, aut quod purior Ecclesia usum eorum*

This decree is unmistakably Calvinist in its theology of church music: though King David indeed used instrumental music, this is not a biblical mandate since it was an Old Testament use no longer required of New Testament Christians; worship after Christ is to be worship in Spirit, without the distracting and superfluous "noise" of instruments such as the organ; and 1 Corinthians 14 is the cited biblical passage against the organ. If this were not enough, the instrument's origin as a human invention, introduced into the church by a Catholic pope, made it automatically suspect to the Hungarian Calvinists.

All evidence suggests that the Debrecen decree was honored by the Hungarian Reformed in this district.[138] In fact, the church possessed an organ, but after a fire destroyed the building and its instrument in 1564, the church was rebuilt, but without a pipe organ.

The Counter-Reformation of the seventeenth century converted most Hungarian nobles to Roman Catholicism. Protestantism suffered setbacks, persecution, and various difficulties at the hands of the Catholic aristocracy until 1781 when Emperor Joseph II promulgated the "Edict of Toleration" granting religious liberty to Protestants. However, when the Protestants regrouped at this time, they relaxed earlier regulations and relinquished the 1562 ban on the use of the organ and musical instruments in worship. Thus, records show that the Debreceni Reformatus Kollegium (Reformed College of Debrecen) commissioned a new portative organ in 1764 for its Oratorium (chapel), and in 1830 commissioned its first large instrument for use in Reformed worship which was completed in 1838 by the Viennese organ builder Jakob Deutschmann.[139]

---

receperit, nisi pontifices delicatim Theatrica Missa tanquam in ludis obscoenis ad saltum histrionum instituerunt. Et Chronica Papistica Vitaliano Papae Organi institutum tribuunt. Et decreta cum Hieronymo Stentorianam vociferationem, Tragaedorum more in templis boantium damnant. In Prophetis rejicit Dominus cantica lyrae, et organa, et iussit Dominus voce humana non umbris, mutisque magistris. Inique faciunt ergo qui horas Canonicas tanquam battalogias supersitiosas, ex opere operato acceptas Deo nugantes demurmurant, item Organa in sanctorum coetu retinent, ut Papistae et alii Mat:15. Quod Dominus non plantaverit eradicabitur. Septies autem Domino laudem dicere significat semper Deum in spiritu et veritate colere, et celebrare, Nam septem significat multipliciter, sine fine. Mat: 18. Luc: 17. August: Hilla: super haec notata loca." Confessio Ecclesiae Debreciensis, 217–18.

138. Voetius also confirms that the Hungarian churches did not use organ music: "in Ecclesiis . . . Hungaricis. . . cultu publico abest Musica Organica." Voetius, PE, 1:561; as did Eubulus, Pointen van nodige reformatie, 186; and Junior, Church-Pageantry Display'd, 10.

139. Fekete, "Debrecen és az orgona," 355–74, and Fekete, "A debreceni Oratorium

Reformed and Christian Reformed Church in America

Ecclesiastical cultures on the European continent were not the only ones to discuss organ and church music. To the west, no less than a thirty-day voyage across the Atlantic Ocean, Reformed churches were laying foundations in the New World. These Reformed, unlike many of their parent churches of Europe, inherited no church buildings appointed with pipe organs. Rather, these immigrants constructed new places of worship that, because of economic need, matched their theological demands for spare simplicity and were barren of all but essential liturgical furnishings. When Jonas Michaelius led the first official worship service for the New Netherland congregation in New Amsterdam on April 7, 1628 it was not even in a church building proper, but in an upper room over a sawmill. In addition to a pulpit, some wooden pews, baptismal font, and Lord's Table, the only other liturgical tool was the *Genevan Psalter* brought with congregants from the Old World.[140] The singing was *a cappella*, in unison by the entire congregation.

Yet however carefully the immigrants set out to replicate their European patterns of worship in America, they could not. First, the American Dutch experienced a new phenomenon after Peter Stuyvesant's surrender of the British fleet in 1664 and New Amsterdam was transformed into the English colonies of New York and New Jersey. Their Dutch language did not—indeed, could not—remain the sole language of life and worship as the Dutch Reformed were joined by German, French, English, and Scottish migrants. Initial conflicts in worship were not of music but of language and resultant concerns of enculturation and "secularization." Ten years later the Governor of New York received instruction from the Duke of York that it would be desirable for all citizens of New York to be of "one faith" and at one with the English church.[141] By the mid-eighteenth century, political tensions began to fade and not only were the Dutch doing commerce in English but they were also intermarrying as well. By the "Great Awakening," which cut across all denominational, cultural, and linguistic boundaries, the Dutch Reformed had lost almost all distinctiveness from their European counterparts, were no longer sitting in worship according to gender, and in 1727 the first pipe organ was

---

első orgonája," 463–66.

140. Brower et al., *Collegiate Reformed Protestant Dutch Church*, 11.
141. Luidens, *Americanization of the Dutch Reformed Church*, 16.

installed and used in a New York Dutch Reformed Church.[142] Astonishingly, in America, Reformed clergy argued proactively for the use of the organ. Thomas Symmes went so far as to label those who insisted on singing the Old Way, that is without the organ, "Anti-Regular Singers," which he not-so-slyly initialized "A.R.S.'s."[143]

During the mid-nineteenth century another wave of Dutch Calvinists immigrated to the United States; Hendrick Scholte and Albertus van Raalte led refugees to Pella, Iowa and Holland, Michigan, respectively. Though these Reformed believers first associated with the Dutch Reformed in America, now planted in American soil for over two hundred years and established as the Reformed Church of America, these new immigrants found the American Dutch too liberal in comparison to their more pietistic ways. Thus in 1857 they formed the "True Dutch Reformed Church," later renamed the Christian Reformed Church.

Despite these political and theological differences, the Christian Reformed Church shared with the Reformed Church of American their love and use of the organ. In addition to the American Dutch having used the organ for quite some time, the immigrant Dutch would have known full inclusion of the organ back from the "old country." Thus organ music on American soil in a Dutch Reformed Church of any stripe was hardly questioned. In fact, unlike the first immigrants to New Amsterdam in 1638, Scholte's first worship space in Pella, Iowa, was furnished with an organ (a harmonium) from its first Sunday. Though the Christian Reformed Church would later debate the inclusion of hymns into its *Psalter*, its synods have never debated nor questioned the use of instruments in worship.

Conclusions

This chapter has set the stage for the historical ascendance of Reformed movements across sixteenth- and seventeenth-century Europe (and beyond) with specific attention to the various ways these communities engaged the pipe organ. Although some ardent anti-Catholics had every intention of being faithful to teachings regarding pure, biblical worship, the permissibility of pipe organs in these localities and regions varied widely: while organs were torn out and burned or sold as scrap in some

---

142. Luidens, *Americanization of the Dutch Reformed Church*, 127–28.
143. Symmes, *Utile Dulci*, 18.

staunchly Protestant cities or countries, other synods, which were equally theologically orthodox in every other way, gave permission to use organs (albeit judiciously) during worship. This chapter has also shown the importance of nontheological factors, specifically questions of political power, property ownership, geographical location, that caused this wide variation of organ use amongst Reformed groups, which were otherwise largely united in matters of faith.

This contextualization is crucial to understanding the unique situation in the Netherlands, particularly during and after independence from Catholic Spain. The Netherlands illustrates also how widely the application of teaching regarding Reformed liturgy diverged even within a very small geographic scale. Further, the Dutch Reformed church authorities were constrained by the rising political powers in the young Republic. The Dutch wanted to assure that the strict, autocratic rule of the Spanish would not be replaced by a strict, theocratic rule of Dutch ministers who hoped to emulate John Calvin's government in Geneva.

So to the Netherlands we now go. The next chapter narrates in depth the theological, political, and pastoral factors behind the organ conflict, one which forced the Dutch Reformed to shape the basic, defining features of their nascent denomination. The acrimony between the two sides of the organ question in the Netherlands, as exemplified by the vicious exchanges, escalated the longer synods dithered and offered ambiguous statements on the matter. Further, chapters 3–5 then examine the laborious chain of events and the most peculiar cast of characters to show how anti-organ sentiments in this supposedly Calvinist country were finally disregarded in favor of other influences that championed the use of these outstanding instruments before, after, and during Reformed worship.

2

THE PIPE ORGAN IN THE NETHERLANDS

The Dutch pipe organ debate was even more nuanced and protracted than the debates surveyed in the previous chapter. The Dutch revolts against Spanish colonial powers did not neatly replace a foreign, Catholic government with a national Calvinist government. Calvinism was not imposed by political fiat, nor did Reformed ideals dominate Dutch Republican life to such a degree that *anti-orgelist* bans simply became state policy. Rather, just as the groups reviewed in chapter 1 developed and adapted organ policies in response to indigenous, unique circumstances, so did Dutch Reformed churches in each province, each town, each church council room, each town council hall, solve the organ question according to their particular history, local culture, immediate needs, and musical abilities.

Further complicating the situation, it is important to note that the Dutch provinces were not religiously homogeneous, as commonly assumed; rather, a religiously heterogeneous populace existed before, during, and after the Reformation and, accordingly, organ use in worship varied widely among the differing Christian denominations within the new republic. As one might predict, tensions arose between the duty of the new Reformed Church as a public institution to serve the spiritual needs of everyone in the country, and the conviction shared by the more orthodox that they were the guardians of scriptural truth, a truth that limited if not prohibited organ use in worship.

The new Dutch Republic commissioned the Reformed church as a public church (*publieke kerk*): critical to note, not a state church. This Reformed Church denomination was given special protection (*bevoorrechte*) and privilege by law, and open manifestations of any faith except for Reformed Christianity were prohibited, but other faiths were tolerated as long as they remained inconspicuous.[1] As a privileged denomination the country's military and prison chaplains were Reformed, its ecclesiastical buildings were used solely by Reformed congregations, its Reformed preachers were paid out of public funds, and public functions and professions were open only to its members.[2] However, equally important was the 1579 Union of Utrecht's article thirteen that guaranteed individual freedom of religion and mandated that no one would be persecuted or questioned about their religion.[3] As a result, this provision gave each province the right to arrange public religious life as it saw fit.

The Reformed Church's privilege came with a cost; namely, the Reformed Church had to serve all citizens upon request where the needs of the state intersected with functions of the clergy. Simply put, Reformed clergy were required to baptize any member of the public who requested it for themselves or their child, and anyone could be buried in the church graveyard. So, with these ecclesiastical "services" available to all, official Reformed church membership was neither necessary nor required. Contrast this freedom of church membership (or freedom from it) in the Netherlands to other Calvinist cultures, such as that of Calvinist Scotland, where membership was compulsory, and every citizen a member of the Kirk and subject to its discipline, save those who specifically opted out.

Given the requirement that the Reformed churches serve the needs of the public and the requirement of official membership, many Dutchmen and -women were long-term visitors, so to speak, at their local church without officially being on the membership rolls (*liefhebbers*), and they had the freedom to visit neighboring churches, even those of another confession, without serious consequence.

For the smaller numbers of Dutch who did wish to become an official member in a Reformed congregation, the process was arduous. Applicants for formal membership would have to subject themselves to an examination by the church elders on their knowledge of Reformed doctrine, have their private life tested for moral purity, and, in cases of moral

1. Israel, *Dutch Republic*, 374–77.
2. Deursen, *Bavianen*, 13–33.
3. *Groot Placaet-Boeck*, 1:7; Boogman, "Union of Utrecht," 5–35; Frijhoff, "Religious Toleration," 38–39; Kossman and Mellink, *Texts Concerning the Revolt of the Netherlands*.

turpitude, submit to church discipline—which might include anything from public censure to excommunication to social shunning. But as a member, they could vote for parish leaders, become an elder or deacon themselves, and have the right to partake of Holy Communion.[4]

Lutherans

In this way, Dutch Christians of all stripes were exposed to a wide variety of liturgical practices and liturgical music that existed in this small, multi-confessional country. One such group was Lutheranism, which started in eastern German lands but also took root amongst the Dutch, although the congregations were far fewer in number and weaker in public influence compared to the Reformed. While congregations in Antwerp (established 1566) and Woerden (1603) held worship services that differed barely from the Reformed, over time the Dutch Lutherans regularly used organ music within worship primarily because they preferred harmonized, four-part chorales and hymns (still a historical characteristic of Lutheran worship) over Psalms, which were considered an Old Testament, Jewish custom not suitable for a Christian faith based on the New Testament. Dutch Lutheran synodical records from this time show no theological or political strife about organ use at all.[5]

Moravians

Another group of German Protestants, the Evangelical Church of the Brethren, also known as *Hernhutters*,[6] the Moravian Brethren, or the Moravian Church, was welcomed in the Netherlands. The Moravians developed their own rich church music for Sunday morning worship as well as for special celebrations of marriage, birth, burial, and their characteristic *Liebesmahle* (meals of love). Lay choirs sang these new Protestant liturgies accompanied by various instruments. The Brethren are famous for trombone choirs, which would play atop bell towers, but their

---

4. Deursen, *Kopergeld*, 38–50.

5. See Duisberg, *Alle welcke psalmen*; Haecht and Duisberg, *CL psalmen Davids*; Kooiman, *Luthers kerklied in de Nederlanden*; Michels, *Wohlklingende Harmonie*; Klepperbein, *Hundert und fünfzig Psalme*; Mützenbecher, *Sammlung der geistlichen Lieder und Psalme*.

6. See *Evangelische liederen*; Müller, *Hymnologisches Handbuch*; Tollefsen, *Catalogue of the Music Collection of the Moravian Congregation*.

four-part chorales were also regularly accompanied by the pipe organ. When some Moravian congregations did later install pipe organs, they were typically smaller by comparison for the organ was only needed as a continuo instrument.

Mennonite and Baptist

Like the Calvinists, Dutch Mennonites and Baptists also sang some Psalms in worship during this time, if a close study of their songbooks from the sixteenth century is any proof.[7] Because these groups were strongly averse to any strong central ecclesiastical authority, no synod or bishop could impose a songbook for use in all of their congregations. As a result, Mennonite and Baptist worship was widely varied and is difficult to characterize. However, since many of these congregations had no organs until the second half of the eighteenth century, their congregations would most likely have sung both psalms and hymns without accompaniment.

Walloons

The French-speaking Reformed churches in Wallonia[8] (today the French-speaking province of Belgium, but part of the Netherlands in the sixteenth century) stressed Psalm singing, as did all other Calvinists, and in 1594 they published a bilingual edition (that is, Dutch and French) of the *Genevan Psalter* for use in their congregations.[9] Research reveals no central policy amongst the Walloons regarding organ use; rather, it seems that they approached the matter with simple practicality. Since most Walloon congregations had no organ at their disposal, they sang without accompaniment, but a few Walloon congregations had appropriated formerly Catholic churches and used the pipe organs if they had been left intact after the iconoclastic riots of 1566.[10]

---

7. See Hoop Scheffer, "Korte geschiedenis van het kerkgezang"; Cramer, "Bijdragen tot de geschiedenis; Visser, "Litanie van een liturgisch stiefkind."

8. Sometimes also called the *Franse Kerk*, French Church. See Douen, *Clément Marot et le Psautier huguenot*; Bovet, *Histoire du Psautier*; Pidoux, *Psautier*; Luth and Smilde, "Melodieën van het Geneefse psalter," 215–31; Cardaux, "Le psautier huguenot," 71–83; Meyjes, "Les rapports entre les Eglises Wallonnes," 1–15.

9. Marot et al., *Pseaumes de David mis en rime Françoise*.

10. For example, the Walloon congregation worshiping at the Court Chapel employed the famous organist Quirijn van Blenkenburg from 1687 to 1702.

English Reformed

Another foreign group of Protestants that found a home in the Netherlands was the English Reformed, who had been driven from Britain in the face of religious violence.[11] English congregations existed all across the republic, with larger congregations in Flushing and Brielle. As greater numbers of English and Scots Calvinists settled in Dutch lands, congregations grew in important cities such as Amsterdam, Leiden, Rotterdam, The Hague, and Utrecht. By the turn of the seventeenth century about thirty congregations were recognized and viewed as the English-language wing of the Dutch Reformed Church. Because of this special relationship, their liturgical practice varied little from that of the Dutch Reformed, which meant they were strongly opposed to organ music, at least during the first generations after the Reformation. What is more, these immigrant congregations were generally poorer than Dutch congregations, which meant practically that, even if they wanted to purchase an organ, their first financial concern had to be buying or building a meeting space.

Arminians

In addition to these foreign groups, a native denomination was formed in the Netherlands after the condemnation of the Arminian heresy by the Synod of Dordrecht of 1618–1619 which excommunicated clergy and their followers who refused to renounce Arminian doctrines.[12] By 1630 the Arminian Remonstrants had formed sizeable congregations in Amsterdam and Rotterdam, and one must infer that these displaced groups sang psalms without accompaniment for a very long time. Indeed, the first known pipe organ in a Remonstrant church was built in Alkmaar in 1659, in Rotterdam in 1690, and in Amsterdam not until the year 1717 and then only because its entire cost was underwritten by a church member.[13]

---

11. Sprunger, *Dutch Puritanism*.

12. Doel, *Daar moet veel strijds gestreden zijn;* Rasch, "Some Notes on the Camphuysen Manuscript," 30–43.

13. Tideman, "Bijzonderheden uit de geschiedenis," 505–6.

Roman Catholicism

The privilege granted to the Reformed church was blended with tolerance for these other Protestant groups, but Dutch tolerance weakened when it came to Catholicism, which still smacked of foreign domination to the victorious republicans. While it was not illegal to be a Catholic in the Dutch Republic, it was illegal to worship as one. In some provinces laws were issued between the 1580s and the 1680s that prohibited any public gathering of Roman Catholics, teaching of Catholic doctrine, lodging of priests, studying at a Catholic university, and having a priest perform sacraments such as baptism or marriage according to Catholic rites, which were declared "popish idolatry."[14] Fines were levied against violators, and priests were apprehended throughout the country.[15]

But if oppression of Catholics was meant to sweep Catholicism out of the Netherlands, it did not succeed; in fact, official sanctions had the opposite effect. Because the Catholics were not necessarily exiled, their faith practice went underground and into hidden house churches (*schuilkerken*), attics, barns, or other obscure locations.[16] In many Dutch cities Roman Catholic worship not only survived, but flourished despite open, sectarian hostilities of the ecclesiastical establishment. Certainly, Catholic tolerance varied from town to town, depending on the sympathies of local magisterial authorities. In cities where tensions existed between political and Reformed elites over local ecclesiastical settlements, Catholics enjoyed a relatively high degree of toleration and learned to negotiate their beliefs within the parameters of a clandestine, shadowy subculture.

A New Denomination in an Old Space

The most significant effect of anti-Catholic maneuverings, and the most important one for an analysis of the organ controversy, is that Catholic

---

14. Calkoen, *Onderzoek naar den rechtstoestand*, 39–67; Rogier, *Geschiedenis van het katholicisme*, 428–73; Nierop, *Beeldenstorm en burgerlijk verzet*, 106.

15. Enforcement of anti-Catholic laws varied considerably across the northern provinces and over the course of the seventeenth century. In general, central and local governments tended to be more lenient in areas with larger demographic concentrations of Roman Catholics such as the provinces of Holland and Utrecht. Scholars also recognize that conditions generally improved for Catholics in the second half of the seventeenth century. See Spaans, "Katholieken en de Vrede."

16. Meijer, "Missie-verslagen," 149, 154.

buildings were expropriated and given over to Protestant congregations for their use. As a result, Calvinists curiously found themselves with large, ornate, and conspicuous pipe organs in their worship spaces. These remaining pipe organs were the products of several centuries of development in art and engineering. In fact, organs were built in churches in the southern parts of the Low Countries as early as the tenth century, and they appeared in the northern parts during the eleventh and twelfth centuries.[17] These rudimentary instruments were mechanically simple and musically crude. For example, the first organ built in the year 1120 for the Oude Kerk[18] of Utrecht had no stops or ranks but twelve pipes that sounded for each note on the keyboard.[19] In Amsterdam, the first organ in the Oude Kerk was only twelve feet tall. Witnesses from these times reported that these organs sounded like blaring, raucous trumpets. Even though curtains were sometimes hung in front of the organs in order to muffle the sound, some instruments were so ear-splitting that they even drowned out the voices of the choir. This might well explain the development of *alternatum* singing prior to the Reformation in which the organ would first play a stanza of a hymn, then the choir would sing the same stanza afterward; this pattern continued until the psalm or hymn was finished. (This pattern of singing would reappear in Reformed churches centuries later, *sans* organ of course, as will be discussed below.)

By the fifteenth century the church organ had become more common, and the southern cities of Antwerp, Bruges, and Ghent had monopolized the organ building industry.[20] Some Dutch churches at this time even had two organs, a choir organ and a great organ. The choir organ was smaller and not very powerful because it was intended to accompany the clergy as they sang the Mass or chanted the pericopes; logically, it was placed on the gospel side of the main altar. The great organ, by contrast, was originally placed on the north wall of the church in the nave. But as the instruments gradually produced greater volume through technical improvements from the middle of the fifteenth century onward, they were built on the west wall, below the spire.

---

17. See Hess; Knock; Praetorious.

18. Also referred to as the Nicolaaskerk, St. Nicolaaskerk, Nicolaikerk, or the Klaaskerk.

19. Kist, "Kerkelijke orgel–gebruik bijzonder in Nederland," 218; Schotel, *Openbare*, 64.

20. Groenveld, "'Speelstryt,'" 260.

The history of the organ in Dutch Catholic worship is important to an analysis of the Protestant organ controversy not merely because Reformed churches gained use of Catholic property; as with most aspects of this controversy, there are few absolutely clear dividing lines between the parties. After independence a significant number of Catholic priests converted to Protestantism, leading their followers into the new faith with them. Although some professed Reformed theology and practiced Reformed worship, these priests were used to chanting the liturgy themselves supported by a skilled organist, and their parishioners were used to organ music and trained choirs. Such use of the organ during the church service was normalized in most places by the sixteenth century; in fact, in 1550, one noted Reformer, Joannes Verstegen (= Johann Anastasius Veluanus, 1520–1570), who was a Catholic priest before becoming a Calvinist, wrote a book in which he pointed out many wrongs of the Catholic Church and its music, but not once did he cite the organ or its use as a sin.[21]

Dutch Pipe Organs

As elsewhere in Europe, church buildings served many important public functions for Dutch daily life. For example, church towers served as manned lookout posts against fire, flood, and other dangers, and they were used to announce the time of day to the citizens. Pipe organs, also, were a favorite—albeit expensive—piece of church equipment that had been paid for by citizens though city subsidies. In a real sense, the citizens owned their pipe organs because of their residency in the town and their status as taxpayers, not because of their membership in the church. Moreover, in many cities the church organ was used to provide secular musical entertainment during the week, when special recitals could be offered; in fact, most Dutch cities employed a professional organist. For instance, a 1490 record from Dordrecht shows that the city decided to "pay the organist of the great church an annual stipend to keep the organ as usual XIIII crowns each and III s[tuivers]."[22] The deep pride taken by the Dutch in their local church organ was tested during the iconoclasm of

---

21. Veluanus, *Cort onderricht*.

22. "*It. noch betaelt meester Zijnen die orgelist ter grooter kerck van een jaerwedde die orgelen te bewairen na ouder gewoonte XIIII croonen 't stuck III S.*" Schotel, *Openbare*, 65.

1566, when rioters destroyed many paintings and statues of saints, altars, and stained-glass windows, but in most towns the organs were protected by city officials. Because of this history, recent religious turmoil, and the popular connection to these beautiful organs, the urge to continue to protect these instruments must have been very great.

But the greatest reason why Calvinists found it hard to avoid using organs during the worship service itself is also the most ironic: the Genevan psalms could not be sung easily in Dutch to foreign French music. In their attempts to model their liturgy after John Calvin's teachings and his own practice in Geneva, the Dutch Reformed churches always sang a psalm during morning worship, although not every church sang the same one, since there never has been a Calvinist lectionary. Instead, the great liturgical unifier of Dutch Reformed worship was Datheen's translation of the *Genevan Psalter*. The original music of this *Psalter* is impressively simple: the range of the melody rarely exceeds a fifth, and the tunes, which to today's ears seem to have difficult syncopation, are simply a combination of long and short notes. However, employing the *Psalter* was a formidable challenge because the French tunes were literally foreign to Dutch Reformed congregants, and the Dutch translations of the French texts were strained linguistically, requiring contractions of syllables and grammatical contortions in order to fit the meter of the music. Above all, the Dutch had no experience in congregational singing; under Spanish rule and before the Reformation, liturgical music was provided for the worshipers by trained musicians and well-rehearsed clergy.

Consequently, it is hardly surprising that Dutch congregations butchered both the rhythm and the music of these beautiful French psalms in their attempts to sing *a capella*. Reformed Church leaders quickly sought a solution for this musical torture. Several congregations allowed a lead singer (*voorzanger*), often the local school teacher or some other musically gifted person of the congregation, to stand in front of the congregation and sing one phrase of the psalm, which the congregation repeated. In some churches the psalm was even sung note by note, with each note held by the *voorzanger* until he ran out of breath. In other words, each word of every psalm was sung twice, once by the *voorzanger* and then again after him by the whole congregation. But congregants in some churches could not see or hear the *voorzanger* clearly, nor were all *voorzangers* musically trained, so this manner of Psalm singing was less than effective.[23]

By all contemporary accounts, the *voorzanger* did not improve Reformed worship, nor grace the service with the musical weight and majesty envisioned by Calvin. Thus after a short time after the introduction of the new *Psalter* even the most dogmatic Reformed leaders gradually began to question the ban on the pipe organ. It seemed increasingly logical to some leading thinkers that there would be no harm in having the organ played during worship as long as it improved congregational singing. Church records from 1566 in De Lier foreshadow the resistance to come and reveal that the pastor, who was an adherent of new Protestant teachings, nevertheless had on "five or six Sundays, both before and after the sermon, sung Dutch psalms in the church together with some boys, *while* the organ was playing."[24] Similarly, the congregation in Maassluis even introduced organ accompaniment for its psalmody because of the "pulling and dragging" (*slepen en trekken*) of the congregation as they tried to sing without accompaniment.[25]

Regardless of the aesthetic problems caused by *a capella* psalm singing, even the suggestion of using the organ for any reason during worship was blankly opposed by the most orthodox Calvinists as contrary to Calvin's own teachings. They equated the sound of organ pipes with the Roman Catholic Mass, which they in turn equated with idolatry. They therefore insisted that organ music should be totally removed from the Reformed church along with all other semiotic reminders of corruption and papistry, such as feast days, religious images, clerical vestments, veneration of the altar, and festal processions.

As is the case with most revolutionaries, the *anti-orgelists* oversimplified their opponent's position. They either did not know or did not acknowledge the fact that organ use had been questioned from within the Catholic Church for some time before the Reformation all across Europe. The fact is, as early as the twelfth century, the abbot of Rievaulx Abbey in Yorkshire lamented,

---

23. Balfoort documents one such an experience in the church of St. Eusebius in Arnhem. *Muziekleven in Nederland in de 17de en 18de eeuw*, 26–28.

24. ". . . *vyf of zes sondagen zoo voor zoo na die preeke, Duytsche psalmen in die kercke met eenige jongens gezongen, terwijl het orgel eronder speelde.*" Vente, *Bouwstoffen*, 196, supplement 147. Emphasis mine.

25. Zwart, *Van een deftig orgel: Maassluis 1732–1932*, 125.

> How comes it that the Church also has so many organs and cymbals? To what purpose is that terrible blowing of bellows, imitating rather the clash of thunder than the sweetness of the human voice? One sings low, another high, a third higher still, while a fourth puts in every now and then some supplemental notes.... The whole body is agitated by theatrical gestures, the lips are twisted, the eyes roll, the shoulders are shrugged, and the fingers bent responsive to every note; and this ridiculous trifling is called religion, and where it is carried out most frequently, there it is maintained that God is served most honorably.... You would think they had come not to prayer, but to a spectacle, not to an oratory, but to a theatre.[26]

Perhaps the abbot had no musical abilities himself and thus could not appreciate harmony and counterpoint, but one bishop of Vienna, Nausea Blancicampianus, objected to organ music in writing to Pope Paul III with the warning that the pipe organ "arouse[s] wantonness rather than piety."[27] The Council of Trent, bellwether of the counter-Reformation, even devoted three sessions to the role of music and decided that instrumental music should be used only in proper ways and in a manner that enhanced singing.[28]

In the Netherlands, Dutch Catholic bishops were also cautious regarding organ use in the decades before the Reformation. A Catholic meeting in Kamerijk actually prohibited organ use in 1548, a decision not officially proclaimed until 1550,[29] and after the Council of Trent another Catholic meeting held in Mechelen in 1570 declared that the bishops must prevent cantors, organists, and bell ringers from playing and

---

26. Aelred of Rievaulx, *Speculum Charitatis*, 571–72, as quoted by Hayburn, *Papal Legislation in Sacred Music*, 19.

27. *Concilium Tridentinum*, 368.

28. Particularly the sessions of September 17, 1562; July 15, 1563; November 11, 1563. Hayburn, *Papal Legislation in Sacred Music*, 25. See chapter 1.

29. "*Organa nihil lascivum sonent, aut saeculare, sed quod ipsa etiam plebs intelligat religiosum ac pium esse. Et praestiterit, symbolum totum cani, similiter Praefationem, et orationem dominicam, quam partem relinqui organis, sicut magno alicubi consuetum est fieri.*" "Organs should produce no lascivious or secular sound, but, as even ordinary people know, should be religious and pious. It is better for the whole pattern to be sung than for part to be left to the organ, as is customarily done in certain places, with great abuse." Schannat and Hartzheim, *Concilia Germaniæ*, 1759–90; Mueren, "Rond het vokaal-instumentaal vraagstuk," 20–28.

singing indecent music on the organ or bells, and that no song or organ should ever suppress the chanting of the priests.[30]

Nonetheless, the most orthodox Reformed could not be dissuaded from their conviction that the pipe organ was inherently Catholic, consequently idolatrous, and thus deserving of the most severe judgment. The problem they had was how to enforce their righteous indignation. They could not turn to the national government; even though it had indeed given public privilege to the Reformed churches, the national government devolved a great deal of authority over civic affairs to provinces and municipalities. Because of this constitutional arrangement, and for one even greater reason, organ opponents had to deal with municipal leaders: while churches in every Dutch town and city had been turned over to Reformed congregations for their Sunday use, the buildings where Reformed congregations worshiped were not owned by the church at all but by the local government. This extraordinary state of legal affairs meant that the organs and the buildings that housed them were actually city property.

The Organ Controversy Ignites

When one keeps in mind the religious diversity of the Netherlands at this time, then the frustrating political effects for the strictest organ opponents of the civic ownership of churches becomes obvious. Since the Reformed were not the majority of the population in the country as a whole or even any given locality, there was no guarantee that the Reformed controlled every city council, or that a "Reformed" magistrate would even know or vote in a "Reformed" manner. Indeed, there is no doubt that Dutch cities had non-Reformed councilors. Thus, any local drive to ban that city's church organ could not be guaranteed of a majority of votes. Rather, Reformed and non-Reformed councilors alike might be opposed to such a ban or be unwilling to impose Reformed policy on a country that had just recently thrown off a foreign government that had tried to impose its religion on public life. The return of such theocratic principles was objectionable to most Dutchmen and -women indeed, including many moderate Reformed. Besides, documents from the

---

30. "... *indeora musica in cantu, organis et campanis*. . . . *ut Praefatio et dominica oratio in solemni Missae officio integra a sacerdote decantetur, nec cantu, nec organis deinceps supprimatur.*" Schannat and Hartzheim, *Concilia Germaniae* , 2:615.

time confirm that most Dutch viewed their local church organs as great sources of public entertainment, which ought to be given "permission to play, so long as the days of the market are continuing..."[31] and most cities had ordinances that allowed just that.

Thus, with no recourse from secular officials, the *anti-orgelists* would have to rely on church authorities. However, constitutional matters here worked against them as well. In Reformed church polity each local consistory has ultimate authority to govern its congregation as it sees fit; it does not have to answer to its minister (indeed, the opposite is true), and no classical or national synod can force a local congregation to do anything regarding the spiritual care of its congregation. (However, synods do have the power to determine orthodox doctrine and to issue authoritative interpretations of Scripture, a power not granted to a local consistory.) Moreover, after the Reformation Dutch Reformed were not a unitary body because there was not yet a central seminary, and a codified systematic theology was still developing, at least in a Dutch social and intellectual context. There were not yet enough competent ministers to provide cohesion to define a Dutch Reformed identity, and there was no single living leader with national stature who could act as the authoritative interpreter of all Reformed orthodoxy. In fact, some congregations retained personal loyalties to their priests who had converted to the Reformed faith and who allowed their parishioners to practice this new faith in less than strictly orthodox ways. This resulted in a surprising degree of syncretism in these congregations.

Still, provincial and national synods could exert a great deal of pressure on local bodies through their deliberations and pronouncements, which were based on biblical interpretations; once those statements were made public, local consistories were eager to identify themselves with the correct interpretation of Scripture in the face of their congregations. Thus, by the 1570s increasing temptation to use organs during worship collided with the *anti-orgelists*'s determination, and they began to demand action from local consistories. When those bodies acted inconsistently or weakly, *anti-orgelists* turned to regional church meetings (a classis), which were made up of ministers and laymen from each consistory, for help. The decisions reached by these regional bodies during the 1570s do not tell the entire story of the organ controversy, which will be discussed more thoroughly in following chapters, but a small number of

---

31. "*Loff te spelen, soe lange de toendagen van der marct duren sullen.*" Vente, *Bouwstoffen*, 52.

synodical decisions during this decade give clarity and specificity to the primary issues in this analysis, such as statements that declared the organ "unseemly" (*onbetamelick*).[32]

Initial Quandaries

One matter the provincial synod had to address immediately was the postlude, an organ voluntary played as people departed the church after the final benediction by the minister. Because this music was technically played beyond the temporal boundaries of the worship service proper, believers could therefore both stay true to Calvin's ideals and enjoy the beauty of the instrument and the skill of the organist at the same time. However, delegates feared that the postlude did nothing but distract the congregation's attention from divine matters and thereby prompted them to forget the teachings of the sermon, which was (and is) of paramount importance in Reformed liturgy. In June 1574, twenty-five representatives from ten congregations in the province of South Holland gathered in Dordrecht. After some deliberation about the organ postlude situation, they published the following declaration:

> Regarding the playing of the organs in the church we are of the opinion that it should be completely discontinued, according to the teachings of Paul in I Cor. 14:19. And although it [the organ] is still used in some of these churches at the end of the service when the people are leaving, it mostly serves to make the people forget what they have just heard, and we need to worry that afterwards it will be used for superstition, just like it now serves for frivolity (*lichtuaerdicheijt*); and if this were to be discontinued, it would be easier to gather in the offerings at the door when the people are leaving rather than to do so in the middle of the service, at which time it greatly disrupts the worship of God.[33]

---

32. *Acta des Sijnodi Prouincialis ghehouden den 15 Iunii a° 1574*, see articles 45 and particularly article 50, Rutgers, *Acta van de Nederlandsche synoden*, 133.

33. "*Aengaende het spelen der Orgelen in de Gemeenten, houd men dat het gantsch behoort afgeset te vvesen, volgens de Leere Pauli I Cor. 14. vers. 19. Ende al hoe vvel men het alsnoch in sommige deser Kercken, alleen in 't eynde der praedicatiën gebruyckt op 't scheyden van den volcke, soo dienet nochtans meest om te vergeten vvatmen te voren gehoort heeft: ende is te besorgen, dat het hiernaer tot superstitie sal gebruyckt vvorden, gelijck het nu tot lichtvaerdigheydt dient; d' vvelck soo 't afgeschaft vvare, men soude de Aelmoessen bequamelijcker aen de deuren in 't uytgaen des volckx, versamelen,*

Incidentally the reference in this decision to First Corinthians is especially noteworthy because it is the same passage that John Calvin himself used to give biblical support for his teachings against instrumental music in the church. In that passage,[34] the apostle Paul insists that whatever is done in worship should contribute to the edification (οἰκοδομήν) of the Body, and whatever is spoken must be intelligible. In verse seven, he refers specifically to music in worship:

> Even in the case of lifeless things that make sounds, such as the flute (αὐλός, tibia) or harp (κιθάρα, cithara), how will anyone know what tune is being played (lit: what is being piped, αὐλούμενον) unless there is a distinction in the notes?

As the next chapters will show in greater detail, this passage would be used by both proponents and opponents of the pipe organ to support their respective positions. In brief, the *anti-orgelists* interpreted Paul's negative reference to the pipe, the αὐλός, as a clear prohibition against instrumental music in general and organ pipes in specific. Clearly, the pipe organ, which was an inanimate instrument—"a lifeless thing" that made sound—could not be used by the New Testament church in worship. But

---

dan datmen sulckx in 't midden der Predicatie, tot groote hindernisse des Dienstes, doen moet." Schoock, *Exercitationes variae*, 538. The Dutch word *predicatie*, usually translated as "sermon," can also refer to the entire worship service, and is so here and elsewhere translated. See Tel, "*Gebruyck of Ongebruyck*," 315n6.

34. "Now, brothers, if I come to you and speak in tongues, what good will I be to you, unless I bring you some revelation or knowledge or prophecy or word of instruction? Even in the case of lifeless things that make sounds, such as the flute or harp, how will anyone know what tune is being played unless there is a distinction in the notes? Again, if the trumpet does not sound a clear call, who will get ready for battle? So it is with you. Unless you speak intelligible words with your tongue, how will anyone know what you are saying? You will just be speaking into the air. Undoubtedly there are all sorts of languages in the world, yet none of them is without meaning. If then I do not grasp the meaning of what someone is saying, I am a foreigner to the speaker, and he is a foreigner to me. So it is with you. Since you are eager to have spiritual gifts, try to excel in gifts that build up the church. For this reason anyone who speaks in a tongue should pray that he may interpret what he says. For if I pray in a tongue, my spirit prays, but my mind is unfruitful. So what shall I do? I will pray with my spirit, but I will also pray with my mind; I will sing with my spirit, but I will also sing with my mind. If you are praising God with your spirit, how can one who finds himself among those who do not understand say "Amen" to your thanksgiving, since he does not know what you are saying? You may be giving thanks well enough, but the other man is not edified. I thank God that I speak in tongues more than all of you. But in the church I would rather speak five intelligible words to instruct others than ten thousand words in a tongue." 1 Cor 14:6–19.

the *orgelists* also used the very same words of Paul to support their contrary position. They argued that organ accompaniment could strengthen congregational song, thereby "making words intelligible," to paraphrase the apostle; in other words, using dignified organ music to support psalmody would actually be consistent with Paul's teaching.

This decision by the 1574 South Holland provincial gathering that attempted to discontinue organ music had consequences that required yet further decisions. Reading between the lines of these minutes, it is easy to conclude that many churches had also allowed organs to play while the offering was collected during the service. However, now that they had prohibited organ music, there would be an awkward silence while the offering was collected that would be filled with the sound of coins clanging and clattering, a noise that would hardly be more worshipful than organ music. The only practical solution now was to receive the offerings at the doors as worshipers departed the sanctuary. The 1574 provincial synod strongly supported that idea, but did not require it:

> 49. Although standing at the doors of the churches to collect the gifts is the most appropriate and suitable, it was decided just the same that the manner of doing this shall remain the option of the churches. However, the ministers should strive as much as possible to avoid the collection during the service.[35]

A month later, meeting in July 1574, a synod composed of forty congregations in the northern part of Holland met in the city of Edam and also debated organ use, putting the onus for implementation upon the civic magistrates who alone had the authority to enforce the organ restrictions:

> [It] is decided that all ministers of the Word of God should diligently and kindly instruct the authorities in this matter (as this does not concern the authority of the ministers, but the power of the [civil] authorities), so that organ playing in the church may be discontinued so that the Word of God may better work its effects in the human heart and abide there.[36]

---

35. 49. "Hoewel het staen voor den deuren der Kercke om de aelmoessen te versamelen het allervoechelixte ende bequaemste is, Soo is nochtans besloten dat de wijse van omme te gaen als noch inde vrijheijt der Kercke staen sal. Doch soo sullen de Dienaers arbeijden, dat sij het ommegaen soo veel mueghelick [moeghelick] is sonder erghernisse afbrenghen." Rutgers, *Acta van de Nederlandsche synoden*, 150.

36. "... is besloten, dat alle die dienaeren des woerts Goids met vlyt ende alle vriendelycheyt die overheyt supplicerende zullen in dese saecke onderrichten (dewyle tselfde

The matters discussed in those meetings of 1574 are illustrative of nationwide issues developing in Reformed worship, as can be seen from decisions taken in a subsequent 1578 national synod that convened in Dordrecht. This 1578 synod, with a large cross-section of delegates, confirmed the Calvinist practice of using only biblical texts for singing in the churches by insisting that "the psalms of David translated by Pieter Datheen shall be sung in the Christian gatherings of the Netherlands churches as has been done until now, excluding the hymns which are not found in the Bible."[37] Further, this body affirmed the disapproval of the use of organs, as the 1574 provincial gathering had done, and insisted on the immediate removal of pipe organs:

> 77. We do not consider the use of the organs in the churches to be appropriate, especially not before the service. And that is why we recommend that the servants [the ministers] should strive as they were tolerated for a while, to have them removed at the earliest and most suitable time.[38]

This decree implies that churches were still allowing preludes or music during the offering or both (both occurred before the sermon) despite the prohibitions of 1574, and they were ordered stopped. This 1578 synod therefore had to repeat the earlier decision about the offering:

> 16. Whether it is better for the Deacons to collect the gifts after the service at the doors, or to go around among the people during the service? The first method is better. However, in those churches where this is not possible, it can be tolerated until the situation can be improved.[39]

---

nyet der dienaeren aucthoriteyt maer der overicheden macht concerneert), ten eynde dat, het orgelspelen in die kercken naegelaten zynde, die dienst des woorts Goids beter zyn effect in die herten der menschen vercryge ende bewaert worde." Reitsma and Veen, *Acta der provinciale en particuliere synoden*, 1:27.

37. "De Psalmen Davids van Petro Datheno overgezet, zullen in de Christelyke t' samenkomsten der Nederduitschen Kerken, gelyk men tot nog toe gedaan heeft, gezongen worden, achter latende de Gezangen die in de Heilige Schrift niet gevonden worden." Hooijer, *Oude kerkordeningen*, 145. Incidentally, Datheen himself was the president of this synod.

38. 77. "Het ghebruyck der orghelen in den kercken houden wij niet voor goet insonderheyt voor de predicatie. Daerom achten wij dat de Dienaren behooren te aerbeyden, ghelyckse voor eenen tyt gheduldet worden, dat se alsoo metten eersten ende op het aldervoeghelijckste wegh genomen worden." Rutgers, *Acta van de Nederlandsche synoden*, 253.

39. 16. "Of 't beter is dat de Diakenen om de Aalmoessen te vergaderen na de

Finally, this synod went even farther and declared that "it shall also be the duty of the ministers to take care that the use of bells (which by the papacy are rung both at the death and the burial of people) shall be done away with."[40]

The Pipe Organ Evolves

One might think that these authoritative judgments would have settled the matter finally, but sources from the next few decades show exactly the opposite. Where pipe organs had been removed or destroyed, they were repaired or replaced, and existing organs were used increasingly frequently. In fact, shortly after these synodical decisions, organ construction began to flourish once again as the Dutch became more prosperous, and descriptions of the pipe organ both as an instrument and as a fixture within the church from the late sixteenth and early seventeenth centuries are not divine at all, but clearly pragmatic. This is because the pipe organ was now no longer functioning solely as a concert instrument, or even as an instrument to support small monastic choirs. Now it was to accompany an entire congregation in song. Thus, the organ's sound, volume, design, and construction had to change drastically for this new task.

The idea of organ builders was that if the instrument was going to be used to support the human voice, then the organ's design should be humanly guided wherever possible. Diameters of organ pipes were scaled to the classic proportions of the human body—its width being one sixth of its height—because, it was thought, by more closely matching the pipe's construction to the classic proportions of the human body, then the organ would be better suited for supporting the human voice.[41] Organ builders even hoped to emulate the human voice with a new solo

---

Predicatie aan de Kerkedeuren staan, of dat zy in de Predicatie omme gaan? Het eerst is beter, doch indien men dat niet kan invoeren, zal men het andere laten, tot dat men het bekwamelyk veranderen kan." Hooijer, *Oude kerkordeningen*, 161.

40. "Het zal ook der Dienaren Ampt zyn, zorge te dragen dat het gebruik der Klokken (dewelke in 't Pausdom, zoo in 't verscheiden, als in het begraven der menschen, geluyd worden) mag weggenomen worden." Hooijer, *Oude kerkordeningen*, 153.

41. The organ's pipes and machinations were given decidedly anthropomorphic terms: for example, the parts of the organ pipe are to this day referred to as the toe, the foot, the mouth, the lips, the ears, the beard, the waist, and organ pipes "sit" on a "chest."

stop, the *vox humana* (human voice).[42] Stories are told of competitions where blindfolded judges heard a solo line of music played on the *vox humana* and an actual human who sang the same line of music. The judge was then asked to discern which was which. Many times the judges were fooled; in one case, a desperate organ builder eager for fame placed a singer inside the organ case, but her performance was too real, and the organ builder was exposed as a fraud.[43]

The organ was made visually and audibly more conspicuous as well. A principal chorus complete with pitches from sixteen feet through the upper work mixtures and solo stops such as the trumpet and the cornet[44] were often placed in a new organ division called the *Rugpositief* (literally "organ at the back") since this division of the organ hung on the balcony rail, against the organist's back, so that the solo pipes were lower than the others and closer to the singing congregation. These new solo stops could trumpet the melody, literally, into the ears of the singers. Organ builders invented the *vogelgesang*[45] organ stop, which mimicked the sound of singing birds, and they brought back the sound of bells into the sanctuary by adding the *zymbelstern*[46] to some organs.

Even more surprisingly, *orgelists* began to see their pipe organs as allegories of the church, the body of Christ, itself. Rows of pipes standing in ranks that praised God with their voices were likened to the rows of church pews filled with worshipers, as Jacobius Revius penned in 1625:

> The organ is properly used for psalms and prayer
> Oh bliss whose throat opens the glory of the Lord!

---

42. To achieve this effect, the pipes were thinly scaled, nasal-sounding reeds. The use of the *tremblant* (a device that wavered the wind supply in such a way to produce a tremulous sound) heightened the simulation.

43. Bolt, "Character and Function."

44. A combination of five ranks at the 8', 4' 2 2/3', 2' and 1 3/5' pitches that, when combined, form a beautiful nasal sound rich in harmonic overtones.

45. This voice was made by three or four pipes that were inverted into a pan of water. When the pressure forced air up through the pipes, it simultaneously made the water gurgle, and the result simulated a warbling bird whistle.

46. The "cymbal stars" are actually complex sculptures that make sound. A paddle wheel is set in motion by air jets when the organist pulls a stop on the console. The paddles move a metal beater, which is surrounded by a set of bells hanging from an outer frame. When the paddles move the beater, the arms of the beater strike the bells, making a charming sound. The whole machinery twirls a glittering decorative star; when the air jets blow the paddles, this air current also spins the star around in circles on an axle.

> But yet the organ plays its song unwittingly,
> And many sing and thank, and the heart does not feel.
> Listen friends, it is only wind, a wind that stays but briefly;
> This keeps us in our life, and that power the organ:
> Just close a pipe, it gives no further sound[47]

One minister from the northeastern region of the Netherlands even allegorized the names of the various organ stops: the Principal (*Praestant*) stop was the Holy Spirit, and the Großgedackt stop supposedly referred to God's covering (*decken*) of our gross (*groß*) sins.[48]

Dutch worshipers also began to view the organ as a work of art to be appreciated. Nothing could be less Calvinistic, to be sure, but the designs and installations of organs from this time period are irrefutable proof of the change in Reformed thinking about the organ. Figurines of angels, reminiscent of the angels who announced the birth of the Christ Child, were painted on some organ cases, while others depicted important characters from the Bible. Less lofty but perhaps more visually impressive were mechanical statues whose arms moved to beat a drum or lift a trumpet to wooden lips. Over time weather vanes, clocks, heraldic imagery, civic mottos, and even sculpted animals and figurines were placed on the organ cases. The least ecclesiastical decoration from this time period is probably the organ at Edam, whose three façade towers were each topped with obelisks sculpted as mounds of cheese, the town's signature export. Some organ builders added an extraordinarily pedestrian invention for the convenience of the organist: a hidden "drink drawer" where a bottle of spirits could be secretly stashed for discreet use as needed.[49]

The debate effectively ended about two generations after the strongly worded decisions of the 1570s: in 1638 the question of whether, when, and how to use the pipe organ in Reformed worship matter was declared *adiaphora* (not a matter of doctrinal orthodoxy) and was left to the choice of each local consistory. In fact, In January of 1638 the Delft Church Council first asked the Burgomaster (Mayor):

47. "Tot psalmen en gebee'n wort 't orgel recht gebruycket, O Salich welcker keel des Heeren roem ontluycket! Maar ach het orgel speelt onwetende sijn liet, En menich singt en danckt, en 't hert en voeltet niet. Hoort vrienden, 't is maer wint, een wint die weinich blijvet, Dit ons bij't leven hout, en die de orgel drijvet: Dout eens een pijpken toe, ten slaet niet meer geluyt." Revius and Smit, *Over-ysselsche sangen en dichten*, 66.

48. Luth, "Orgel," 32–38.

49. It is unclear whether the spirits were used to brace the organist against the cold, damp Dutch weather in these unheated churches or to dull their musical senses against the horrible unaccompanied congregational singing that resulted from the organ ban.

... whether he would not consider it edifying and proper to reinstate the use of the organs and to use them during the singing of the psalms?[50]

The Burgomaster did deem it "edifying and proper" and wrote:

> In the year 1638, on 25 January, being the day of the conversion of Paul, they have started in the city of Dordrecht to play the organ during the singing of the psalms, before and after the sermon. In the Groote Kerk they played in the morning, during the singing, and in the afternoon in the church of St. Augustine, and as well during the entire week during the evening service.[51]

With civic approval in hand, and with precedent set in Dordrecht, the council then brought their request to their regional meeting. Here the Provincial Synod of South Holland, which met in Delft on August 2–14, 1638, decided that playing the organ to support the congregational singing of psalms was "a matter of medium importance [best left] to the decision of the churches." Further, they declared that "those that use this organ playing can best judge whether it happens in an edifying way in their churches or not."[52] On July 26, 1638 the Classis of The Hague discussed the same question and agreed with the delegates of Delft:

> It is determined that the playing of the organ is a matter of medium importance (*middelmaetijge zaecke*) and is therefore left to the freedom of each church for the purpose of edifying (*stichtinge*) [the congregation].[53]

These decisions implied that there was no longer any official objection to the sound of organ pipes in Calvinist worship within their classis.

---

50. "... *of hij niet stichtelijck en oorbaerlyk en soude achten het gebruik der orgelen wederom te herstellen en onder het zingen der Psalmen dezelve te gebruiken?*" Schotel, *Openbare eerdenienst der Nederl*, 69.

51. "*Int jaer 1638, op den 25 jan. zyjnde Pauli Bekeeringe, heeft men begonnen, binnen Dordrecht, op den orgel te spelen, onder het singen der psalmen vóór en na de predikatie. In de Groote Kerk speelde men sondachs smorgens, onder het zingen, en na den middag in de Augustyne, en voorts de gantsche week in d'avondpredikatie.*" Schotel, *Openbare eerdenienst der Nederl*, 69–70.

52. "... *dat de classis dese zaecke als middelmatich zijnde dern kercken bevolen laet, welcke did orgelspelen gebruijcke, als best connende oordelen off het met stichtinghe in haere kercken gebryckt wert ofte niet.*" Knuttel, *Acta der particuliere synoden*, 175.

53. "... *is geoordeelt, dat hetselve is een middelmaetijghe zaecke; en wert daeromme gelaeten in de vrijheyt van yedere kercke, omme to doen tot stichtinge.*" K. A. 48 fol. 629.

Thus it is undeniable that a little more than a century after the ascendance of Protestantism in Dutch public life, the path was now clear for the use of pipe organs in Reformed worship. By the eighteenth century, in fact, organ music was expected in all Dutch Reformed churches. English eyewitness John Evelyn was struck by the contrast between the Dutch Reformed and the Protestants of his country. He stated the case well:

> Generaly, there are in all the Churches in Holland Organs, Lamps, Monuments &c: carefully preserved from the fury, and impiety of popular reformers, whose zeale has foolishly transported them in other places rather to act like madmen, then religious.[54]

Evelyn confirms the fact that pipe organs were used without fail in almost every region of the Netherlands by the end of the eighteenth century.[55]

It is a minister and musician, Joshua van Iperen (1726–1780), minister at Lillo and later in the Dutch East Indies, that might be credited with the end of the controversy. In 1773 he was asked to help curate a new Psalter, the *Statenberijming* (Authorized Versification). This psalter included four-part notation for the congregation; that is, not just a melody line as had been the case in previous psalters. This "new manner" of singing was a bit more complex for the congregation, and so the use of the organ helped introduce the newly notated tunes, even as the organ was then fully reintroduced into all parts of the worship service. The organ was no longer undesirable, idolatrous, nor Roman Catholic, but a "necessary appliance." Van Iperen explains:

> The introduction of the improved versification led, here and there, to the installation or improvement of the organs in the church buildings. At Bemmel, in classis Nymegen, the nobles and upper classes, which graced that pleasant village with their presence during the summer, and many others had contributed their gifts to that end: and the organ was consecrated there on the fifteenth of October 1775, and its sound was blended during the singing of the psalms with that of many other musical instruments. At Zierikzee, at Hoorn, at Nymegen, and elsewhere, many expensive organs were installed: and in other congregations, even in Zeeland, people greatly lamented the judgment of

---

54. Evelyn, *Diary of John Evelyn*, 49.
55. For an exhaustive list with documentation, see Kist, "Kerkelijke orgel–gebruik bijzonder in Nederland," 283–94, 297; Vente, *Proeve*.

our forefathers who, because of incorrect prejudice, or because of fear of maintaining an organist, had omitted to provide their House of God with such necessary appliances.[56]

Rutgers[57] explains thoroughly this "new manner of singing" introduced by the 1773 *Statenberijming*. First, the *Statenberijming* set the first and last note of every phrase as a whole note, but within the phrase the notes were made rhythmic. This became to be known as the *korte zingtrant* (short singing style) because it took less time to sing a Psalm that it had before.[58] Second, as noted previously, while the original Genevan book showed only the melody for unison congregational singing, the *Statenberijming* provided notes for all four voices, which encouraged rich congregational harmony. These changes in the 1773 Psalter definitely depended on instrumental accompaniment both to introduce the rhythmic and harmonic changes and to sustain them. Indeed, multiple accounts confirm that organ support became normative in Reformed churches after the introduction of the *korte zingtrant*.[59] In some regions,

---

56. "Ook gaf de Invoeringe van het verbeterd Psalmrym, hier en daar, aanleidinge tot het maaken of verbeteren der Orgels in de Kerkgebouwen. Te Bemmel, onder de Classis van Nymegen, hadden de Edelen en Aanzientlyken, welke dat aangenaam dorp, des zomers, met hunne tegenwoordigheid vereren, en ettelyke anderen daar toe liefdegaven verstrekt: en het Orgel werd 'er ingewyd, op den vyftienden van Oogstmaand 1775, gaande deszelfs deklank vereenigd, onder het Psalmzingen, met andere Musyktuigen. Te Zierikzee, te Hoorn, te Nymegen en elders heeft men zeer kostbare Orgels doen toestellen: en by andere gemeinten, zelfs in Zeeland, beklaagt men zich thans zeer, over de denkenswyze onze voorouders, die, door een verkeerd vooroordeel, of uit vreeze voor het onderhouden van eenen Organist, verzuimd hebben, hunne Godshuizen, van zulken noodig huisraad, te voorzien." Iperen, *Kerkelijke historie van het psalmt-gezang der christenen*, 443.

57. Rutgers and de Jong, *Verklaring van de kerkenordening*.

58. According to the 1773 Psalter committee the proper way of singing in "the short style" was to hold only the first note of line, but successive notes could be sung quickly ("short"), the last note was to be held long again. This was different from the old way of singing, which was *isometric*: all notes were sung equally long and without a rest between them. Iperen offered this advice to sing these new Psalms well: "1. Stretch the notes; 2. Turn them in the mouth; 3. Chew; 4. Through numerous raisings and elevations between the teeth and in the palate move it back and forth like a snake; 5. Make them whirl." "(1. De noten uitrekken; 2. in den mond draaien; 3. kauwen; 4. door ettelijke verhogingen en de verheffingen tussen de tanden en 't gehemelte slangswijze henen slingeren; 5. ze doen dwarrelen)." The committee also made the picturesque comment that the old manner of singing led to a very dragging and slow singing, which (in Zeeland) was compared to the waves and murmuring of the sea. Iperen, *Kerkelijke historie*, 442–43.

59. Ypeij and Dermout, *Geschiedenis der Nederlandsche Hervormde Kerk*, 84; Luth,

the government even instituted mandatory rehearsals in the evenings so that congregants could practice this "new manner of singing"; those who did not attend were fined.[60]

Any final vestiges of any organ prohibitions were swept away in 1817 when a national synod addressed the problem of declining worship attendance. As a remedy, this synod published a pamphlet that ordered churches that were not already doing so to begin using the organ on a regular basis by 1818. Leaders recommended excellent congregational singing supported by regular organ accompaniment as a way to attract new members:

> The Synod desires that in those churches where there are organs, the organ always accompany the singing, and the custom, which exists here and there, and because of which during some worship services the organ is silenced or [where] such [silencing] is permitted, [this custom of silencing the organs] will be discontinued immediately. [The synod] further desires and requests the preachers, that in their public and private teaching, the listeners and pupils are always to note the importance of this part of the worship service; and to encourage them to practice this; warning them against all shrill and undisciplined shouting; to have the congregation stand occasionally to sing a song; [and] to introduce at solemn occasions antiphonal singing, for example, men and women, and [then] by everyone together; and even where this can be done on the High Feast days of Christianity, to dedicate an occasional service almost entirely to Song and Music.[61]

"Psalmzingen in het Nederlandse," 195; Bernet Kempers, "Meerstemming psalmgezang," 176. Even then, there was a new revolt not against organ music, but against the newly introduced rhythms of the psalm tunes. Ypeij retells a situation that occurred in Maassluis in 1776 when public worship was disrupted by congregants who screamed out loud against the new manner of singing and "raved, ranted and cursed the government, ministers and consistory" before they threatened to murder them. They were summarily thrown into jail. Ypeij and Dermout, *Geschiedenis der Nederlandsche Hervormde Kerk*, 84–85.

60. Iperen, *Kerkelijke historie van het psalmt-gezang der christenen*, 450.

61. "*Met opzigt tot het Godsdienstig gezang wenscht het Synode, dat in Kerken waar Orgels zijn, het Orgel het gezang steeds vergezelle, en het gebruik, hier of daar bestaande, en waardoor bij sommige Godsdienstoefeningen aan het orgel het zwijgen is opgelegd of vergund wordt, dadelijk worde opgeheven. Het wil, daarenboven, de Leeraars hebben uitgenoodigd, om, bij hun openbaar en bijzonder onderwijs, hunne toehoorders en leerlingen, telkens het gewicht van dit deel van den gemeenschappelijken Godsdienst te doen opmerken; om hen tot oefening in hetzelve aan te sporen; om hen te waarschouwen tegen*

This chapter has challenged earlier historical interpretations that the Dutch Republic was religiously homogeneous; historiography shows that the country had a more complex religious composition than popularly assumed. This chapter has also shown that the pipe organ was an important feature of Dutch cultural and musical life for centuries before the Reformation and war with Spain. Despite the destructive iconoclastic riots of 1566, the stern suppression of open Catholic worship, and the conversion of existing churches to Reformed usage, the pipe organs often survived intact or were even reconstructed. Despite the privilege given to the Reformed church and its signature aural iconoclasm that it inherited from its theological father, political realities and religious pluralism meant that doctrinal priorities seldom produced the political action necessary to remove, destroy, or even permanently silence Dutch pipe organs as they were ultimately under civic control. Finally, from a purely pragmatic viewpoint, organ music was needed to help congregations, which were often made up of poorly educated folk with limited musical skills, to sing the tunes and read the poetry of the Dutch version of the *Genevan Psalter*. Thus at this time a linear development of church dicta to ward off the evils of organ sound during worship did not develop, nor did a unilateral counter-movement to use the organ affirmatively.

By the turn of the eighteenth century, proscriptions on organ use during worship were all but ignored in the Low Countries, and almost all Dutch Reformed churches were using the organ to assist their singing, which inspired a "Golden Age" of organ construction not seen since the baroque age. This new adaptation in the design and construction of organ brought about by the organ's need now to accompany a singing congregation. A new 1773 Psalter set the Genevan tunes to four-part harmony, and such an innovation all but required organ accompaniment.

Some Reformed communities, as was illustrated earlier, heeded synodical calls to silence the pipe organ during the worship service for a very long time, but in most Dutch territories magistrates and ministers compromised or ignored the bans of 1574 and 1578 for a host of different reasons and at different tempi. Recent interdisciplinary urban studies (*Städteforschung*) have studied the complex make-up of Dutch

---

alle hard en ongeregeld geschreeuw; om nu en dan de Gemeente een vers staande te doen zingen; om, bij plegtige gelegenheden, beurtzangen, bij voorb. van mannen en vrouwen, en van alle te zamen, in te voeren; en om zelfs, waar dit geschieden kan, op de Hooge Feesten der Christenheid, eene enkele Godsdienst-oefening, bijna geheel, aan Zang- en Toonkunst toe te wijden." Besluiten van het algemeen, 3–4.

cities during the sixteenth and seventeenth centuries. The complexities revealed by these studies—the differences from region to region, from city to city, even the differences between social strata within the same city—account in large part for the wide variations within the Netherlands to the organ proscriptions of the 1570s. Having given a general picture of the organ controversy on a national scale in this chapter, these widely varying local stories will be the subject of the next.

3

REGIONAL MODELS OF REFORM

Theme and Variations

The previous chapter explained how political authority in the Netherlands devolved onto cities and towns after the revolt against Spain. Thus, it is hardly surprising that organ use varied widely within even such a small country as the independent Republic of the Netherlands. This chapter will show that not a few Reformed churches ignored the organ ban by singing their psalms with organ accompaniment during worship, and nearly all congregations with organs used the instrument to provide voluntaries before and after worship. Elsewhere, ardent *anti-orgelists* tried to enforce organ proscriptions wherever they had power to do so using the rule of the secular government or the authority of Church Order. However, almost all Dutch churches lay somewhere in between these two extremes. Local history, the religious pluriformity of city councils, and the comity between civic and ecclesiastical governments influenced each locality's use of the organ. The clarion call against organ use by orthodox Calvinists fell on deaf ears.

Recent research from the field of urban studies (*Städteforschung*) confirms how different the people in one Dutch province were from those in another at the time of the Reformation. As a result of these local differences, each province, indeed each city and town, responded to the ascendance of the Protestant Reformation at different speeds and with differing degrees of favor and fervor. The conclusions support the fact that the Dutch organ controversy was played out primarily on the stage of local city halls rather than the floors of Reformed synods or around consistory tables. This local autonomy allowed Dutch civic authorities to ignore the national synods of 1574 and 1578 ban on organ music (described in the previous chapter), and especially the 1578 synod's demand to remove organs from Reformed churches as soon as possible. As J. W. Smit remarked:

> ... because every province, even every town, to a large extent constituted an autonomous system, each with its peculiar socio-economic and political structure, revolution or internal war can be studied and explained only in local terms.[1]

This chapter details the situation further by showing that the same is true for the use of organ music among the Dutch Reformed. When orthodox *anti-orgelists* tried to enact these synodical directives in their respective locales, they encountered differing political configurations of power that were complicated by military, national, and even feudal interests that had been shaped by each city's history.[2] As a result, the country had a liturgical "map" during the sixteenth century that was just as jumbled as the theological landscape.

Friesland

Perhaps the most musically liberal and yet most socially conservative province in the Netherlands at this time was Friesland, where a rich organ culture existed before the revolt.[3] The Frisians' reputation for being stubbornly autonomous may be the strongest explanation why organ use continued after the revolt despite the dicta produced by Dutchmen in southerly provinces. Recently Wiebe Bergsma has examined this culturally and linguistically unique province, and he argues convincingly that Friesland's political and social structures led to uncommon homogeneity

---

1. Smit, "Netherlands Revolution," 149.

2. An excellent overview of this historiography of Protestantization can be found in Elliott, "Protestantization in the Netherlands," and Smit, "Present," 11–28.

3. Hess, *Dispositien der merkwaardigste Kerk-Orgelen*; Hess and Enschedé, *Dispositiën van Kerk-Orgelen welke in Nederland worden aangetroffen*; Knock, *Dispositien der merkwaardigste kerk-orgelen*; Komter-Kuipers, *Muzyk yn Fryslân oant 1800*. Generalities, obviously, can be overstated. For example, though the church of Winsum had an organ, it did not accompany psalmody until 1875. Oosterhof and Penning, *Orgelbouwkundige bijdragen*, 199.

and stability compared to other Dutch provinces.[4] For instance, suffrage was granted only to those Frisians who owned the province's ten thousand or so farms, and this right could not be bought or earned but only inherited. According to Bergsma, this electoral practice granted much greater influence to rural areas of the province than was given to city dwellers. It also ossified Frisian politics because those who had the right to vote had no interest in swift or broad social changes. Also, each Frisian locality managed its own affairs quite independently of its neighbors, a behavior that continued after the arrival of the Protestant Reformation, as Bergsma describes:

> The circumstances differed between the cities and villages, the appointment of ministers happened in varying tempo, the establishment of the classis meetings did not happen equally quickly everywhere, the number of members differed from place to place, as did the nature of the competition from other denominations.[5]

Although Protestantism did color Frisian society, Bergsma estimates that about 25 percent of Frisians remained religiously neutral during the mid-seventeenth century, identifying as neither Calvinist nor Catholic. That is to say, while the Frisian Protestant churches were theologically and politically Reformed, the prevailing culture was not purely Calvinist, Zwinglian, Lutheran, nor Catholic. It was distinctly Frisian.

This independent spirit of the Frisians as well as their love for their church organs is eminently clear during the iconoclastic riots of 1566. When a certain Asinge van Ripperda and his brothers decided to participate in the "purification" of their local Reformed church in the Frisian village of Winsum, they indiscriminately smashed Catholic images and removed other popish pollutions alongside the rest of their neighbors. The delightful Frisian streak of this rampage, however, is that the men were urged on in their plunder by Mevrouw van Ripperda, the wife and mother of these men, who played popular "beggars's songs" on the church organ itself![6] Apparently, these plundering Frisians did not view

---

4. Bergsma, *Tussen Gideonsbende en publieke kerk*.

5. "De omstandigheden verschilden tussen de steden en de dorpen, de benoemingen van predikanten gebeurden in wisselend tempo, de realisatie van de classicale vergaderingen ging niet overall even snel, het aantal lidmaten verschilde van plaats tot plaats, evenals de aard van de concurrentie van andere denominaties." Bergsma, *Tussen Gideonsbende en publieke kerk*, 240.

6. Kleijntjens, "Beeldenstorm in Groningen en in 'de Ommelanden," 181.

the organ as a Catholic appurtenance but as an element with some kind of inherent value to be preserved. In fact, many new church organs were built for Frisian churches during this time. Jan Luth, a preeminent scholar on the history of Psalm singing within the Dutch Reformed Church, argues that these new organs would not have been built only for concert use, but were surely commissioned for liturgical use as well.[7]

No evidence appears of vociferous opposition to the organ in Friesland. On the contrary, the *Rekeningenboek* of the province's capital, Leeuwarden, recorded in 1580–1581 that Ritscke Janssen paid Petrus Christianij for playing the organ in the Grote (Jacobijnen) Kerk.[8] Another *Rekeningenboek* entry records expenditures in 1580 to repair the organ of the Grote Kerk of Leeuwarden, a directive completely at odds with the order of the 1578 national synod that such instruments be removed. The city even hired Peter Joachim Brandenbourgh to be organist and *voorzanger* of the Grote Kerk; further, as Mr. Brandenbourgh was blind, the city hired Gerardo Lambertz to serve as his assistant.[9] After Brandenbourgh's tenure, Matthias Mercke became organist in 1597 so that the church was not without organ use before, during, or after the revolt.[10]

In another Frisian city, Sneek, the city government hired (as one might expect) the local school teachers, including the rector of the school, but they also hired the minister, the *voorzanger*, and even a calcant, a person to pump the bellows for the organ.[11] The existence of a calcant along with many documents from the church shows that the organ in the Martini Church of Sneek could be heard at worship before, during, and after the revolt.

Pipe organs were not just permitted in larger Frisian cities like Leeuwarden and Sneek; Frisian villages also used their organs after the defeat of Spanish forces. In Stiens, for instance, Lambertus Sipkes was appointed organist in 1555, and his successor Jacobus Adama was appointed on March 23, 1567. Adama's tenure continued unchallenged even after

---

7. Luth, "Music of the Dutch Reformed Church," 35.

8. "*Betaelt Ritscke Janssen cedulscriver ses carolus gls van twintick stuivers t stuk ter cause dat hij Petro Christianij betaalt had de uijt zaecke van het spelen op het orgel in de Reformeerden kerck gedaen nacomende ordinantie.*" Oosterhof and Penning, *Orgelbouwkundige bijdragen*, 4:160.

9. Oosterhof and Penning, *Orgelbouwkundige bijdragen*, 4:161–62.

10. Oosterhof and Penning, *Orgelbouwkundige bijdragen*, 4:217.

11. Bergsma, *Tussen Gideonsbende en publieke kerk*, 239–40.

Stiens's first Reformed minister, Regenerus Falco, arrived in 1580.[12] In the village of Burgwerd, church officials commissioned a new organ even as they tore down Catholic altars and swabbed whitewash over the colorful church murals. Similarly in Gouw, Catholic shrines (*schrijne*) were sold off in order to finance organ repairs.[13] Maarten Vente, a scholar of Dutch organ building practice, makes a very good point that these smaller towns would not have appointed organists nor installed such expensive instruments only for concertizing.[14]

Widespread use of the organ in Friesland during this period is also confirmed by contemporary church records. Documents from the church in Catrinabandt, for example, a small village in the county of Engwierum, suggest that the faithful there found organ accompaniment desirable and so they commissioned an instrument "following the example of several churches and communities in this province" that the "Lord God Almighty can be praised with more devotion and worship" and properly thanked for "His uncounted blessings already received and still being received daily."[15] The pro-organ reputation of Friesland was known still further away in Arnhem, of the province of Gelderland; after the riots of 1566, the ministers inquired of the synod of Harlingen whether they should have the organ played during the singing of the psalms, *as was done in Friesland*.[16]

Indeed, the Frisian classis of Leeuwarden formally and boldly declared on March 31, 1580 that organ music would be permitted in Reformed worship. Their conspicuous pronouncement would surely have drawn the ire of any organ opponent:

---

12. Romein, *Naamlijst der predikanten*, 69–70.
13. Vente, *Bouwstoffen*, 52.
14. Vente, *Bouwstoffen*, 52.
15. "... datter nae het exempell van verscheijden Kercken ende Gemeenten deser Provincie wierd gesticht in den Dorpe Catrinabandt een orgell omme also met meerder devotie ende Godsdiensticheijt Gode almachtich te komen loven prijzen ende dancken voor soe velle ontelbare weldaeden alreeds aen ons gedaen ende daegelijcks noch bewesen wordt." Oosterhof and Penning, *Orgelbouwkundige bijdragen*, 3:94.
16. *Off men na de gewoonte van die van Vrieslandt onder 't zingen van de psalmen, niet mede het orgel zoude doen spelen*, as cited by Luth, "Daer wert...," 6; Oldenhof, *In en om de schuilkerkjes van Noordelijk Westergo*, 72. Emphasis mine.

About the organs: Playing organ during the singing before and after the service is understood to be allowed, as long as there is nothing unedifying [*onstichting*] to fear.[17]

Emden

No discussion of organ use in Friesland would be complete without examining the situation in the German city of Emden, which was a refuge for expatriate Protestants from all over Europe, especially Calvinists from the northern Dutch territories during Spanish rule. It is estimated that two to three thousand Dutchmen lived in Emden in 1564, and this number increased to five thousand between by 1579.[18] These refugees would have heard an organ used during worship in Emden as organ use there was never banned outright.

This is not to suggest that all worshipers of Emden were pleased with the organ's liturgical use. In fact, several persons were outraged by the organ. For instance, the "Council Minutes of Emden 31 December 1565" noted that

> Johann Kuell declared his innocence against the congregational complaint that he made pompous, unnecessary expenditures for the baptismal font, the pulpit and the organ, while there were more necessary things to spend money on."[19]

Later, in 1579, the Emden minister Jean Polyander fumed: "I really marvel that, when other idols were removed, this noisy idol [i.e., the organ] was retained."[20] Other ministers joined Polyander in 1593 as they drafted a "Counterargument by the orthodox ministers"[21] and they reported there that a group of refugees living in Emden exhibited a "strange zeal

---

17. "*Van de Orgelen: Het orgelspelen onder 't singen voor en na de Predikatie wort verstaan geoorlooft te zijn, als 'er geen ontstichting te vreesen is.*" Oosterhof and Penning, *Orgelbouwkundige bijdragen*, 4:143.

18. Schilling, *Niederlandische Exilanten im 16. Jahrhundern*, 66; Nauta et al., *De Synode van Emden*, 7–21; Smid, *Ostfriesische Kirchengeschichte*, 193–96.

19. "*Ock heft Johann Kuell bysunderinge syn unschuilt gedhan tegen der gemene klachte, de pompoese unnoedige unkosten in der doepstheen, predickstoel unde oergell kostlicken uutthoputzende, dar dar woll voele noediger kosten tho doende wheren....*" *Kirchenratsprotokolle der reformierten Gemeinde Emden*, 1:224. I thank Mr. Jouke Sjaardema for his help with this particular English translation.

20. Pettegree, *Emden and the Dutch Revolt*, 179.

21. Ligarius, *Warhafftiger Gegenbericht*.

against organs."[22] When the neighboring town of Bardowick constructed an instrument, the minister Christophorus Friccius (= Christoph Frick, 1577–1640) offered a dedicatory prayer in which he prayed to God that their new instrument would be protected from Calvinists,[23] suggesting that at least some Calvinists in the vicinity had established themselves as zealous *anti-orgelists*.

Yet despite these protestations against organ use, the "Church Regulations of Emden of 1594" condoned organ music, and even went so far as to suggest exact repertoire appropriate for the organist—psalm tunes, the melody used for the Ten Commandments, and, astonishingly, Christmas carols. After the turn of the sixteenth century, a 1617 document that was intended to address the unruly behavior of local miscreant youth who used the church building for recreation, indirectly confirms that the organ continued to be used in Emden:

> As there are complaints about the great unorderliness and fooling around that is carried on by the youth in the Great Church before and on Christmas day, so it is decided that the custodian will lock the church on Saturdays and that the organist will stop his playing on those days.[24]

Groningen

This analysis of the liturgical life in Emden is a crucial focus because of the independent worship style that developed here at the mouth of the River Ems, and because of Emden's proximity to other Dutch provinces such as Groningen and East Friesland.[25] After Groningen was liberated

---

22. "*Dass sie einen sonderlichen Eifer gegen Orgeln, Altäre, Chorröcke etc. zeigten. Aber von einer wüsten Orgelstürmerei, wie sie auswärts vorgekommen, hören wir hier nichts.*" "'They showed a strange zeal against organ, altars, choir robes, etc. But we do not hear anything about a wild 'organ storm,' as happened in other countries." Ligarius, *Warhafftiger Gegenbericht*, 29.

23. For the complete prayer with an English translation, see *Sound Theology: A Reader*.

24. "*Dewile geklaget worden wegen der groten unordnung und raserey, so van der jöget gedreven wert in der Groten Kercken vor und up christdach, so iss beslaten dat de koster de kercke am saterdage sall thoholden und de organist dat spelent up der orgel am sulvigen dage sall instellen.*" *Kirchenratsprotokolle*, 2:1110; Booma and Gouw, *Communio et mater Fidelium*, 478.

25. See Brucherus, *Geschiedenis van de opkomst der kerkhervorming in de provincie*; Pont, *Geschiedenis van het lutheranisme in de Nederlanden*; Lorgion, *Geschiedenis*

from the Spanish, many Groningers returned from Emden, bringing to their Dutch city worship practices experienced in Emden. When the first Reformed service was held in Groningen on July 24, 1594 in the Martini Church, led by the Emden pastor Menso Altinga, the organ was used. In fact, the organ was apparently overused because article 28 of the 1595 Church Order for the Ommelanden of Groningen tried to limit excessive pre-worship organ music:

> On Sundays, before the nine o'clock service while the people are assembling, an elder shall read one or two chapters from the Bible in place of playing the organ pipes.[26]

Despite this directive, the organ pipes continued to play. A second decree followed a year later:

> While the servants [i.e., the elected leadership of the classis] have come to understand that it is not yet possible to remove the organ pipes, nor to install the diaconate or presbytery in every village, [it] is resolved in the mentioned synod that everyone must do his best to bring it to pass, and since it is still not possible to establish such [a presbytery and diaconate] in every village, they should set up as soon as possible a presbytery and diaconate in two, three, four or five villages until the good Lord grants more grace, and that they may also sponsor Communion in the united villages each in turn.[27]

---

van de kerkhervorming in Friesland.

26. "*Op den Sondagen, voor de negen ures predige sall een Olderling in stede des orgell pijpens, een ofte twee Capittelen wt den Bybel lesen, bett dat dat volc al tho samen komt.*" *Christlicke und Schriftmetige Kercken Ordenung* (Franeker: Gillis van den Rade, 1595), art. 28. Far to the south over a decade later, a similar suggestion was made in Amsterdam. On January 15, 1609, a consistory member stated that "many of the congregation would like to see that the playing of the organ before the service be banned from the local churches and that instead a few chapters from the Word of God be read." "*Veelen van de Gemeente geerne sien souden dat het orgelspel voor de predicatie uitter kercken alhier soude moghen geweert worden ende in plaetse van dien eenige capittelen uit Gods word mochte gelesen worden.*" *Archief Nederlands Hervormde Gemeente te Amsterdame; Kerkenraad, 1578–1899,* 3:202.

27. "*Dewile die dieneren tho erkennen gegeven hebben, dat noch nit mögelich ijs de orgelpipen aff tho schaffen, offte die diaconatum und praesbiteratum ijn allen dörpen ahn tho stellen, is ijn gemeltem synodo resolvirt, dat ein jeder sin utherste beste dohn sall, dat ijdt geschehn möge, ende so ijdt ijmmer nith mögelick ijs in ein jeder dörp solches tho vorrichten, dat se dan ijn twe, dree, 4 oder viff dorpern einen diaconatum ende praesbiteratum, sobalde ijdt geschehn kan, ahnstellen willen, beth solange de gudige Godt bether gnade vörlehnet, ende dat se ock dat avendtmael ijn den vöreenigeden dörpen per vices holden mögen.*" Reitsma and Veen, *Acta der provinciale en particuliere synoden,*

This decision is striking enough because some churches of the classis appear unable or unwilling to follow orders to remove their organs, but even more noteworthy is the ecclesiastical priority established in this directive: first remove the organs, then install a ruling church council in each locality. These examples demonstrate how strongly *orgelist* the Reformed churches in the north of the country were, reflecting *orgelist* practice of sister churches in the northwest of Germany in cities such as Emden, despite the antagonism provoked by a minority of Calvinist clergymen and laymen.

North Holland

Evidence from North Holland shows that several congregations in that province likewise ignored the national synodical organ bans, although their *orgelist* action caused some discord. As a result, a provincial classis met on June 2, 1586 to address an ancillary problem associated with organ use. From the minutes of this meeting one can infer that organs were used, but its use led to a new problem of appropriate repertoire for the Reformed service of worship. While civic organists had been allowed to play before and after worship as "entertainment," this classis now judged that the time before and after worship on Sundays was not an acceptable context for offering secular music:

> Art. 19.1. Concerning the playing of frisky [*lichtvaerdige*] and worldly songs on the bells and organ, it is unanimously decided that every church in which this is done will insist to its authorities that such be improved.[28]

Once this issue was settled, the organ was supposed to provide only "sacred" melodies. But the issue apparently continued for quite some time: when the Monnikendam organist Dirck Jansz. Velsen requested a raise in salary in 1642, city officials would only do so if he promised to cease playing "papist" and "lighthearted ditties" on the organ and bells.[29] Yet organ use as such is not contested on the church record.

7:6.

28. "*Art. 19.1. Belangende het spelen van lichtvaerdige ende weereltlycke gesangen op klocken ende orgelen is eendrachtelycken besloten, date een yeder kercke, die daervan gebruyck heeft, zal aenhouden by haer overheyt, dat zulcx gebetert werde.*" Reitsma and Veen, *Acta der provinciale en particuliere synoden*, 1:136.

29. ". . . . *mits dat d'heeren Burgermrn. hem vermanen sullen geen papiste ofte*

Overijssel

Compared to these northern cities, the church organ was accepted more slowly amongst Calvinist congregations in the city of Kampen, which is in the province of Overijssel.[30] Like most Dutch cities, Kampen inherited a rich organ culture from the time before the Reformation.[31] Both the Bovenkerk (St. Nicolaas Church) and the Buitenkerk (Onze Lieve Vrouwe Kerk) had pipe organs that were played by Catholic priests prior to the revolt.[32] In 1524 the Bovenkerk commissioned a new organ specifically to accompany the "Sunday service of praise"[33] and other weekday services.[34] Before the revolt, three-year appointments of these organists were the responsibility of the church council with the approval of the municipal council.[35] Archival research by Maarten Seijbel shows continuous records of appointments of organists from the sixteenth century through the revolt, unimpeded by *anti-orgelist* pronouncements from early Reformed church synods.[36]

The unbroken stream of organ music was most likely enabled by the placement of two *burgomasters* (civic authorities) on the Reformed church council in Kampen that allowed city leaders to check any

lichtvaerdige deuntjes op d'orgel ofte op de clocken te spelen...."

30. Vente, *Brabanter Orgel*, 41, 49–50, 60–64, 66, 84, 131, 150, 174, 177, 191, 207; Vente, *Proeve*, 102–3.

31. Mey, "Orgels en organisten van de St. Nicolaaskerk te Kampen," 46–76; Kleij and Zwart, *Orgels en organisten in Kampen*; Seijbel, *Orgels in Overijssel*, 7–10.

32. Mey, "Orgels en organisten van de St. Nicolaaskerk te Kampen," 54; Vente, *Brabanter Orgel*.

33. "*Sondaechs loff.*" In February 1565 an agreement was made with the organist Mr. Willem, and in 1580 the church trustees paid Mr. Willem "*voor dat sondachs loff to spelen eer de kerke gereformmyert worde....*" "for the playing of the Sunday praise before the church became Reformed." City Archives of Kampen: OA 1332, fol. 92, as cited by Pol, *Reformatie te Kampen*, 35.

34. "*Meister Jacob Zyll als orgniste ... sal van des hilligen Sacramentsmemorie wegen sijne dachlixe presencie offte loen ... geboirt hebben ende des sall hie spolen ende dienen der memoriën voirss., als die selve sijne voirvaderen gedaen hebben.*" "Mr. Jacob Zyll, the organist ... shall frequently have received wages from the holy Sacramentsmemorie for his daily presentations ... and therefore shall play here and serve the aforementioned memories, in the same way his predecessors have done earlier." Pol, *Reformatie te Kampen*, 35.

35. The organist was included in the registers and instructions of municipal servants, the *Ordinaris Campenisis Conditiones Officiatorum*. Mey, "Orgels en organisten van de St. Nicolaaskerk te Kampen," 51, 63.

36. Seijbel, *Orgels in Overijssel*, 7–10.

ecclesiastical decisions that would be provocative.[37] Contemporary records from Kampen suggest that this kind of cooperation ensured that organ music continued, albeit to a limited extent, even after independence from Spain. Such *orgelist* practices in Kampen influenced localities in Overijssel after a "particular" (regional) classis was formed together with the churches in the neighboring cities of Drenthe, Twenthe, and Lingen. When this coalition of churches first met in Kampen on April 10, 1581, it essentially brushed away entirely the 1578 national instruction to ban the organ when it decided that the use of the organ in their classis was left to the discretion (*vrijheitt*, freedom) of each congregation.[38]

In Kampen organ music was not relegated to an ancillary role as prelude and postlude music provider only. Rather, Kampen exercised its *vrijheitt* and incorporated organ playing throughout the worship service to accompany the congregational psalms and hymns. When the Kampen Reformed first worshiped in the Church of the Holy Spirit in 1574 organist Gerrit Lucasz accompanied the service, where sermons where now heard "according to the Reformation of the holy Gospel."[39] Interestingly, the songs he accompanied were definitely not the strict psalm book of Geneva as the congregation sang hymns[40] and the Lord's Prayer, but only at Sunday services and not at the weekday service.[41] That the organ was viewed as indispensable in Kampen is proved by the fact that they would not worship without one: when the Kampen congregants of the Church of the Brethren (Broederkerk) vacated their space for an interim while it was being "adapted" for Reformed worship, explicit arrangements were

---

37. Pol, "Religious Diversity," 28; Pol, *Reformatie te Kampen*, 312–14. This practice of burgomaster-elders seems to be normative in other Overijssel cities such as Deventer, Hasselt, Oldenzaal, Steenwijk, Vollenhove, Zwartsluis and Zwolle; see Reitsma and Veen, *Acta der provinciale en particuliere synoden*, 5:207, 215, 226, 233, 242, 247, 248, 260, 267, 277, 293. Burgomasters were named as elders on consistories as late as January 20, 1748; Pol, "Religious Diversity," 28.

38. 6. "*Off niet datt gebruick der orgelen sall und behoertt te staen in die vrijheitt van een jegelicke kercke.*" Booma, "Acta van de Overijsselse," 174.

39. Pol, "Religious Diversity," 257.

40. "*Dat eenighe selecte lofsangen uth den osterschen psalmboeken bij unsen psalmen sall laeten drucken. Dien van Overyssel is uut seker respect toegelaten eenige der lichste psalmen Davids, tot XII oft meer toe, besonder te drucken, ende daer by eenige oostersche uutgelesen gesangen.*" Rutgers, *Acta van de Nederlandsche synoden*, 421.

41. "*Dat gebedt O Godts, die onse Vader bist, sal men in der weecken te singen naelaten.*" Pol, *Reformatie te Kampen*, 272.

made to move the chapel organ from the Church of the Holy Spirit so these Reformed could continue to worship with organ music.[42]

South Holland

Reformed churches in Friesland, Groningen, and Overijssel accepted the pipe organ for use before, during, and after worship services, and the examples from these cities illustrate the different ways Dutch civic and ecclesiastical authorities at various levels shared authority over Reformed liturgy, especially its organ music. However, not all *orgelist* churches used the organ to promote a "new," Reformed manner of organ use to accompany their Genevan psalmody. Some churches continued to use organ music because it was an "old" Catholic practice. Such was the case in Leiden, a university city that did not embrace Calvinism easily or quickly. This once solidly Catholic city's council had served simultaneously as the parish council prior to the revolt, and this arrangement continued after independence from Spain. Despite their responsibility to uphold the public, Reformed church, the Leiden council never enforced prohibitions on organ music. In fact, in 1593 Cornelis Schuyt was instructed to play before and after the service in addition to weekly evensong in the Pieterskerk in Leiden; further, sometimes the choristers of the church sang with the "adornment of the organ."[43] As if organ-accompanied choirs were not enough of a vestige of the Catholic worship, the Pieterskerk went so far as to commission a painting of the Trinity on its organ case doors, and then even installed extra lighting so that worshipers could see the

---

42. The Benedictine Church (*Minderbroeders* = Lesser Brothers) is called the Church of the Brethren (*Broederskerk*) after the Reformation. The accounts of the church trustees of the Benedictine church include an amount for two organ builders who came from Zwolle, a distance of about fifteen miles. They stayed overnight with schoolteacher Trymen Albertzen and collected forty Earl's pounds to move the organ from the Church of the Holy Spirit to the Church of the Brethen and to tune it. Pol, *Reformatie te Kampen*, 305.

43. ". . . *tot verschiereinge onder de organen wel meezongen*." Seiffert, "Cornelis Schuijt," 246–47, 251. Wouter Jacobsz., in a fragment of his journal from 1578, attests "*dat in sinte Pieterskerck op die orgelen gespeelt ende van de gemeent nae Calvinus maniere met groot geluyt gesongen werde. . . .*" "that in the St. Peters Church [of Leiden] the organs had been played and the congregation had sung with a resounding voice in the manner of Calvin." Jacobsz, *Dagboek van broeder Wouter Jacobsz*, 728. The city magistrates also believed that organ music in the church would draw people out of the taverns and bars.

paintings clearly.⁴⁴ Nothing could be less Reformed than the preservation of such images, much less their intentional emphasis on an organ case, yet a large, sympathetic (albeit underground) Catholic populace all but ensured that sweeping Reformed liturgical change would not happened quickly nor conclusively in Leiden.

Protestants in Gouda similarly ignored the organ ban and were just as independent from national decisions as those in Leiden. No doubt this was because Gouda's oligarchs merely tolerated the Reformed church's privilege in their city. These powerful men insisted that freedom of religion would be absolutely guaranteed,⁴⁵ so they were not generous in their financial support of the city's Reformed congregations. Moreover, they insisted on calling and appointing of "suitable" ministers,⁴⁶ a direct violation of Reformed polity, according to which each congregation's elected elders chose and supervised the life and work of its pastor. Worshipers in Gouda must have seen organ music as an integral part of worship because after Gouda's St. John's Church was damaged by fire in 1552, the city restored the church and offered a contract to organ builder Heinrick Niehoff. Gerbrant van Blankenburg was appointed organist once the instrument was installed. The great amount of resources put into organ construction, and particularly into the new organ stops added at this time, suggests that this was a liturgical instrument used to accompany congregational song.⁴⁷

While these examples suggest that the pipe organ was gradually but regularly reintroduced into Dutch Reformed worship shortly after the organ bans of the 1570s, there are also examples of staunch opposition to any use of the church organ. For example, the city of Maassluis in the province of South Holland initially introduced organ accompaniment after the revolt in an attempt to remedy the pulling and dragging (*slepen en trekken*) of the congregation as they sang the psalms. But just seven years later, organ accompaniment in Maassluis ceased because it did not result in singing that had more weight and majesty; rather it cause a musical chaos, a "slurring" of congregational singing that was intolerable to all concerned.⁴⁸ Placing a higher priority on intelligible praise of God than

44. Deursen, *Plain Lives*, 244.
45. Hibben, *Gouda in Revolt*, 102–3.
46. Hibben, *Gouda in Revolt*, 114–20.
47. Muylwijk, *Vervolgd en toch overwinnars*, 172 as cited by Deursen, *Plain Lives*, 270.
48. Zwart, *Van een deftig orgel: Maassluis*, 125.

on adherence either to strict Reformed practice or even popular practice, the Reformed in Maassluis decided not to use the organ during worship.

However, after a century of *a capella* singing, congregational song apparently still did not improve in Maassluis. The situation was remedied when Govert van Wijn generously donated an organ for the Grote Kerk of Maassluis. The church's minister, Ægidius Francken (1676-1743), actually preached a sermon at a service of dedication for the new pipe organ. Using the 150th Psalm as his text, Francken complained in the sermon of confused (*verwart*) singing, inattentiveness (*onaandachtig*) in worship, and in general all around irreverence (*oneerbiedig*) during the hour of worship.[49] Though Francken was keenly aware of the dangers of organ use, and that it might even be used of the devil for musical frivolity or the playing of secular ditties, in the end he preached that organ use during worship had the ability to beautify worship and enable better singing. Insincere worship replete with poor singing posed a greater threat to worship than did possible organ misuse.

Gelderland

While the previous examples described how church leaders and city leaders found consensus regarding organ use in their communities, organ use in the city of Arnhem, in the province of Gelderland, was bitterly contentious. Arnhem's citizens demanded that organ music begin again during worship[50] and Arnhem's city registers show that on February 14, 1589 the church council informed the magistrates that members of the church wished to restore the organ. The magistrates agreed, and the church repaired the organ without using city funds.[51] A certain Mr. Pronk was hired

> as organist of this city at a salary of three hundred and fifty gulden per year, starting when he has moved to this city and with such instruction to play during the singing of the psalms, the same after the preaching, and to play in the evening during the winter and at such other times as the council will tell him.[52]

49. Francken, *Heilig*; Mastenbroek and Bosman, *Grote kerk Maassluis*.

50. *Bijdragen en Mededeelingen*, 60; Hasselt, *Kronijk van Arnhem*, 193; Vente, *Bouwstoffen*, 103.

51. Hasselt, *Arnhemsche oudheden*, 257-58.

52. "... *tot organist deser stat angenomen tegens een tractement van driehondert en vijfftich gulden jaerlix, an te vangen te lopen wanneer hy sich alhier sal nedergesett*

However, this record simultaneously notes that the organ music greatly displeased the ministers:

> In this year the ministers submitted a petition to the magistrates against the playing of the organ, and it was determined that at all times when there is a religious service the organ will be played, similarly as is done in the neighboring provinces, at such times the worship service is not disturbed by it, and the ministers were advised of this with the additional note: that the organ will not be used for church purposes but rather for political [civic] functions.[53]

Though no *anti-orgelist* minister is mentioned by name in this record, the next entry clearly indicates that the protestor was pastor Johannes Nijken, who was a delegate to the national synod of 1578 held in Dordrecht; civic authorities quickly reminded him that the pulpit was not an appropriate way to make his objections to the organ known. This record is astonishing and goes directly to the heart of the issue: the civic council wielded control, and they were not only monitoring the use of the organ but also lecturing the pastor on his conduct. The Arnhem magistrates did defer a bit to Nijken when they instructed Mr. Pronk not to commence his postlude until Nijken had left the pulpit:

> This happened on 21 July [1589], but as Reverend Nijken preached against the playing on the organ, it was pointed out to him on 15 August that he had gone too far, and that if he or Fontanus were of the opinion that the magistrates had not dealt well with this, they should have instructed the magistrates of

hebben ended at op alsulcken instructie van onder het singen van de psalmen, item na de predication en bij wintertijt des avondts te spelen en anders, als hem bij een eerbaer raeth sal gegeven worden." Das, "Strijd over het orgelgebruik in de protestantse kerken," 76.

53. "*In dit jaar door de Predikanten een gescrhift overgegeven sijnde aan de Magistraat tegen het spelen van de Orgel, zoo is verstaan: dat op alle tijden, als ser Godsdienst gepleegd wordt, op het Orgel zou gespeeld worden, gelijk in de naburige Provintiën, op zulke tijden, dat de Godsdienst daardoor niet gestoord wordt, en is daarvan aan de Predikanten kennis gegeven, met bijvoeging: dat het Orgel niet tot den Kerkendienst, maar als eene politieke zaak soude gebruikt worden.*" Portheine Jr., "Orgels," 188. The petition, entitled *Bedenckens des Kerckenraets deser Gemeinten, off die reparatien der Orgelen raetsam, om hernamals dieselue in der Reformerter Kercken alhier, als einich deil des Goedesdienst to gebruycken*, is reprinted in Hasselt, *Kronijk van Arnhem (1310–1789)*, 245–60. The petition has four sections: biblical teaching about the use of organs, a review of the early church fathers sentiments on the use of the organ, the opinion of the consistory on the matter of organ music, and finally, arguments and reason for why the organ is not edifying.

that fact. The organist was instructed the next day to play some psalms on the following day, both before and after noon, after the service, but to wait until the ministers had left the pulpit, and not to play anything that could create offense.[54]

In other words, Nijken's sermon against organ music was fruitless, cemented secular control, and rendered the conflict insoluble.

Holland

Not all ministers were overruled by their respective city councils, as were Nijken and Fontanus in Arnhem. In Delft, as in Kampen, the same men were often members of both city council and the local consistory. However, unlike Kampen, Delft was not as friendly towards its resident Roman Catholics. At the outset of the rebellion, Delft's province of Holland was religiously pluralistic. However, the worsening military situation of the early 1570s cast suspicion on Catholic loyalty, and Beggar troops (*Gueux*) fractured any religious peace when they plundered churches and monasteries, murdered priests, and purged town councils of Catholic sympathizers.[55] In the end, the Reformed got the upper hand: in 1573 Catholicism was officially suspended and by 1581 Catholic worship was outlawed.[56] Still, no more than 10 percent of the province officially belonged to the Reformed church in Holland in the 1580s.[57] Nevertheless, the Reformed church became the privileged church of the country and

---

54. "*Dit geschiedde op den 21 Julij, maar Dominus Nijken daarna gepredikt hebbende tegens het spelen op den Orgel, zoo werdt hem op den 15 Augustus onder het oog gebragt, dat hij daaraan te veel gedaan had, en dat, indien hij of Fontanus meenden, dat hieromtrent van de Magistraat niet wel gehandeld was, zij daarvan de Magistraat in het particulier hadden moeten onderrigten. En werdt den volgenden dag de Organist geordonneerd, om des anderen daags, voor en na de middag, na de Predicatiën, eenige Psalmen op het Orgel te spelen, maar so lang te wagten, tot dat de Predikanten van den stoel souden sijn, en niets te spelen, dat ergernis verwekken kan.*" Hasselt, *Kronijk van Arnhem*, 3:249.

55. Parker, *Dutch Revolt*, 132–98; Groenveld et al., *Kogel door de kerk?*, 87–108.

56. Knuttel, *Toestand*, 2–6.

57. A substantial percentage of the population retained associations with the faith in which they were raised, and Catholic and Reformed adherents might be found even within the same family into the seventeenth century. See Kok, *Nederland op de breuklijn Rome-Reformatie*, 10–11; Duke with Jones, "Toward a Reformed Polity in Holland," 373–93.

in 1591 the province of Holland endorsed a church order for the public church that allowed magistrates a larger role in patronage.

This political situation meant that in Delft the ministers' concern of organ use was respected by the magistrates: the organ was used before and after worship, but not during the service to accompany congregational psalm singing. Some ministers were so averse to the organ that they tried to avoid hearing even the first notes of the organ postlude by escaping the pulpit before the singing of the closing psalm was finished. Apparently, such ministerial exits were not subtle enough and so a decree of the "Order of worship" (*Ordonnantie op de predicatie*) put a stop to such unseemly habits. The decree threatened a fine of three nickels for ministers who left their pulpit before the last psalm was completely finished.[58]

Such a mitigated use of the organ lasted in Delft until April 1634 when a contract was signed by organist Jan Cornelisz. Schoonhoven to play the organ during psalmody, the first city of the province of Holland to do so (other cities soon followed: Leiden in 1636 and Dordrecht in 1638).[59] In fact, in just four more years Delft would be the site where the supposed "end" of the organ controversy would be referenced when the

58. Jaanus, *Hervormd Delft ten tijde van Arent Corneliz*, 246–47.

59. Oosterhof and Penning, *Orgelbouwkundige bijdragen*, 5:139; Bleyswijck, *Beschryvinge der stadt Delft*, 173, 201; Vente, *Bouwstoffen*, 112–19, 195. The actual contract for was quite specific: "Op den 15en April 1634 sijn kerckmrn veraccordeert met mr. Jan den organist, dat hij voor sijnen dienst jaerlycx trecken ende genieten sal de somme van vijfhondert guldens, te weten voor 't ordinaries spelen volgens voorgaande accort, de somme van vier hondert guldens, en voor 't spelen op 't orgel des winters sondagsavonts twintich guldens en voor 't speelen voor en nae de predicatie onder 't gesang soo sondags als in de weecke tachtich guldens, bedragende seamen als vooren de somme van vijfhondert guldens daer van 't eerste termijn sijnen ingang sal nemen op den eersten april deses jaers 1634, doch indien naermaels goet gevonden mochte werden 't spelen onder 't gesang aft e schaffen, sal in soodanige gevalle in plaetse van de vijfhondert guldens trecken ende genieten de soma van vierhondert en twintich guldens. Actum bij kerkmrn. ten dage en jaere als voren." "On April 15, 1634 the church wardens made an agreement with Mr. Jan the organist, that in payment of his services he will annually earn and get the sum of five hundred gulden, that is for the regular playing following the previous contract the sum of four hundred guldens, and for the playing of the organ during the winter on Sunday evenings twenty gulden, and for playing before and after the sermon, during the singing both on Sundays and through the week eighty guldens, amounting in total as stated the sum of five hundred guldens, for which the first term will start on the first of April of this year 1634; however, if it is later decided to discontinue the playing during the singing, in that case instead of the five hundred guldens he will earn and receive the sum of four hundred and twenty guldens. Actum by the church masters on the date stated." Vente, *Bouwstenen*, 3:104–5.

provincial classis declared that organ music was best left to the discretion of each church, a decision analyzed in the previous chapter. After this provincial permission to use the organ was in place, Delft commissioned new instruments for the Nieuwe and Oude Kerk, both built in 1545 by the famous organ builder Henrik Niehoff but soon expanded and reconstructed in 1632–35 by Jan Morlet III. In 1657 Delft's *Heilige Geest Gasthuiskerk* commissioned a new instrument whose case was boldly inscribed with the following lines for perpetuity:

> Ter Eeren Van Godts Soon
> Ten Dienste Van Godts Kercke
> Tot Hulp Van Sangers Toon
> Staet Hier Dit Orgel-Werck[60]

Zeeland

Events in a nearby province were not so easily controlled by the local ministers in some cities. South of Delft lies the coastal province of Zeeland. After the defeat of Alba's troops, representatives of the Reformed churches in Zeeland came together in Middelburg on May 29 to June 21 1581 to write a Church Order for the province. But even before the classis could meet, the church in Middelburg queried its sister churches if organ use should continue. Classis replied

> It is not considered advisable, especially not before the worship service. Therefore the ministers should work that it will be discontinued at the first opportunity, as has been counseled for a long time.[61]

This orthodox reply was not well received in Middelburg by the city magistrates, who in turn formed a committee to study this decision and all the other orders that affected Middelburg which had been issued by the classis.[62] The committee's work, "Order for Ecclesiastical and Civil

---

60. "To the honor of God's Son/ for the service of God's church / to the aid of the singers' sound / this organ stands here"

61. "*Particulare ofte byzondere vragen verhandelt en verantwoort in deze synode. . . . Offt het ghebruyck der orghelen inde tempelen te houden zy? Antw. Het wordt niet voer ghoet gehouden: insonderheyt voer die predicatie. Daarom die dienaers arbeyden sullen, dat dselue ghelyck het eenen tytlanck geduldet wort mitten aldereersten afgestelt worden.*" Rutgers, *Acta van de Nederlandsche synoden*, 409.

62. Hooijer, *Oude kerkordeningen*, 225–46.

Government," was sent first to the provincial court for advice; the legal opinions with the provincial *Order* were sent then to the cities. Conspicuously, the advice of Reformed ministers was not sought, needed, nor wanted. But because this draft circulated through so many hands, the ministers became aware of the *Order* before it was made public, and they expressed their firm objections to it and their lack of involvement in defining its shape. They were so disturbed at the prospect that this drafted *Order* would be forced upon them that they warned in 1583 that their acceptance of it would not be forthcoming. Wisely, the magistrates delayed the publication of this *Order*. This example shows that control of the organ in Zeeland's capital ultimately belonged to the magistrates, though they were influenced by the clergy, and the shape of the liturgy was the magistrates by right also.

Utrecht

The debate as to whether and how to use church organs was arguably nowhere more fractious than in Utrecht. In most of the country the largest religious tension was between Calvinists and Catholics, but in Utrecht the constellation was more cluttered. In the 1570s the city gave sanction to a "Libertine" church that followed the teachings of Hubert Duifhuis. Among other things, the Libertine churches welcomed anyone to partake of Holy Communion, and they did not practice excommunication, which Reformed theologians taught was a defining sign of the true church.[63] Practices such as these were so unacceptable to orthodox Calvinists in Utrecht that they demanded from the city council a separate church that would adhere strictly to Reformed doctrine. When their request was denied, the Calvinists then simply occupied the Minderbroederkerk, which had been expropriated from the Franciscans. There, in March 1579, one hundred and eighty-five members of the Reformed Church received Communion for the first time.[64] But the Utrecht city council exercised its rights over all church spaces and swiftly installed an organ even in the Minderbroederkerk. Then, as if to pique their Calvinist constituents, the

---

63. Kaplan, *Calvinists and Libertines* (1995), 156–288.
64. Dunthorne, "Dramatizing the Dutch Revolt," 32; *Archief voor Kerkelijke*, 3:254; *Caecilia*, 118; Vente, *Bouwstoffen*, 172.

council hired a Roman Catholic organist, Peter Claesz. Wijborgh, to play it.[65]

Further such action by the Utrecht councilors was checked after the *stadtholder* appointed a number of Calvinists to the town council in 1585. Thereafter, the religious climate in Utrecht changed swiftly. In July 1586, the Libertine congregation meeting at St. Jacob's Church was officially dissolved, and the magistrates worked quickly to ban such activities as prostitution, profanation of the Sabbath, the ringing of church bells, use of choirs in worship, and the celebration of folk festivals. One might assume that such a bold blueprint for "Protestantization" in Utrecht would have extended specifically to a ban on the use of organ music, but records confirm that three of the four parishes—the Oudekerk,[66] Jacobskerk[67] and the Geertekerk[68]—used organ music nevertheless, though in an ancillary role. For instance, in 1593 Gijsbert van Groenenberg was paid to perform recitals from ten o'clock in the morning until noon each Tuesday and Friday at the church; similarly, in St. Jans church, which was used by the Walloon congregation of Utrecht, after the altar and paintings were removed, the organist played on St. John's feast day to honor the patron saint of the church, as well as after every worship service.[69] The Buurkerk, the site of the magistracy's own chapel, was governed not by a church council but by civic officials chosen directly by the magistrates and here the organ was fully used.[70] The Buurkerk's organist, Jacob van Schendel, was ordered to accompany the psalms during worship, but also to play other pieces before and after worship and at the evening services[71] as long as they were "honest musical composition, free of idolatry and superstition."[72] Though the Calvinists of Utrecht did work dutifully to

65. Vente, *Vijf eeuwen*, 88.

66. *Archief voor Kerkelijke*, 6:321; *Caecilia*, 3, 81, 178, 181; Vente, *Bouwstoffen*, 169–71. This church owned an organ as early as 1478, a rudimentary instrument built by Peter of Utrecht. Moseley, "Marcussen Organ in the Nicolaïkerk Utrecht," 102–4; Riemsdijk, "Orgel van de Nicolaikerk te Utrecht," 195–99.

67. Riemsdijk, *Geschiedenis van de Kerspelkerk van St. Jacob te Utrecht* (1882), 20; Vente, *Bouwstoffen*, 168–69.

68. *Archief Aartsbisdom Utrecht*, 9:259–46; 11:307; Vente, *Bouwstoffen*, 171–72.

69. Vente, *Bouwstoffen*, 114.

70. Kaplan, *Calvinists and Libertines* (1995), 283; *Archief voor Kerkelijke*, 6:307; *Bijdragen en Mededeelingen*, 3:25–224; *Caecilia*, 147; Vente, *Bouwstoffen*, 166–68, 197.

71. ". . . zoe voer als near die predicatie een bequame tijt die psalmen ende anders te speelen." Vente, *Bouwstoffen*, 2:301.

72. ". . . den psalm eenighe veersen near de predicatie over gespeeld sijnde, sal hij

ensure a new Protestant order, organ control was relegated to a lower priority than other reforms.

Meanwhile, some *anti-orgelists* of the city felt they had no choice but to display their displeasure publicly. When the organist at the Dom church in Utrecht began to improvise organ "diversions" (*per intervalla*) between the stanzas of the Psalmody during one 1606 service, some worshipers stopped singing, put their hats back on, and sat down until the "diversion" was over. Yet at the same time those worshipers who found the organ playing pleasing remained standing and sang—hats removed, of course.[73] This *per intervalla* practice, actually a vestige of organ alternation used in Catholic liturgical practice, was challenged in 1608 along with the use of choirs in worship, but again it must be underscored that organ use itself was no longer questioned.[74]

"Calvinist" Practice?

The survey presented so far in this chapter attests to an *orgelist* majority in the Netherlands before, during, and immediately after the 1579 Union of Utrecht, despite synodical bans to the contrary. Though Calvin championed Reformed services that were based on the Word of God as the unmistakable centerpiece of worship, God's Word spoken, read, and preached was supplemented by the congregation's sung prayer. The texts for these prayers were to come only from the book of Psalms, a sanctioned psalter lifted from the pages of Scripture itself were to be offered by the most beautiful of all instruments, the God-created human voice using dignified tunes of weight and majesty unobstructed by any musical instrument. While instrumental music and even polyphonic hymnody could be enjoyed privately in the home, in public worship the risk of misuse outweighed any potential benefit for the gathered body of Christ at worship.

Dutch *orgelists* were willing to set aside these clear directives for church music in their country in order to ensure musical dignity; as reviewed in the previous chapter, Calvin's foreign Genevan tunes had

---

moghen enighen anderen psalmen, hymne off eerlijcke musyckstuck, geen afgoderije oft superstitie daerin gelegen sijnde moghen speeldn." Das, "Strijd over het orgelgebruik in de protestantse kerken," 73.

73. Vente, *Utrechtse orgelhistorische verkenningen*, 289; Vente and Vlam, *Bouwstenen*, 230–33.

74. Vente and Vlam, *Bouwstenen*, 112.

neither majesty nor weight when they were sung *a capella* and so the ban of instrumental music was therefore ignored by most Dutch Reformed. But organ music was not the only exception to Calvinist liturgical ideals, other worship issues were likewise ignored, altered, or adapted that distinguished the Dutch Reformed from Calvinists elsewhere.

Ironically, Calvinism itself may help explain the apparent divide between Reformed theory and actual, varying practice. While Calvin did set forth clearly his liturgical ideals, he worked equally as hard to underscore the necessity of democratic church governance that could accommodate cultural and local variations of practice. Further, Calvinists distinguished the essence of worship from those things which are the circumstances of worship. That organ music fell into this latter category was generally assumed, indeed, affirmed by the Provincial Synod of Delft 1638 when it attempted to put the organ controversy to rest for the churches in its classis. In addition to organ music, other liturgical issues such as funeral rites, hymns, and the time of day for worship were also regulated as circumstance of worship, and considered a matter of local preference, and thereby set by the discretion of each church council.

Funeral Customs

For example, funeral customs of the Dutch is another example of liturgical adaptation and disregard of synodical liturgical guidelines.[75] Calvin had decried all funerary observances as superstitious and Catholic. In fact, to this day, Reformed Church Order has no requirement of funerary rites for its members as the matter is relegated entirely to the family's discretion, a drastic change in theology and practice from its status held by the Catholic Church. Attendant funereal issues such of place of burial, the preaching of funeral sermons, the erection of memorial markers, the ringing of bells at the graveside, and offering prayers for the dead were repeatedly addressed by local and national gatherings.[76] The repeated

---

75. Boge and Bogner, *Oratio funebris*; Dooren, "Leichenpredigten"; Bosma, *Woorden van een gezond verstand*; Karant-Nunn, *Reformation of Ritual*; Koslofsky, *Reformation of the Dead*; Lenz, *Mortuis nil nisi bene?*

76. *Classicale acta*, 1:6, 37, 148–49, 225, 227 245, 248, 476, 485; 2:68, 177–78, 496; 3:139, 237, 242–43; 6:5, 47, 61, 78, 102, 103; De Gier, *Dordtse kerkorde*, 316–20; Knuttel, *Acta der particuliere synoden*, 2:237; 3:283; Reitsma and Veen, *Acta der provinciale en particuliere synoden*, 1:4, 7, 137; 2:133–34, 199, 329, 346, 372, 405, 454; 3:92, 110, 132, 144; 4:2, 29, 84; 5:7, 99, 263; 6:54, 69, 136; 7:13, 43, 54, 113, 157; Rutgers, *Acta van*

discussions and multiple entries in synodical minutes alike suggest that funeral customs were not so easily dropped and that the issue was not easily dismissed.

One example not only illustrates the reluctance of families to dispense with age-old funereal customs, but also points to their tenacity in appealing to the authorities. In 1587 in Leiden, the heirs of Abraham Merten, a deceased schoolmaster, insisted that the Reformed consistory allow a funerary sermon (*lijckpredicatie*) to be preached at Abraham's funeral. Because praying for the dead or even preaching to the faithful in the presence of a corpse was considered to be too Catholic, and because the synod had ruled against *lijckpredicatien*, the elders refused the family's request. The Merten family appealed to the church consistory, reminding the elders of the late Abraham's high esteem amongst the lords of the city. Unwilling to risk antagonizing city leaders, the elders acquiesced, but only as long as Merten's body was already interred under the church floor by the time the *lijckpredicatie* was preached.[77] This incident is but one example that the Dutch did not immediately nor uniformly cease funerary rites, even in the face of Reformed doctrine to the contrary.

Other anti-synodical moves

Beyond funeral rites, other examples also show how the Dutch Reformed liturgy grew in decidedly anti-synodical, indigenous ways. For example, when the Kampen church renovated their space for Reformed worship, they repaired the organ in 1625,[78] and, as did many Dutch churches, moved the pulpit to the center of the church, installed a sound board over it to ensure the intelligibility and audibility of the sermon, and placed a candlestick stand near the pulpit. The organist played for Sunday worship services, accompanying both psalms and hymns. What is more to the point here, Kampen then continued weekday evening prayer liturgies; city

---

de Nederlandsche synoden, 142, 248–49, 393, 501.

77. *Archief van de Nederlands-Hervormde Gemeente, Kerkeraadsacta*, vol. 1, as cited by Kooi, *Liberty and Religion*, 82.

78. "*25 januari 1625: Synnen die Cameners de Ecclesiastique guederen deser Stadt de Schepenen ende Raedt geautorisiert om met Meester Gerrit, Orgelwercker soe nae enighsins doenlicken wegen die Reparatie ende Verstellen vant grootste Orgel in de Broederkercke too veraccordieren op alsuck besteck als hy daarvan geconcipiert ende een Erb.*" *Raedt voorgesteld heft*, cited by Seijbel, *Orgels in Overijssel*, 45.

ledgers for 1583 record the expenditure for candles for such meetings.[79] The national Synod of Dordrecht 1578 had warned its churches against instituting these services because it smacked of Catholicism and because it might lead to people skipping a Sunday service in favor of these simpler, shorter weekday vespers.[80] In addition, the synod feared that these evening prayers in the church could displace "the necessary use of family prayers" at home. However, in defiance of the national synod, Kampen's Classis Overijssel, as it had done with the organ issue, claimed independence regarding liturgical decisions and left the institution of evening prayers to the discretion of each church.[81] In addition to this representative record from Kampen, synodical records from this period from all provinces are replete with decisions about weekday services, festivals, and the celebration of holy days. Again, the very fact that documented decisions are recorded about weekday services suggests that it was not only those in Kampen who were questioning Sunday-only services, or absorbing Reformed liturgical ideals into their local worship practice.

Psalms or Hymns?

But perhaps the biggest Dutch liturgical difference from Calvinist liturgical ideas, after organ use, funerary rites, and weekday services, was the addition of hymns to the canon of repertoire. The early meetings of the Dutch Reformed in Emden decided to use a hymnal in addition to the Psalter, another direct contradiction of Calvin's approach to liturgy. Because Emden was in German-speaking lands, it is hardly surprising that

79. "*Item anno 1583, op den 24 february, heb ick afgerekent met kaarsenmaker Helmick Jansz . . . in den Broederkercke als men wintertijt het aventgebet predigest.*" "Ditto, anno 1583, on February 24, I have made payment to the candlemaker Helmick Jansz . . . in the church of the Brethren when in the wintertime the evening prayer is preached." Pol, *Reformatie te Kampen*, 282.

80. Article 57. See also for example Provincial Synod of Middelburg 1581 art. 47; National Synod of 1586 art. 57; Provincial Synod of Middelburg 1591 art. 54; Church Order of Ommelanden 1595 art. 30; Provincial Synod of Utrecht 1612; National Synod of Dordrecht 1618–1619 art. 64; Church Order of Drenthe 1638, arts. 79–82; Deursen, *Plain Lives*, 169; Benedict, *Christ's Churches*, 490–518.

81. "*Voor het gebed in de eredienst in algeméne zin gaf de gecombineerde synode van 19 en 20 januari 1580 aan, dat de formuliergebeden voor en na de predikatie uit het Kerkboek van Datheen als richtlijn gelden.*" "Concerning the prayer during the worship service in a general sense the combined synod of January 19 and 20, 1580 indicated that the formula-prayers before and after the sermon from the Churchbook by Datheen would serve as a guide." Pol, *Reformatie te Kampen*, 273.

the 1567 hymnbook used in Emden (which was published by someone with the arch-Frisian name of Sybout Aysma) included hymns penned by Martin Luther; further, its liturgical forms varied from those used in Dutch Reformed congregations elsewhere. But the 1578 National Synod of Dordrecht called for such hymns to be discontinued: it had decided that the one hundred and fifty Psalms should be the sole source of Reformed worship music, the only exception allowed was for biblical canticles and musical settings of the Ten Commandments and the Lord's Prayer. Even then, there is little evidence that congregations that were using hymns at this point ceased to do so; indeed, many added hymns to their repertoire, just as Emden had done before. Perhaps the most egregious example of disobedience to this directive comes from Utrecht shortly after the turn of the seventeenth century. When the "Christian Church Order of the City, Towns and Territories of Utrecht Ratified in Utrecht on 28 August 1612"[82] was approved, this order stated the following "Concerning Hymns Approved for Worship":

> The custom of singing songs of praise as practiced in our and other Reformed churches shall be maintained, for the purpose of honoring and praising God as well as for the edification of the congregation the following shall be sung: the hundred and fifty Psalms, called the Psalms of David, the Songs of praise of Mary, Zechariah and Simeon, the Apostles' Creed, the Ten Commandments, the Lord's Prayer and the Evening Song *Christ, who art both day and light*; also the prayer before the sermon, *O God who art our Father*, as well as many other Scriptural songs of praise and Christian songs related to the birth of Christ, his circumcision, baptism, suffering, death, resurrection, ascension into heaven, the outpouring of the Holy Spirit, etc., in so far as they, following the custom in certain other evangelical Reformed churches where they are correctly established, fittingly and for the development of spiritual devotion as this is worked by Jesus Christ our Savior, can be introduced and practiced, after a preceding inquiry by those whom we will assign for this purpose, and with our knowledge, the local Magistrates and the consistory of every place where it is edifying to use them.[83]

82. "*Christelijcke Kercken-Ordeninge der Stadt, Steden, ende Landen van Utrecht, ghearresteert binnen Utrecht den XXVIII Augusti XVIc XII.*"

83. "*De ghewoonte van de Lof-sangen te singhen in onse en andere Ghereformeerde Kercken gebruyckelijck, sal men onderhouden, ende ten selven eynde tot Godts lof ende prijs, mitsgaders stichtinghe der Ghemeynte singhen; de hondert vijftich Psalmen ghenaemt: de Psalmen Davids, de lof-sangen Mariae, Sachariae ende Simeonis, de Articulen*

This declaration is noteworthy for many reasons. First, it gives evidence that psalmody was not everywhere the norm; rather, it twice mentions that hymn singing is established as a "custom" in some Reformed churches. Second, this Church Order not only recognized hymn-singing practice, but also sanctioned hymns for every season of the liturgical year. Third, the synod's permission to sing "Christ, who art both day and light" (*Christe qui lux es et dies*), a vesper hymn from the earliest centuries of the church and sung in Catholic churches, is simply startling. Finally, and just as groundbreaking as the introduction of a hymn from apostolic times, this Church Order declares that hymns are useful for the "development of spiritual devotion."

Once this decision to allow a well-defined corpus of hymns was taken, Utrecht city leaders appointed a committee to compile these songs, and the hymnal was published.[84] Voetius mentioned that the product was a collection of fifty-eight songs published in 1615 in The Hague by Hillebrant Jacobsz under the title *Hymni ofte Loof-sangen op de Christelijeke Feest-Dagen ende Andersins. Met privilegie*.[85] It did not receive immediate or unanimous praise; when the hymns were used for the first time in Utrecht, the congregation "did not sing along with the cantor, and even showed their aversion and disagreement so that the introducers were compelled to give up."[86] Apparently, the hymnal fared no better on following Sundays because extensive archival research reveals no other evidence of *Hymni of Lof-sangen* being used, and no extant copy survives. Nevertheless, that a hymnal was used in Emden as early as the 1580s, that multiple synods had to give an official opinion on the subject, and that

---

de gheloofs, Thien Gheboden, t' Vader onse, ende het Avont-leidt, Christe, die ghy zijt dach en licht, oock t' Ghebedt voor de Predicatie, O Godt die onsen Vader bist, mitsgaders soo veleandere Schriftuyrlijcke Lof-sanghen en Christelijcke Liedekens, handelende van Christi gheboorte, Besnydenisse, Doop, Lijden, Sterven, Op-standinghe van den Dooden, Op-vaert ten Hemelen, Seyndinghe des H. Gheestes etc. als men naer ghewoonte van sommighe andere Euangelische ghereformeerde Kercken bequamelijck in-ghestelt zijnde, naer voor-gaende visitatie der gener, die wy daer toe sullen committeren, ende met kennisse van ons, de Magistraet ende Kercken-raedt van yeder plaetse daer men die sal goet ende stichtelijck vinden te ghebruycken, ghevoechgelijck ende tot meerder opweckinghe in gheestelijcke aen-dacht vande Euangelische weldaden, den menschelijcke gheslachte door Jesum Christum den Salichmaeker gheschiet, sal connen in treyn brenghen ende oefenen." Hooijer, *Oude kerkordeningen*, 384.

84. De Jong, "Utrechtse Hymni van 1615," 263-76; Huet, *Over den gezangen-strijd*, 40-41.

85. Voetius, PE, 1:528. Voetius decried also that the Utrecht hymnal was Arminian.

86. Hooijer, *Oude kerkordeningen*, 385.

Utrechters and Dutch in other cities published their own hymnal all lead to the conclusion that hymns were used in many Dutch Reformed places of worship in addition to psalms.

Who Plays the Organ?

These examples demonstrate that in many locales during the late sixteenth century the organ did not stop playing, and that the Dutch Reformed liturgy evolved apart from the ideals of Geneva. Even though organ practice was irregular and chaotic, the Dutch Reformed moved inexorably toward allowing full organ use in their church. Therefore, opponents of organ music took a different tack: they began questioning the qualifications of the organist himself. Naturally, before the Reformation and independence, organists were all Catholic. But after the Reformation not all of these Catholics converted, nor were there skilled organists amongst the faithful Reformed. Consequently, it was not uncommon to have the organ played in a Reformed service by a Catholic musician. This drove some *anti-orgelists* to submit formal grievances, or gravamina, to their provincial classis through the local consistory such as the gravamen received by the Provincial Synod of Groningen held in the city of Loppersum in April of 1599 which asked

> whether the papist organists should not be dismissed as much as possible and that in their place should be appointed adherents of the true Reformed religion.[87]

No longer questioning whether the organ could be used, this gravamen asked rather for permission to inquire of the religious loyalties of church employees.

The men who were subjected to this questioning perceived such inquiries as intrusive, and they disassociated their art from their religious belief. Cornelis Helmbreeker of Haarlem, for example, who lost his post

---

87. "25. *Ofte niet die Papistische organisten sooveel mogelyc afgheschaft ende in haere plaetse sullen gestalt warden die waere Gereformeerde religie toegedaene.*" Reitsma and Veen, *Acta der provinciale en particuliere synoden*, 6:135. Classes Kampen and Vollenhoven asked the same question using similar language: Classis Kampen, 20: "*Of oock niet die papistische organisten soeveel moeghelick afgheschaft, ende in de plaetse ghestelt die waere ghereformeerde religie toeghedaene.*" *Classicale Acta 1573–1620 VI*, 122. Classis Vollenhoven, 25: "*Ofte niet die Papistische organisten sooveel mogelyc afgheschaft, ende in haere plaetse sullen gestalt warden die waere Gereformeerde religie toegedaene.*" Reitsma and Veen, *Acta der provinciale en particuliere synoden*, 5:309.

as organist because he refused to sign his agreement with the Reformed confessions, defended his action believing that his art "had nothing in common with one doctrine or another,"[88] and that he played in church but did not preach there, and therefore he should not have to declare his doctrinal positions. Further, organist Helmbreeker suggested that if the ministers wanted to set the confessions to music he would then gladly play them on the organ, for that would be in agreement with his contract. Not amused, the ministers summarily dismissed Helmbreeker from his duties.

The church of Deventer was bedeviled not just by an organist but also by the sextons (*kosters*) it employed. According to a decision by the city magistrates on November 6, 1598, the nomination and appointments of the church sextons was put in the hands of the church council; the magistrates only had to give their approbation,[89] and they rarely challenged the church's choice.[90] These sextons were supposed to follow the instructions of the consistory that hired them, a consistory that enforced the organ bans of the early synods.[91] However, the sextons proved to be insubordinate, and their behavior spoiled peace in the town. Deventer's Catholic citizens were known to perform funerals inside the Reformed church at times. Consequently, the church council asked the sextons to lock the church doors in order to be "on guard against the actions of the

---

88. "... geen gemeenschap hadt met deze of die leere." Brandt, *Historie der reformatie*, 3:939.

89. Deventer Kerkeraadsarchief, November 6, 1598.

90. Deventer Kerkeraadsarchief, October 30, 1598; April 9, 1598; July 16, 1598; September 21, 1598; October 8, 1621.

91. Mr. Willem ter Clocke, *voorzanger* of the Groote Kerk, died in 1622, and organist Claude Bernard was then appointed the new *voorzanger*. Bernard was instructed to play the organ prelude, and then serve as unaccompanied precentor during the service before he returned to the organ bench to improvise the postlude. Deventer Kerkeraadsarchief, March 25, 1622; April 1, 1622; April 15, 1622; April 18, 1622; April 29, 1622; May 6, 1622. No doubt this limited use of the organ was championed by Deventer minister Caspar Sibelius (1590–1658), an outspoken *anti-orgelist*. In his expansive autobiographical narrative, *De curriculo totius vitæ et peregrinationis suæ historica narratio*, Sibelius opposed organ use in Reformed worship for familiar reasons: the organ had pagan origins (Sibelius cites Plato, *Ligibus* 1.3 and Plutarchus, *Musica*), instrumental music was a Jewish custom that New Testament Christians no longer needed, and organ use was a Catholic practice first introduced by Pope Vitalianus. Sibelius, "Curriculo," 361–69; Sibelius and Scheibe, *Zeittafel der Geschichte der Lateinischen Schule*, 53–86; Slee, "Gereformeerde gemeente van Deventer," 19:1:3–58; Tydeman, "Caspar Sybelius, in leven predikant te Deventer," 481–533.

papists in the Bergkerk."[92] However, the sextons defied these instructions; they unlocked the Reformed church's doors not just for Catholic funerals, but also so that Catholics could visit the graves of their dead who were interred under the floor or in the stone walls of the building. In what is perhaps the most egregious violation of church and council orders, it is recorded that at one funeral mourners rode into the church on horseback as part of a funeral cortege, all to the beating of drums and blowing of trumpets. It is little wonder, then, that Deventer's church minutes are replete with requests that the magistrate forbid such profanity.[93]

As a result of the city's repeated inability to make the sexton's conform to the Reformed consistory's orders,[94] the Deventer church asked its classis to require that all church employees confess the Reformed faith, and that the personal lives and moral deportment of all church employees in their region be above reproach.

Apparently, Deventer was not the only city of the classis dealing with difficult employees. For example, Article 4 of the July 18, 1620 classis meeting made an unusual pronouncement about one church employee in Boorn [Borne]:

> [T]he honorable deputies . . . should consider the life of the organist at Boorn, as he sets his hat according to the wind: with the papists, he is papal; with the Lutherans, Lutheran; with the Reformed, Reformed. And that he does not live with his wife but has left her. And having deliberated about this, to depose him and to discontinue his salary as the schoolteacher, which is very necessary in that place, as [he has] vacated the school position and the youth run around wild.[95]

92. ". . . tegen het bedrijf der Papisten in de Bergkerk." Deventer Kerkeraadsarchief, February 26, 1627, November 8, 1630.

93. ". . . te willen verbieden dat sodanige profanatie niet weder geschiede." Deventer Kerkeraadsarchief, December 22, 1620; April 23, 1620; July 30, 1621; September 13, 1624.

94. According to the church minutes, the sextons were unable to control miscreant youth who vandalized the cemetery, sat on chairs reserved for council members, operated a very loud oil mill (*oliemolen*) next to the church during services, and repeatedly stole money from the marriage box (*trouwbus*); Deventer Kerkeraadsarchief, February 26, 1627; November 8, 1630; December 29, 1595; November 1, 1624; October 11, 1602; December 3, 1621; August 30, 1624; October 13, 1628, respectively.

95. "4. To versoken aen den Edelen heeren Gedeputerden dat haar believe t'overleggen het leven des organisten to Boorn, alsdat he mit alle winden wayet, mit den papisten papas, mit den luthersen luthers, mit den reformerden reformert is, ende dat he sine huisvrouwe nit bi sich, maar verlaten heft. Ende sulckes overlecht hebbende, dessulvigen

However, this wild organist of Boorn was not tamed quickly or easily. The minutes from the classis meeting of October 10–11, 1620 reveal that he was exercising some sort of diaconal functions, which he was instructed to cease forthwith: "the organist of Born [sic] will be prohibited from visiting the sick."[96]

The Reformed churches in Haarlem also tried to control the private lives and religious belief of their church employees. Records from July 16, 1628 show that the organist Johan Heeres was admonished by the church because of a despicable life (*ergerlicken leevens*). A month later, despite the admonishments, it appears that Mr. Heeres was censured again for his licentiousness (*ongebondenheit*) and was finally dismissed.[97] The Church Order for the Ommelanden of Groningen (article 33) attempted to ward off such judicial cases when it stated up front that "organists and other church servants cannot and should not be keepers of public houses."[98]

But perhaps the most clear attempt to ensure the quality and character of the organist comes from Sneek, where, in 1602, civic authorities actually formulated qualifications for the position of organist. Besides merely playing only approved church music on Sunday, with the now-requisite warning never to play "frivolous" repertoire, he had to be available to play on all weekday preaching days for a half hour before and after worship. Further, he had to serve as general curator of the instrument, and he must never frequent public houses.[99]

Even as the Reformed tried to regulate the private life and religious confession of their organists, at the same time, they still wrested for control over their church organ during and outside of worship. In 1630 the Frisian classis of Franeker queried its member churches "whether it is permissible for individual congregations to use the playing of the organ

to deporteren end emit sin tractament een schoolmeister te gasyren, diewelke in die plaatse seer nodich, overmits die schooldients aldaer vacert ende die juget in't wilde loopt." Reitsma and Veen, *Acta der provinciale en particuliere synoden*, 6:92.

96. "24. . . . Item, dat den organist von Born [sic] het besoeken der kranken mogte verboten warden." Reitsma and Veen, *Acta der provinciale en particuliere synoden*, 6:103.

97. *Acta Consistorii 1595–1637*, 334–336, Gemeente Archief Groningen, as cited by Luth, "*Daer wert . . .* ," 212.

98. "33. Item noch geresolvirt, dat kosteren, organisten und kerckendieners nene krögers konen offte behören tho sin." Reitsma and Veen, *Acta der provinciale en particuliere synoden*, 6:27.

99. The Dutch text and English translation of this notice is found in *Sound Theology: A Reader*.

during the singing before and after the service, without prior knowledge and permission of the entire church."[100] Note that organ use was clearly not in dispute, the question of Franeker was the control of such a decision. The classis answered simply, "[As it] has been answered, that it may be done, as long as there is no fear of impropriety."[101] Apparently the answer was sufficiently vague, for the very next year this very same classis of Franeker raised the question yet again because "a few churches" veered "from the old way," meaning that the organ was being used during the service and not just as a provider of prelude and postlude music. The Franeker classis was careful to allow room that such *orgelist* action was involuntary disobedience when it concluded "but we think it to have happened accidentally."[102] The classis went on to declare that in those places where the organ assisted the singing, care should be taken to ensure that it happened in an edifying manner; but where the use of the organ was not customary, it did not have to be introduced.[103]

The Second Generation

The increasing use of pipe organs in Reformed worship, singing of hymns, and relaxation of other worship norms were only the liturgical symptoms of what was viewed by many Calvinists as a dangerous departure from true Christianity. A subsequent generation of *anti-orgelists* railed against the instrument from university lecterns and church pulpits in an attempt to convince magistrate and church member alike that the evils of pipe organ use had not diminished over time or merely with widespread use within the Reformed church. Thus the cause was taken up again after the turn of the seventeenth century when some more zealous believers feared that Protestantism was straying too far from its roots, and promoted a

100. "... *off het particuliere gemeinten geoorloft is onder het singen voor ende near de predicatie het orgelspelen te gebruijcken sonder voorgaende kennisse ende approbatie van de gantsche kercke?*" Orgelgebruik bij de kerkzang (A 4385) of the provincial archives of Friesland, as cited by Kalma, *Mensen in om de Grote Kerk*, 50.

101. "*Is geantwoort, daet het wel mach geschieden, als geen ontstichtinghe te bevresen is.*" Kalma, *Mensen in en om de Grote Kerk*, 50.

102. "... *maar aghten 't uit eenige toevalligheden geschiedt te wesen.*" Kalma, *Mensen in en om de Grote Kerk*, 50.

103. Kalma, *Mensen in en om de Grote Kerk*, 50. At this time many churches in Friesland had their organs repaired or built new ones. The organ in Dronrijp was altered no less than nine times in 1630. Oosterhof and Penning, *Orgelbouwkundige bijdragen*, 1:196–97.

return to orthodox theology and practice.[104] Indeed, stress was placed on *reformatio vitae*, a reformation of life, which meant strict personal piety in all aspects of life. As to the use of the pipe organ in worship, they felt that organ use was a misapplication of the *adiaphora* principle, for if it were decided that Reformed worship was completed by both the organ and the mouth—that the organ was to be part of worship—then this matter was foundational, i.e., not *adiaphora*. Further, *anti-orgelists* found organ use to be of the puerile epoch of the church, a human invention without biblical warrant, and a needless distraction.

Anti-orgelists were not afraid to assert themselves into the shaping of civic policy also. For example, by the middle of the seventeenth century the use of the organ and printed hymnals in Utrecht became so contentious that on January 29, 1655[105] the city leaders asked Gisbertus Voetius (1589–1676) and two other professors from the university, Andreas Essenius (1618–1677) and Matthias Nethenus (1618–1686), to advise them

> whether the Christian Civic Authorities have the power, during this time of the New Testament, to institute the playing of the organ during the public singing of the psalms, all the more and principally since this had not been the custom previously.[106]

These three men were all ardent *anti-orgelists* who must have savored the opportunity to assert their views to the municipality and thereby persuade their fellow citizens of the truth revealed in biblical instructions. They concluded that, while psalms and hymns could freely be accompanied if they were sung in private (*in 't privé*),

> the playing of the organ in the public worship of the New Testament is a useless and unedifying practice, which draws the thoughts of the majority of the Christians from appropriate attention toward human entertainment, and thus prevents rather than promotes true worship, which must happen in spirit and in truth. Note then that the apostle teaches us in which way we should conduct the meetings of the believers and to which end

---

104. Graafland et al., "Nadere Reformatie," 108; Hof, *Gereformeerd piëtisme*; Israel, *Dutch Republic*, 474–77; Lieburg, "From Pure Church to Pious Culture," 409–29; Lieburg, *Nadere Reformatie in Utrecht ten tijde van Voetius*.

105. Duker, *Voetius*, 351; Broeyer, "Franciscus Burman," 105–6.

106. "*Of de Christelike Overheyd ten tijde des Nieuwen Testamentz vermoegende het speelen van den Orgel onder het openbaare Psalmsinghen in de kerckn in te voeren, te meer en voornamelick als sulks te vooren in geen gebruyck is geweest.*" *Theologisch Advys op 29 januari 1655*. Vente and Vlam, *Documentaet et archivalia*, 234–5.

> all public acts and practices that are carried out there should be directed, when he writes this way in 1 Cor. 14:26 . . . .[107]

There is little evidence that their advice was ever implemented nor that it had any lasting effect on Reformed liturgy in Utrecht. Rather, organ music continued and possibly became even more widespread after this 1655 statement by Voetius and his associates, a fact that then prompted the ministers to address the city council about the issue again in 1683:

> . . . we cannot consider anything but a totally new and uncommon occurrence here, diverting from the old and simple custom in the church of Utrecht, about which long ago the Theological Faculty rendered a unanimous judgment. You the honourable Lords, as supervisor of the church are to please leave the church of God here at peace with its old and simple singing of the Psalms, without the organ being played during that, just like from the time of the Reformation until today had generally been done, not without some edification of simple Reformed Christians.[108]

Thus the minister invoked the "theological Advice" nearly thirty years later, but still with no change. Accompaniment had already been ordered by the authorities whose very right to make that decision had been disputed in the *Advies*. In fact, in another fifty years, the magistrates of Utrecht would actually declare which stops the organist was to use,[109] even as all evidence suggests that organ practice in Utrecht continued, if not increased.[110] The magistrates instructed the organist of the Dom Kerk to play the organ before and after each Sunday's morning worship services, at afternoon services, and in the winter also at the evening services. What is more, the instructions are not only to provide prelude and

---

107. Theologisch Advys, January 29, 1655.

108. ". . . *tselve niet anders hebben kunnen aanmerken als een gansch nieuwe en tot noch toe hier ongewone saak, afwijkende van het aloude eenvoudige gebruyck in de Utrechtse kerken: van welk hoe veeleer door de Theologische faculteyt alhier eenparig geoordeeld is. U. Ed. A. A. als voedsterheeren der kerke believen toch de kerke Gods alhier gerustelijck te laten blijven bij haar oud en eenvoudig psalmgezang, sonder eenig orgelspeelen daaronder, evengelijk het van den beginner der Reformatie af tot heden toe niet sonder algemeene stichtinge van de eenvoudige gereformeerde Christnen is gebruyckt geweest.*" Das, "Strijd," 78.

109. Vente, *Bouwstoffen*, 171. From the directive, it is clear that a full organ plenum, from 8' principal foundations through mixtures and reeds, was the norm. However, if fewer people were in church the upper manual was to be uncoupled.

110. See Vente; Kist; Moseley; Riemsdijk.

postlude music, but the organist was instructed now to play the organ when the congregation sang the Psalms.[111] Furthermore, the organist was to play on festival days; the only limit to organ use during worship was that the organ was to play neither during Communion services nor on the previous Sunday, because those services in the strictest Reformed communities always included a special exhortation to devoted spiritual preparation to receive the sacrament in one week's time.[112]

Anti-orgelists had some success in smaller villages where magistrates were more easily influenced by a majority. For example, in Abkoude, a village near Utrecht, when city officials did not silence their organ, the Reformed consistory petitioned the council in advance of Christmas 1649 to issue a clear organ moratorium.[113] Their piquant letter argues not just that the organ was being played in direct violation of the previously adopted ban, but also that the church murals were not even fit for a brothel. The consistory recommended a fine of one thousand "double riders" (*dubbele rijders*) should the organist even so much as sound a pipe, and that the custodian be ordered to lock the church doors in order to assure that "no new superstitions should be introduced into our holy Reformation, so that the weeds that are being sown this way will not grow, and the kingdom of the Antichrist be increased." Ironically, the consistory of Abkoude ended its request by demanding that the re-issued ban be announced with the ringing of the church bells. The magistracy agreed to the requests, though the fine was reduced.

Likewise, in the village of Sluis, the minister Jacobus Koelman (= Christophilus Eubulus, 1631–1695),[114] a protégé of Voetius, attempted to silence the organ there, but with a markedly different outcome than that of Abkoude. According to the minutes of Classis Walcheren, the classis to which the congregation of Sluis belonged, the council of the Sluis church decided to censure worldly sins. Therefore they attempted to stop such evils as violating the Sabbath, playing cards or dice, skipping public

---

111. ". . . onder het singen der psalmen personelyk de orgelen deeser kerke sal bespeelen." Water, *Groot Placaatboek*, 8:507–8.

112. *INSTRUCTIE voor den Organist van den Dom, den 24 Decemb MDCCVI.* Water, *Groot placaatboek*, 8:507–8.

113. *Archief voor de Geschiedenis van het Aartsbisdom Utrecht*, 44:37. See *Sound Theology: A Reader* for the full decree with an English translation.

114. See Theophilus Parresius (= Jacobus Koelman), *Historisch verhael van de Proceduuren tegen D. Jacobus Koelman, Predicant tot Sluys in Vlaenderen*; Israel, *Dutch Republic*, 694–95; Krull, *Jacobus Koelman*.

worship services, and using pipe organs in church. To enforce these bans, the consistory of the church in Sluis petitioned Classis Walcheren to rule against the organs. The background to this overture was not only the situation in Sluis, but also of another church in the classis, the church of Veere. In Veere, in 1646, the magistrates approved organ use but they faced opposition both from the church council and from the classis. Thus Classis Walcheren wrote to the Veere magistrates of "the great offense that will be given over the introduction of the organ in the church of this city [Veere], especially during the worship service."[115] Nevertheless, the magistrates of Veere commissioned Willem Degens to build a new organ on July 1, 1646. This action aroused the ministers' ire so acutely that on July 23, 1646 they filed their objections again, and later two of the ministers were reprimanded for preaching publicly against the acquisition of the organ.[116]

Thus, with organ use so dangerously close to home, Sluis's church council authored another *anti-orgelist* statement and sent it to the city fathers, a statement supported by a petition signed by fifty-three of Sluis's citizens. The statement's concerns were similar to those expressed previously:

> 13 November 1672
>
> We request in unity and sincerity, that Your Honors will ban from the service of God in our area the use of the organ, as being a fallacious novelty, unknown to the Apostolic and the old church giving the sense of Jewishness, heathenism, and Papistry, and which does not serve to further and encourage the spiritual involvement, but rather to prevent and diminish that, and as the Synods state, to make us forget the good and giving more occasion to cause at some time or other more ceremonies in the church, and more musical instruments in the worship service, and to fall into other superstitions, which were also rejected in the first reformation, in all Swiss, French, Scottish, Hungarian, German and Dutch churches, as is obvious of the latter, and is shown fully by two of our National Synods, held in Dordrecht, in the years 1574 and 1578, art. 50 and art. 77.[117]

---

115. ". . . het groote ergernisse dat gegeven sal werden over het invoeren van den orgel in de kercke deser stede, ende specialijck onder den godsdient." Luth, "Daer wert . . . ," 224.

116. Vente and Vlam, *Bouwstenen*, 2:236.

117. "Wij versoeken ook eenpaariglijk en ernstelijk, dat toch door U U A A geweert worde van ontrent onse Godsdienst het gebruyk van het Orgel, sijnde een quade

The reference to "the first Reformation" underscores Sluis's understanding that their Reformation was second wave. Notable also are the indelible and unmistakable brush marks of *anti-orgelist* theology in both gravamina. The reference to Jewishness (i.e., Old Testament practice), heathenism, and Catholicism are three arguments posited by Koelman's teacher Voetius's in his *De Organis*, remarks that will be examined in full in a latter chapter. The gravamen asked for a return to the teachings of the apostolic fathers and the decrees of the synods of 1574 and 1578 because those assemblies rightly judged that "superstitious" organ music only served to make people forget what they had just heard, namely the Word of God preached in the sermon.

In the end, the authorities in Sluis did not acquiesce to either request to remove the organs. The only outcome was that Koelman was perceived as insubordinate and summarily deported in 1674. Neither the church authorities nor the city magistrates would make organ usage a matter of doctrinal importance. Even in exile, Koelman's continued his *anti-orgelist* insistence; four years after being thrown out of Sluis, he published this paragraph against organ use:

> In several large cities, it is accepted, without objections by the ministers (yes, some even are starting to endorse it) that the people at and around, before, during, and after the service use the organ to somewhat entertain the ears, although this is quite objectionable to others. Before they begin to sing the organ plays for quite a while, and the organ plays also during the singing, although that is not done in some places, and after the singing and once the blessing has been pronounced, the organist resumes his playing, plays the tune of a psalm or hymn, or of a ditty, for the entertainment of those present or who stay in the church a while. It appears they are copying this from the Jewish tradition, from the heathens or from the papistry, however it was unknown to the Apostolic and old churches; and it does not serve

---

nieuwigheidt, de Apostolische en oude Kerk onbekent, smaakende na 't Joodendom, Heydendom, en Pausdom, niet dienstigh sijnde, om de geestelijke beweegingen te bevorderen ofte te verwakkeren, maar wel om die te verhinderen en te verswakken, en gelijk de Synoden seggen, om het goede te doen vergeeten, gevende gereede occasie, om daar door teeniger tijdt tot meer Ceremonien in de Kerk, en meer musicale instrumenten in den Godsdienst, en tot andere superstitien te vervallen, ook verworpen in de eerste Reformatie, in alle de Zwitsersche, Fransche, Schotsche, Hungersche, Hoogduytsche, en Nederlantsche Kerken, gelijk van de laatste klaar, en ten vollen blijkt in twee van onse Nationale Synoden, tot Dordrecht gehouden, in 't Jaar 1574. en 1578. art. 50. en art. 77."
Parresius, *Historisch verhael*, 16.

to the enhancement and awakening of Spiritual movements, as some are wont to say, but rather to hinder and weaken them, and as the synods say, to have us forget the good things, which the synods, particularly those of the years 1574 and 1578 held at Dordrecht Art. 50 and 77, have rejected, just like was done by the Swiss, French, Scottish, Hungarian and German. However, now the synods of The Netherlands do not strive against this any longer; the evil is now established and they don't want to touch it any longer.[118]

Koelman's diatribes against the organ continued until 1688 when he wrote an "Address to the supervisors of the Reformed Churches of the Netherlands" in which he argued that the Reformed ought not to sing with the organ, nor any instrument, for it smacked too much of Jewishness.[119]

A contrasting example of magistracy cooperation can be found in the province of Zeeland's capital city of Middelburg. As mentioned above, the unique political arrangement in Middelburg resulted in the magistrates respecting an *anti-orgelist* decree put in place by the ministers. But by 1640 the magistrates of Middelburg challenged this state of affairs; they ordered that organ accompaniment now begin "under" the psalmody during the holy hour of worship.[120] The ministers of the city, with fifty years of *anti-orgelist* precedent on their side, warned the magistrates to stop any such reckless and intrusive move.[121] Such pleas

---

118. "*In verscheyde groote steden wordt zonder tegenspreeken der Leeraeren verdragen (ja zommige beginnen het voor-te spreken) dat men by en ontrent/ voor/ in/ en na den Godsdienst/ het orgel gebruykt/ om de ooren wat te vermaeken/ hoewel het andere zeer aenstoot; voor dat men begint te zingen/ speelt het orgel een tijdt lang; en alsmen zingt/ speelt het orgel mede/ hoewel dat in zommige plaetsen wordt nagelaeten/ en na datmen gezongen heeft/ en den zegen is gegeven/ vangt den Organist zijn spel wederom aen/ speelt den toon van een Psalm of Liedeken/ ofte ydel gezang/ tot verlustiging van die present zijn/ of noch wat in de Kerk te blijven; dit heeft men/ zo 't schijnt van 't Joodendom, Heydendom/ en Pausdom gehaelt: doch 't was by de Apostolische en Oude Kerk onbekent; 't dient niet tot bevordering en verwakkering van Geestelijke beweegingen/ gelijk zommige voorgeven/ maer om die te verhinderen/ en te verswakken/ en gelijk de Synoden zeggen/ om het goede te doen vergeeten; welke Synoden/ byzonder dat van 't jaar 1574. en 1578. tot Dordrecht gehouden Art. 50. en 77. die hebben verworpen/ gelijk mede de Zwitsersche/ Fransche/ Schotsche/ Hungersche en Hoogduytse. Doch nu wordt van de Synoden in Nederlant daer tegen niet meer geyvert: dat quaedt legt nu vast/ en men wil 'er niet aen roeren.*" Eubulus, *Pointen*, 186–187.

119. Koelman, *Sleutel ter opening*, 225ff.

120. Schotel, *Openbare eerdenienst der Nederl*, 70.

121. "*... dat men wilde interdiceren en nalaten het spelen van den orgen, gedurende*

were delivered from the pulpit of Hermannus Faukelius (= Herman Faukeel, 1560–1625) when he preached a sermon in Middelburg on the 45th Psalm to remind his congregation that

> the people of the Old Testament were truly urged in Psalm 150: Praise the Lord with the trumpets, the psalteries and the harps, praise him with tambourines and dancing, with strings and pipes, and with the bright sounding cymbals, because God had ordained such playing of instruments in that age in the ceremonial worship service, but now in the New Testament it would be great foolishness to prescribe them for the people of God as a part of the external worship service: and in this way we correctly criticize the papists which retain the sound of the organs in their sanctuaries, as well as chimes and bells....[122]

Nevertheless, the magistrates proceeded, and organ accompaniment began in 1640. The magistrates incidentally mentioned that two of the city's ministers opposed this new ordinance, surely one of these pastors was Abraham van de Velde (1614–1677). As Faukelius, Van de Velde preached against the use of the organ with unmistakable anti-Catholic fury:

> With one word, we judge this [organ use] and other novelties in these forgettable days a useless hindrance. This we also say of the introduction of new forms of songs and human hymns and present day ditties which we do not find in God's word, as also the playing and peeping of organs in the Church which things are all against the resolutions and decisions of the synods of our Fatherland.... It is known from Church history that those who are after novelties by introducing man-made hymns and errors have corrupted the congregation, so warned Arius, Samosatenus and Valentianen in Nichephor vol. 9, chapter 24; Eusebius in vol. 7, chapter 24; and Tertullian in *Carne Christi*, chapters 17

---

date de psalmen, naar gebruyck van Godts kercke alhier, in de kercken warden gesongen." Schotel, *Openbare eerdenienst der Nederl*, 70.

122. "... daerom wert seer wel het volc des ouden Testaments Psal. 150. vermaent: Looft den Heere met Basuynen, Psalters ende Harpen, looft hem met Tamboerinen ende Reyen, met Snaren ende Pijpen, met hellen ende clinckenden Cymbalen, om dat toe der tijt / God sulcke instrumentenspel in den Ceremonialischen Godtsdienst verordent hadde / alsoo souder nu groote dwaesheyt zijn / in het Nieuwe Testament / die den volcke Gods voor te schryven / als een deel der uytterlycke Godts-dienst: ende in desen deele berispen wy met recht de Papisten / welcke in hare Tempels / het gheluyt der Orghelen houden / mitsgaders der Clocken ende Bellen...." Faukeel, *Bruylofts-liet, ter eeren Jesu Christi gesonghen; inden 45. psalm*, 18. More excerpts are include in *Sound Theology: A Reader*.

and 20 of vol. 2. Although these people have no wrong motives, it is nevertheless not advisable to follow in their steps, since we may receive from them copper instead of gold as the pious Peter Martyr witnessed about the time hymns were introduced into the Roman Church.... Humanly speaking, it would be better if this and other novelties were not mentioned.[123]

But, as Faukeel before him, Van de Velde's invectives imparted no lasting change. The presbyterian system of church governance at the root of the Reformed church order ensured that laymen and not clergy controlled each church. So despite the biblical protestations proclaimed by two ministers, the magistrates declared in this clear, punitive, and succinct resolution:

> It having been proposed by the Lord Mayor that two of the ministers of this city on behalf of the church council had contacted them and on behalf of those mentioned before that [we] would prohibit and discontinue the playing of the organ during the singing of the psalms in the churches, as was customary in God's church here, and it having been deliberated, it is decided that the aforementioned officers [ministers] will be advised that we cannot find that there is anything disruptive for the congregation in that; on the contrary, it encourages and supports many people in their singing, and also prevents inappropriate singing; and that, therefore, we cannot understand the request to discontinue, but that we will instruct the organist to play with every proper and sweet tone daily on days of preaching, both on weekdays and Sunday.[124]

123. "*Met een woort dan / wy oordeelen dese en diergelijcke voorslagen en nieuwigheden in dese forgelijcke tijden gansch ondienstigh / gelijck oock het in-voeren van nieuw Formulieren van gesangen en menscheliche liedekens / buyten de ghene die wy vinden in des Heeren woort / en daer onder het gespel en gepiep der Orgelen in de Kercke: welch een en ander strijt tegen de resolutien en besluyten van de Synoden onses Vaderlandts. . . . 't Is bekent uyt de Kerckelicke Histozien / dat door nieuwe menschelicke gesangen / de nieuwigheden in 't hooft hadden / de Gemeynte door dwalingen hebben verborven / soo van ARIUS, SAMOSATENUS en van de VALENTINIANEN wort verhaelt / Nichephor lib. 9: cap. 24. Euseb. Lib. 7. cap 24. Tertull. Lib 2. de carne Christi. Cap 17 & 20. Daerom of schoon uyt geen quade meyninge van dese of die sulche nieuwigheden mochten worden geoppert / soo is sulcx doch gansch ongeraden in desen tijt te practiseeren / op dat wy door dese menschelijcke gesangen geen koper voor gout krijgen / soo sulcx de Geleerde PETRUS MARTYR getuyght van de gesangen inde Roomsche Kerck ingevoert. . . . Menschelijck dan waer het / dat dese en andere nieuwigheden niet wierden geoppert.*" Velde, *Wonderen des Alder-Hooghsten*, 410–11.

124. "*Sijnde door de Heeren Burgemeesters voorgedragen, dat twee van de Predikanten binnen dese stad, uit den name van de consistorie, haer hadden aangedient,*

This resolution acknowledged that impetus for such change was the horrid singing that occurred without the organ, and that organ music greatly improved psalm singing. This resolution shows that city magistrates controlled church buildings, organs, the ministers, and, in this case, even the liturgy of the public church in Middelburg. Thus in Middelburg the question of power led the magistrate to curb through a variety of means the Reformed Church's potential ability to monopolize liturgical decisions.

Thus even with attempts by *anti-orgelists* to stop organ use during worship, the organ use trajectory did not wane. By the time *anti-orgelists*, such as Faukeel and Van de Velde reviewed above, rose to preach, teach, and write against organ use, the organ was too far entrenched into the public and church life of most Dutch cities as to be stopped.

Improvisations

Records from the 1630s forward, the antecedent decade of the publication of *orgelist* Constantijn Huygens book that is the subject of the next chapter, paint a picture of organ music now normative in most every Dutch church. As the early organ bans became ephemeral, the organ was playing in many Reformed churches before and after worship; what is more, psalm accompaniment was expected. In 1638 the organ in the Nieuwe Church in Amsterdam was installed, in 1639–1641 an organ was built in the St. Pieters Church in Leiden, in 1639–1645 the St. Laurens Church of Alkmaar built their organ, and in 1656 the organ of the Gasthuis Church in Delft was dedicated, to cite just four landmark instruments built during this decade.[125] In the city of Hoorn, located in the province of North Holland, the church, not the magistrates, cautiously asked in 1644 if the organist could now begin to "play also during the

---

en uit den name als voren versocht, dat men wilde interdiceren en nalaeten het spelen van den Orgel, gedurende dat de Psalmen, near gebruijk van Godts Kercke alhier, in de Kercken wierden gesongen: waerop gedelibereerd sijnde, is verstaen, dat men voors. Gecommitteerde sal tot antwoord toevoegen, dat men niet kan vinden dat daarinne eenige ontstichtinge voor de Gemeente is gelegen; maer tot contrarie vele menschen opwekt en stijft int singen, oock het inordentelijck singen voorcompt: dat men daeromme tot het afschaffen niet en kan verstaen, maer dat men de Orgelist sal gelasten met alle ordentelijkheijt en soeten toon daegelijks op de preekdaegen, sowel in de week als sondagh, te spelen." Cited by Kist, "Kerkelijke orgel–gebruik bijzonder in Nederland," 263.

125. Hess; Knock, *Dispositien der merkwaardigste kerk-orgelen*; Schotel, *Openbare*, 68–69.

singing of the psalms in the great church, in the event this would now, or in the future, please this assembly and would not be offensive to the consistory and community."[126] It was agreed, and from that time forward this church, like so many of her sister churches, used organ music before and after worship, and now, even during the hour of divine worship.

What is more, it is clear that in many places the organ was now being used without any repertoire restriction. For example, in Kampen, where the organ was used during worship ever since the Reformed church began there, the church instructed organist Alewijn Pietersz de Vois of the Pieterskerk in 1636 to

> entertain the congregation there with his art and that in addition he shall play, both on Sunday and during the week, whenever there will be preaching in that church, both before and after every sermon to play on the large organ the psalm that is being sung, whichever the minister shall request to be sung.[127]

Interestingly, in De Vois's response, he complains that congregational accompanying was not a rewarding task. He also mentions that his colleague in the Hooglandse Kerk of Leiden was given more salary because of his accompaniment duties. Though De Vois's was complaining of remuneration, his comment reveals that in Leiden organ accompaniment was introduced even earlier than in the Pieterskerk.[128]

Additional evidence supports this journey toward full organ use from the mid-seventeenth century onward. For example, city archives of Leeuwarden of the province of Friesland confirm continued use of the organ, which is hardly surprising given the *orgelist* culture present there already reviewed. What is of interest now is that two organists of the Jacobijnen Kerk, namely the "old" Gysbert Harmensz and the "young" Jan Apkes Benting, were summoned before the city council in 1637 because they had failed to play during the church service. They were summarily

---

126. "*Oock gehouden sal sijn te spelen onder 't singen van de psalmen in de groote kerck, of misschien 't selve thans of morgen mocht aen genaem sijn dese vergaderinge ende niet aen stootelyck, onzen kerckenraet ende gemeente.*" Vlam, "Hoornse organisten en klokkenisten."

127. "... *met sijne conste de gemeynte trachten te vermaecken ende dat hij bovendien soo wel des Sondaechs als in der weecke telckens als in de voorsz. kercke sal worden gepredict, soo voor als nae yder predicatie onder het singen op het groote orgel sal speelen den psalm, die telckens de predicant verclaren sal, dat gesongen sal werden.*" Doove, "Prestanten en fusten," 342–43.

128. Luth, "*Daer wert* ...," 216–17.

suspended and were requested to turn over the keys to the organ to their successors. The organists had not anticipated that, and responded with a polite letter to the civic council where Benting indicated that he had, indeed, accompanied the singing of the Psalms

> since a few years ago . . . trusting that the congregation and the Honorable Lords would be served with that [the Psalm accompaniments] in an edifying way.[129]

Thus the issue of termination was not that the organ was being used during worship and "under" the Psalms, but of remuneration. When Benting initiated the added duty of accompanying the psalms, he had hoped "to receive gratuitous recompense for his service beyond the call of duty."[130] But when this extra compensation for this added duty was not forthcoming, Benting concluded that his service was not appreciated and so he simply stopped playing.

Orgelist cultures were certainly not *fait accompli*, and organ use most certainly continued to raise the ire of some Reformed leaders. But in the end, neither synodical organ bans, *anti-orgelists*, preachers, nor the passing of time were able to prevail against inevitable magisterial lassitude in upholding the "true" church. One final example from the minutes of the Hooglandse Church documents the struggle:

> 2 May 1636
>
> It was proposed that the Honorable Gentlemen of the court had agreed with the church trustees to order the organist to play on the organ, before the sermon, the psalm which is to be sung and [they] deliberated if there should not be further communication about this with the honorables so that there would be no hindrance because of this in the reading of the holy scriptures or to the worship service. It was approved to approach Mister van Alphen to negotiate further with him and to acquaint him with the inconveniences.[131]

---

129. ". . . *onder het singen der Psalmen [te spelen] met vertrouwen dat de gemeente ende myn E. Heeren tot stichtinge daer meede souden worden gedient.*" Luth, "*Daer wert . . . ,*" 217.

130. ". . . *op hope om voor deszelfs vrijwillige Extraordinaris dyenste gratieuse beloninge te genieten.*" Luth, "*Daer wert . . . ,*" 217.

131. "*Den 2 Meij 1636*
Is voorgestelt dat de Achtbaere Heeren van Gerechte met de Kerckmeesters voor hadden de Organisten te lasten op het Orgel te spelen, voor de Predicatie, de Psalm die gesongen sal worden, ende gedelibereert of men daer over met Achtb. niet en behoorde naerder

9 May 1636

Mr. van Alphen has proposed that the Honorable Gentlemen of the Court, before they make any decision about the piece to be played by the organist, [and he] has agreed to hear the advice of this meeting to see if it were better to have a psalm played before the beginning of the service, or during the singing, or not to do so at all. It was approved, although the meeting was small, to meet next Sunday about this.[132]

11 May [1636], special meeting

Having deliberated about the aforementioned matter of the playing of the organ before the sermon, the brothers have given the advice that the reading of the scriptures before the sermon should not be hindered or omitted; and for that reason if they would approve the playing of the organ before the sermon then such should take place reverently during the singing of the psalms. The president and the clerk will let Their Honors know of this decision.[133]

Conclusions

This chapter presented contemporary evidence of the wide divergence of local policies regarding church organ music amongst Reformed

---

to communiceren, dat daer door geen verhinderinge gedaen en worde aen het lesen van Heilige Schrifture ofte van den Godsdienst; is goedgevonden te versoecken mijnheer van Alphen, met deselve hierover nadir te handelen en de inconvenientien voor te houden." Kist, "Kerkelijke orgel-gebruik bijzonder in Nederland," 259.

132. *"Den 9 Meij 1636*

De Heer van Alphen heeft voorgestelt, dat de Achtb. Heeren van Gerechte, eer deselve op het stuk van het spel van den Orgelist eenige resolutie wilden nemen, goetgevonden hadden, het advijs van dese vergaderinge te hooren, of het beter ware dat sij voor het beginnen van de Godsdienst een Psalm souden spelen, ofte onder het singen, oft gansch nalaten. Is goetgevonden, alsoo de vergaderinge cleijn was, toecomende Sondach daerover eens te vergaderen." Kist, "Kerkelijke orgel-gebruik bijzonder in Nederland," 259-60.

133. *"Den 11 Meij, extraordinaris vergaderinge*

Is gedelibereert over de voorgaende saecke van 't Orgelspelen voor de Predicatien, ende is der Broederen advijs geweest, dat het lesen der Heilige Schrifture voor de Predicatie niet en dient verhindert ofte nagelaten: ende daarom, soomen immers voor de Predicatie soude goetvinden op den Orgel te laten spelen, dat dan sulcks stichtelijkst soude geschieden onder het singen van de Psalmen. 'T welck de Praeses en Scriba hare Achtbaarheid sullen bekent maken." Kist, "Kerkelijke orgel-gebruik bijzonder in Nederland," 260.

congregations in the Netherlands under the influence of the fluid courses of local politics. During the first fifty years of the Netherlands independence, the Dutch Reformed put into place a presbyterian form of church government that absorbed local custom. The result was that the provinces' true rulers, the urban regents, opted for local liturgical preferences even as church councils sought to place theology over local custom. Their motives were as varied as their actions. Consequently, the experiences of confessional groups and the role of the pipe organ differed from province to province and from city to city.

What is more, Reformed liturgy had no uniform shape amongst the Dutch, sometimes not even within the same province; Reformed liturgical practice developed in insular ways unique to each civic environment. Theologically, the Reformed left indifferent, non-salvific issues such as organ music to local discretion along with other liturgical decisions such as funereal practices, weekday services, and the use of hymns. As Reformed theology met entrenched, local customs, congregations, consistories, organists, and theologians jostled for power against each other. They in turn wrestled in some way with secular powers who demanded equal control over the religious lives of their citizenry.

That organ use was given adiaphora status did not go unchallenged. By the mid-seventeenth century *anti-orgelists* attempted to impose the ephemeral organ bans of 1578 anew, and reasserted that organ use was a needless, distracting, Old Testament and Catholic accoutrement of worship. In short, organ use was an issue of importance that compromised the essence of worship. Yet at the same time, evidence shows that organ use continued, if not increased, as churches expanded the role of the organ to include the accompaniment of the psalms during worship.

However, the examples given in this chapter do not relate the most intense chapter of the organ controversy yet to be told. One might expect that anti-Catholic (and thus anti-organ) sentiments would be the strongest as the Dutch gained their independence from Spain. However, as the next chapter will show in a singular test case in Dordrecht—where the organ controversy played out at the exact same time as an international theological controversy over predestination and free will. Clearly, nearly a century of accommodation and debate on the matter only made the organ controversy more acute, all the while sharpening the arguments of organ proponent and opponent alike.

4

THE CURIOUS CASE OF DORDRECHT[1]

After a bloody political break with Spain and a theological break with Rome, liturgical decisions became just as bloody within the United Provinces. In the first days of reformation, Dutch church musicians were expendable, organ pipes and choirboys silenced, and human-composed liturgical texts discarded. Biblical texts from the book of Psalms were to be sung only to tunes worthy of the dignity and weight of the Creator. As a result, historians unfailingly stereotype the nascent Dutch Reformed as a group of angry, tone-deaf, dyspeptic Protestants huddled together in their cold, silent churches, save for a black-robed dominee wagging a finger as he delivered a two-hour sermon on the evils of the papacy.

This chapter shows us that this caricature needs to be challenged, as we know this perception was not entirely the case—partially, but not entirely. In fact, history shows that the early Reformed did indeed have musicians serving in their churches who respected Protestant ideals even as they challenged them musically. One example is Jan Pieterszoon Sweelinck (1562–1621), organist of the Oude Kerk of Amsterdam, a composer and sought-after teacher. Curiously, Sweelinck wrote little music solely for the church; then again, why would he if organ music was not used in Reformed services proper? One of Sweelinck's contemporaries was Hendrick Joostenszoon Speuij,[2] the city organist and harpsichordist of Dordrecht, and the composer of the first published organ music

---

1. This chapter is adapted from Engle, "Song of the Synod."
2. Speuij's name varies in spellings: Speuy, Spey, Spuiy, Spuy, and even Spruyt. I shall use the commonly referenced Speuij.

written exclusively for the Dutch Reformed Church.³ Although Speuij was not an official delegate to the international Synod of Dordrecht (1618–1619), he nonetheless played a formative role there as the city and church musician.

Merely one year before Speuij was born in Den Briel, a town outside of Rotterdam, the Dutch Reformed church planned their first public meeting on Dutch soil. Prince William of Orange called civil authorities to meet him in Rotterdam on June 1, 1574. While he asked for money for his militia, he also requested that Reformed preachers receive an annual salary from the government.⁴ By September Prince William wrote to his brother, Jan van Nassau: "The number of Reformed clergymen has increased so much here during these last years through an exceptional grace of God that only few, if any, differing convictions are left."⁵

Meeting separately from the civil authorities in June 1574, these Reformed clergy "of few differing convictions" designed rules and regulations by which the new churches of the provinces of Holland and Zeeland would be governed. Speuij grew as a man and as a musician within a strictly defined liturgical environment that was governed by several of the decisions made then. For example:

> 45. The congregation should be left free during the gathering on Sunday morning or afternoon to read as well as to sing or to sing only. However, where there is reading only the Canonical Books shall be read to the people, and such as are considered by the consistory to be most edifying to the congregation. But they should see to it that the singing or reading stop by the time that the service begins.⁶

> Margin Note

> In the recording of the Articles [Articulen, minutes] the brothers have decided about the playing of the organs in the churches, that it is unseemly [*onbetamelick*, improper], and they have

---

3. Van den Borren, *Origins de la musique*, 55; Eitner and Springer, *Biographisch-bibliographisches*, 307; Molhuysen and Blok, *Nieuw Nederlandsch Biografisch*, 2:1349, 5:786; Bol, "Hendrik Joosten Speuy."

4. Pettegree et al., *Calvinism in Europe*, 163–64.

5. Hooijer, *Oude kerkordeningen*, 86.

6. "Acta Ofte Handelingen des Provinciale Synodi der Kerken van Holland en Zeeland, gehouden binnen Dordrect, den 16 Junij begonnen, ende den 28 geeindigt Anno 1574," art. 45, in Kersten, *Kerkelijk Handboekje*, 72.

made an article [Artikel, motion] about this which is number 1: Regarding the playing of the organs, etc.[7]

The secretary continues the Margin Note by making clear that "number 1" refers, in fact, to article 50, which reads as follows:

> Regarding the playing of the organs in the church we are of the opinion that it should be completely discontinued, according to the teachings of Paul in I Cor. 14:19. And although it [the organ] is still used in some of these churches at the end of the service when the people are leaving, it mostly serves to make the people forget what they have just heard, and we need to worry that afterwards it will be used for superstition, just like it now serves for frivolity [*lichtuaerdicheijt*, superficiality]; and if this were to be discontinued, it would be easier to gather in the offerings at the door when the people are leaving rather than to do so in the middle of the service, at which time it greatly disrupts the worship of God.[8]

In brief, this synod stated that organ playing distracted worshipers from those things for which people attended worship, and organ playing would lead to superstition. Their citation of Paul's letter to the church in Corinth[9] echoed John Calvin's commentary on Corinthians, where he also wrote against the use of instruments in worship.[10] One month after these decisions were made in Dordrecht, the Provincial Synod of Edam met in July 1574 and likewise discussed the use of the pipe organ. They agreed with Dordrecht but went even further to warn the civic authorities:

> Art. 3. About the organ playing: art. 50 of the aforementioned Synod regarding the discontinuation of the organ playing in the churches it was decided that all ministers of the Word of God should diligently and kindly ask [and] instruct the authorities in this matter (as this does not fall under the authority of the minister, but concerns the power of the authorities) to the end that, if the playing of the organ were to cease, the service of the word of God would gain a better and lasting effect in the hearts of the people.[11]

---

7. *Acta Ofte Handelingen des Provinciale Synodi*, art 45 marginal note.

8. Schoock, *Exercitationes variae*, 538.

9. "But in the church I would rather speak five intelligible words to instruct others than ten thousand words in a tongue." 1 Cor 14:19.

10. See chapter 1; Taylor, "John Calvin and Musical Instruments," 248–69.

11. Reitsma and Veen, *Acta der provinciale en particuliere synoden*, 1:27.

The civil authorities were involved in this synod because the church organ itself was the property of the city, and the municipal organist's salary was paid from public monies. Therefore, the question of whether to use the church organ was necessarily a matter of public policy. And in specific regard to organ use, it is clear that the established culture of pipe organ music among the Dutch was stronger than the new coalition of Reformed ministers.

This setting was Speuij's liturgical world, a collision of power between clergy and civic councils that resulted in a worship service where the pipe organ played before and after, but not during, the liturgy proper. Indeed, Speuij's situation in Dordrecht was even more complicated than the general Reformed context because attempts in Dordrecht to limit or prohibit the use of the pipe organ failed quickly and quietly. For example, only five years after the 1574 ruling against the organ (that is, in 1579), Dordrecht archives reveal a payment of nine pounds to organist Gherrit van Grippe to play the organ at the Augustine Church and another payment of twelve pounds to calcant Cornelis Jansz. van Tongeren to pump the organ bellows. Organist Van Grippe was replaced the next year by Adriaen Servaessen.[12] As time went on, the city purchased a new harpsichord in 1604 and a decade later, in 1614, it even commissioned Albert Kiespenning of Nijmegen to build an organ for the Groote Kerk. Clearly, the citizens of Dordrecht had no intention of limiting instrumental music in their churches; they wanted it increased. Much later, Dordrechters even petitioned their councilmen to allow the new Groote Kerk organ to be played on Sunday afternoons.[13]

Hendrick Speuij succeeded Servaessen as official city organist in 1595[14] with an astonishing increase in pay, no doubt because Speuij was to play at both the Augustine and Great churches. But with the increase of pay came increased stress: Speuij was to be a musician for a city that was just as loyal to the organ culture as it was to the new Reformed religion.

Initially, Speuij's career as Dordrecht's organist and harpsichordist pleased the organ culture crowd in the city. Apparently young Speuij offered flashy organ postludes after the worship service, which piqued the ire of local church authorities. On August 27, 1598 the church council

12. Vente and Vlam, *Bouwstenen*, 2:121–22.

13. *Dordrecht Consistorie Boeck*, no. 9, June 17, 1621. The next week, however, the consistory clarified that this would happen only in the Great Church (i.e., not at the Augustine Church).

14. *Dordrecht Kerkelijke Rekeningen* 1595–1596, fol. 108.

decreed that no more "frivolous pieces" would be tolerated from the organ loft. Indeed, if the organist wanted to play a postlude while congregants enjoyed talking in the ambulatory, the consistory directed the organist to offer only serious, pious pieces (*grave stichtelicke stucken*):

> August 27, 1598. Both the organists (Adriaen Servaessen and Henderick Spueij) will be admonished to appear here and they will be told to start with the psalms immediately following the service and once they have played them 5 or 6 times in succession, if they then want to play musical pieces they are to play serious pieces.[15]

Apparently the organists had difficulty giving up their frivolous organ music because the admonishment was repeated a mere four months later on Old Year's Eve, 1598:

> December 31, 1598. Both organists are to appear and they will play psalms or motets in the church, and will refrain from frivolous pieces.[16]

One year later, yet again:

> December 30, 1599. Rev. Demetrius and Jacob Frans Witten will speak to the mayor about the organists, that they are to be reminded to avoid all frivolous music on the organ.[17]

On February 3, 1600 the uncontrollable, unrepentant organist is identified for the record not as the elderly Servaessen, but the young Speuij:

> February 3, 1600. Andries de Meester has reported that he spoke to the mayor, as Jacob Frantzen had done earlier, and has given the honorable person counsel about the frivolous music

---

15. "Den 27 Augusti 1598. Beyde de organisten (Adriaen Servaessen en Henderick Spueij) sullen vermaent worden hier te verschijnen ende sal haer aengeseet worden terstont na de predicken met de psalmen te beginnen ende die 5 oft 6 mael achtervolgt hebbende, so sij dan musicale stucken willen spelen dat se grave stichtelicke stucken spelen." Vente and Vlam, *Documentaet archivalia*, 2:93.

16. "Den 31 December 1598. Beyde de organisten verscheyden worden ende sal men se vermaenen dat sij in de kercke willen spelen psalmen ofte motetten ende lichtvaerdige stucken achterweghen laten." Vente and Vlam, *Documentaet archivalia*, 2:93.

17. "Den 30 December 1599 D. Demetrius met Jacob Frants Wittens sullen den heer burgemeester aenspreken van de orgelisten dat sij vermaent mogen werden om alle lichtveerdige musique op d'orgel te vermijden." Vente and Vlam, *Documentaet archivalia*, 2:93.

being played on the organ. Upon which the Mayor has promised to summon the organists, and particularly the young man [that is, Speuij], in order to reprimand them about that. The next day he was summoned to appear before the Lords and was severely reprimanded by the Official and Mayor.[18]

After quite a few years passed, Speuij learned his lesson and proved that he could meet the criteria for serious and dignified pieces appropriate for use in the Reformed Church.

In 1610, Speuij's *De Psalmen Davids, gestelt op het Tabulatuer van het Orghel ende Clavecymmel met 2 Partijen* was published, a folio of twenty-four bicinia (a composition of two parts) based on Genevan Psalm tunes for organ. The published collection is the first of its kind for the Reformed Church, and the music was received with acclaim. On February 25, 1611 the States General awarded Speuij "sixty pounds of forty groats each" to honor his "sekere Musyckboecken" (certain music books),[19] and the towns of Middelburg and Gouda awarded him similar gratuities.[20]

Around the same time that Speuij matured and tempered his musical exuberance, serious theological trouble arose in the Dutch Reformed churches—not in the form of Roman heresy but rather from a homegrown heretic, Jacobus Arminius, who tested and then broke the bounds of Reformed theological thought. An international synod would be called to settle the "Arminian controversy," as well as other matters of church doctrine and praxis. Providentially for Speuij, the international synod would convene in his home church, the Groote Kerk of Dordrecht, on November 13, 1618. Though no written accounts or diaries specifically mention that organ music was offered by Speuij at the opening service of the synod, evidence allows us to conclude that this was the case. Still further, a convincing argument can be made as to exactly what music was offered. Documented and anecdotal evidence from four hundred years ago, the date of the international Synod of Dordrecht, paints this

---

18. "Den 3 Februarij 1600. Andries de Meester heeft ingebracht dat hij den borgmeester heeft aengesproken gelijc Jacob Frantzen tevoren ooc eenen E. Raedt heeft aengegeven het lichtverdich spelen op d'orgelen. Daerop den borgmeester belooft heeft de organisten ende insonderen den joncman Spueij te ontbieden om daervan vermaent te worden. 's Anderdachs werd hij voor de heeren ontboden ende heftich van Schout ende Borgmeester vermaent." Vente and Vlam, *Documentaet archivalia*, 2:93.

19. Curtis, "Henderick Speuy," 19:147.

20. Curtis, "Henderick Speuy," 19:147.

tantalizing musical picture. First, as previously mentioned, it was an established practice in Dordrecht at the time of the international synod to play the organ before and after Sunday worship services. In fact, the city and church shared an organist expressly for that purpose.

Second, Speuij had already composed a collection of pieces for use solely in the Reformed church. Surely, with international delegates flooding the city, Dordrecht would have wanted to impress her visitors by offering the finest worship service, replete with newly composed music by her prized organist.

Third, just two years before the arrival of the international delegates, Albert Kiespenning fulfilled his contract to build a pipe organ for the Groote Kerk of Dordrecht.[21] The stop list of this particular instrument has been lost, but comparisons of Kiespenning's other work at this time with Dordrecht's contract shows that the Groote Kerk received a good-sized two-manual organ, plus pedal. Surely this newly acquired, expensive marvel of Dordrecht was not merely seen, but heard, by all foreign guests on November 13, 1618 at the opening worship service. The Rev. Balthasar Lydius preached a sermon on Acts 15 (the Jerusalem Council) in Dutch at the Groote Kerk, while the Walloon minister Rev. Jeremias de Pours preached a sermon in French at the Augustine Church for the sake of the foreign delegation.[22] Both churches had pipe organs (the Augustine Church its one-manual positive, the Groote Kerk its new Kiespenning), and Speuij's new Psalm settings were composed in such a way that they could be offered beautifully on either instrument.

Finally, there are two accounts that indisputably record that the organ was played at the conclusion of the synod six months later. Delegate Eduard Poppius (1577–1624)[23] described the scene when the Canons of Dort were publicly presented at the closing service at the Groote Kerk:

> On the 6th of May those attending Synod, after they had come together in their usual place (where also his Grace Count Ernst was present) with great pomp, two carriages with ladies preceding them, have gone to the Great Church in Dordrecht; first the honorable gentlemen delegates from the States General, then the ecclesiastical persons and finally the Mayor of Dordrecht.

---

21. Dordrecht Kerkelijke Rekeningen 1614, no. 582, fol. 49.

22. Kaajan, *Pro-Acta der Dordtsche Synode*, 21–23; Sinnema, Moser, and Selderhui, *Acta et Documenta*, 1:9–10, 190; Brandt, *Historie der Reformatie*, 3:13–14.

23. Lieburg, "Participants at the Synod of Dordt," 1:105–6.

> Having been seated in the choir section, the chairman, *after the organ had been played*, made a long prayer in Latin.[24]

And Scottish delegate Walter Balcanquel wrote from Dordt to Sir Dudley Carleton:

> After the whole service was ended, *the organs pulsated* and so all the delegates of synod returned home in pretty much the same order in which they had come to the place of the synod.[25]

Still further, we know that instrumental and vocal music was enjoyed after the synod at the closing banquet on May 29, 1619. This festival overflowed with "Rheinish" wine—actually it more than overflowed: according to one source, the synodical delegates had been deprived of their "cures" for so long that they drank so freely that several of the foreigners ("even the most grave among them") went "reeling home to their lodgings."[26] For the entertainment at this post-Synod banquet

> they all went to dinner, where the whole Synod was plentifully treated with meat and drink, and a noble dessert of all sorts of sweet meats, and their ears entertained with agreeable music, both vocal and instrumental for which purpose several musicians were sent for out of the adjacent towns, and women who sang behind the curtains.[27]

No doubt Speuij was part of this entertainment, putting the town's harpsichord to the test, but surely not playing his Psalm settings.

This composite sketch gives us the facts that the city employed Speuij as a civic and church organist, that Speuij published a collection of Psalm settings in 1610, that the new organ of the Groote Kerk was played for preludes and postludes after 1614, that the Augustine Church owned a positive organ, that the opening worship of synod was held in churches that had pipe organs, and that two witnesses attest that the organ was played at the May 6, 1619 closing service. It is a small logical leap to say that Speuij played the organ at both the opening and closing worship services at the synod. He surely offered his newly composed repertoire based on Genevan psalm tunes.

---

24. Poppius, *Aanteykeningen ofte historisch verhaal*, 88–89. Emphasis mine.
25. Hales, *Golden remains of the ever memorable Mr. John*, 166. Emphasis mine.
26. Brandt, *In and About the Low Countries*, 3:307.
27. Brandt, *In and About the Low Countries*, 3:306–7.

This conclusion is supported by the examination of Speuij's extant musical score. Only two copies of the score exist, one at the London British Library and the other at the University Library of Glasgow.[28] Tellingly, the collection was dedicated to King James VI/I. Speuij prefaces the music score with a verbose dedication in French to the king. On the next page appears an acrostic poem in Dutch that extols the art of music and compares the musical skills of Hendrick Speuij of Dordrecht with King David of Israel, who played the harp and wrote psalms. These manuscripts appear to have been prepared after Speuij's death because a eulogy also appears, written by Gerard Voss. All in all, the score was so treasured that the pages' edges were leafed in gold, and the volume bound in white calfskin embossed with King James's coat of arms in glittering gold, surrounded by the Order of the Garter's motto, *Honi soit qui mal y pense* ("Shame on him who thinks evil").

The Jacobean connection might not be immediately obvious, so we must recall that James I of England was first James VI of Scotland until he inherited the English throne from his childless cousin, Elizabeth I. With James I's scepter of state came the scepter of the church, and so he became Defender of the Faith and Supreme Governor of the Church of England. A son of Scotland, James was a student of the Reformation; he knew the work of Calvin and was supportive of the Scottish Kirk. As such, King James not only urged the international gathering of Protestants in Dordrecht, but he also selected the English delegates and maintained an interest in the synod's work and conclusions.

Had Speuij's Psalm settings not been offered at the synod, they never would have been so elaborately bound, nor dedicated to such a notable patron of the synod.

Unfortunately there is no subsequent published organ music by Speuij.[29] Nonetheless Speuij blazed a trail for the inclusion of organ repertoire into services of Reformed worship. Speuij died in Dordrecht in 1625, six years after the synod adjourned, coincidentally the same year that King James died. Speuij must have known of his impending death

---

28. British Library K.1.i.14. University Library of Glasgow Special Collection G.e.14. Frits Noske has edited and published them under the title *Psalm Preludes* (Amsterdam: Heuwekemeijer, 1962). See also Curtis, "Henderick Speuy," 143–62.

29. Huygens, *Musique et musiciens au XVIIe siècle*, 225; Koninklijke Bibliotheek MS no. 3629 mentions a *Certains Pseaumes de David par Henry Spuy Organiste à Dordrecht, 1621*. If true, this second volume of Speuij is lost; however, most likely this was a second edition of the 1610 *De Psalmen Davids*.

because on August 26, 1625 he and wife Abigael finalized a will; he died on October 1. Memorialized as one who "joined divine things to musical modes" (*Divina organicis adsociando modis*), records indicate that he was buried in the Groote Kerk, no small honor—particularly for an organist whose work was, technically, still prohibited by the very church that honored him![30]

In 1638, the Synod of Delft interrupted the Dutch organ controversy with its sweeping declaration that the use or nonuse of the organ in the worship service was *adiaphora*; that is, an action neither proscribed nor prescribed by the denomination, but best left to the judgment and taste of local congregations. But Speuij was prescient in 1610 when he put pen to score, determined to show that music and art could be used in a God-glorifying and edifying manner. After all, if the Reformed championed God's sovereignty over all things—a theological foundation later trumpeted by the synod—then surely church music was not to be exempt. With this conviction, equipped with musical gifts, Speuij blazed the trail and lived his epitaph: he gave his life to art and, in turn, his art gave life.[31] For these reasons, Hendrick Joostenszoon Speuij deserves a rightful place as the first musician in the Reformed musicians' hall of fame.

The cast of characters in the next acts of this drama includes: an erudite member of the Dutch aristocracy and secretary to the prince of Oranje, Constantijn Huygens; a precise Calvinist layman, Jan Jansz. Calckman; an esteemed professor of theology Gijsbert Voetius; and a host of his *orgelist* and *anti-orgelist* colleagues. These men used baroque-era rhetoric of the highest order and the increasing affordability of books and pamphlets to bring the Dutch organ controversy very much into the public square.

---

30. Dalen, *Groote Kerk*, 132. But the exact location of Speuij's grave is no longer known.

31. "*Ydele Const versmaet Godtlijcke, Const doet leven. / H. S. Const doet leven.*" Speuij, *Psalmen Davids*.

5

CONSTANTIJN HUYGENS

His Friends and Foes

Constantijn Huygens[1] (1596–1687) was an important figure in the politics, religion, and literature of the emergent Dutch Republic during and after its struggle for freedom from Habsburg rule. He was born in The Hague on September 4, 1596 to Christian Huygens, the secretary of William II. Because of his relatively aristocratic standing, Christian could offer his son an excellent education. By the time he was a young man, Constantijn had developed into a skilled gymnast, musician, and artist. In 1616 he enrolled with his elder brother in the University of Leiden, but he stayed there only one year. In 1618, he went with the English ambassador Dudley Carleton to England, where he was presented at court and even played the lute for James I.

An interesting feature of his time in England was the relationship that developed between the young Huygens and John Donne. Huygens

---

1. Huygens's name varies in spelling: Huigens, Huygens, Huighens, and Huyghens. I shall use the commonly referenced *Huygens*. For the historical biography of Huygens, see Hofman, *Constantijn Huygens*; Van Deursen, Grootes, and Verkuyl, *Veelzijdigheid als levensvorm*; Strengholt, *Constanter*. Huygens himself composed a substantial, poetic autobiography, *Vita propria sermonum*, and though Huygens never meant for the poem to be published ("*Nil datur hic vulgo, nil cui tot caetera, famae.*" "The work is not destined for the people, nor for my name, for whom so much other work was destined." *Vita* II §1290), the work was translated and published under the title *Mijn Jeugd*, trans. Heesakkers and Schenkeveld-Van der Dussen.

praised Donne's work and vowed to translate Donne's work into Dutch. In 1618 Huygens returned home in the company of the English delegates to the Synod of Dordrecht, and in 1619 he proceeded to Venice in the diplomatic service of his country. In 1621 he returned to London, this time as secretary to Ambassador H. Jacob van Wijngaerden, and made a third diplomatic visit to England from 1621 to 1623.

Upon his return to the Netherlands, Huygens, who was already an artist, musician, and diplomat, evolved into an author and influential government leader. In 1625 he published a large volume of poetry and in the same year was appointed private secretary to Prince Frederik Hendrik of Oranje. He advised the prince on many artistic matters. Indeed his influence on the art and architecture of the northern Netherlands in the seventeenth century was considerable: Huygens was one of the first to recognize the talent of the young Rembrandt van Rijn and commissioned him to create a series of paintings of the passion of Christ for the prince's Noordeinde Palace in The Hague.

In 1627 Huygens married Susanna van Baerle and settled in The Hague. Four sons and a daughter were born to them; the most famous, Christiaan Huygens, became a noted astronomer and physicist. In 1630 Huygens was granted the title "Lord of Zuilchem" and appointed to the Privy Council where he exercised great influence over affairs of state. In 1634 he completed his long-promised Dutch translation of John Donne's poems, fragments of which still exist. From 1639 to 1641 he occupied himself with the building of a magnificent house and garden outside The Hague (now the modern Huygens Museum) and celebrated its beauty in a poem entitled *Hofwijck*. Because his government service required him to travel throughout Europe, Huygens became acquainted with such notable contemporaries as René Descartes, John Bacon, Marcus Zuerius Boxhorn, and Claudio Monteverdi.

Throughout his lifetime Huygens published poems, books, and reportedly more than eight hundred musical compositions, though only the collection *Pathodia sacra et profana*[2] (1647) survives along with his book *Gebruyck of Ongebruyck van 't Orgel in de Kercken der Vereenighde Nederlanden*[3]—the subject of this chapter. In addition to these musical

---

2. From a letter dated March 19, 1676. *Pathodia* contains twenty psalms, twelve arias, and seven airs for solo voice and basso continuo. This collection is available in Huygens, *Musique et musicians,* and in Huygens, *Pathodia sacra et profana.*

3. Leiden: Bonaventuer ende Abraham Elsevier, 1641; Amsterdam: Arent Gerritsz. Vanden Heuvel, 16592, 16603. Hereafter *Orgel Gebruyck* with all page references to the

works, Huygens was also a famous poet. He was often invited to write "threshold poems" (*drempeldichten*) as introductions to a book. No one knows whether he was asked because of the quality of his poetry or because the publisher wished to have the secretary to the prince endorse the book. It is clear, though, that Huygens's musical talents, his reputation as a poet, his pivotal place between the government, his notable colleagues, and his access to the prince put Huygens in a unique position to influence and guide the organ controversy. And that he did.

Huygens entered the organ controversy on November 24, 1639 when he accompanied Frederik Hendrik to the northern city of Groningen. Frederik Hendrik had been chosen to succeed Prince Willem Lodewijk as governor of the province, so he traveled there to present himself to the Estates (parliament). A grand reception was held in the Hall of the Estates and was followed by a daylong celebration. The music that was performed was not exceptional, according to Huygens, but he added that "His Highness remained in a friendly mood, even when the flutes added their *furieux accords*."[4] That Sunday the new governor, accompanied by Huygens and the magistrates of the city, worshiped in the Martini Church, where they heard the famous organ built by Agricola, newly renovated just that year.[5]

This single church service was revelatory for Huygens, and affected church music for centuries to follow. The same day Huygens conveyed his enthusiasm in a letter to Princess Amalia, Frederick Hendrik's wife:

> 25 November. This morning, S. A.,[6] surrounded by a large number, went to the preaching at the large Church and heard there, with much satisfaction, the beautiful organ that accompanied the singing of the people with such gravity and majesty that it is a wonder the entire world would find edifying. This positively animated me to have printed this winter what I have written on this matter, that I cannot suffer, that our flourishing churches remain frustrated from not having such a beautiful aid for their order and devotion.[7]

1659 edition. Huygen's extant manuscript is archived at the Koninklijke Bibliotheek, The Hague: Hs KA XLVIII.

4. Poelhekke, *Frederik Henrik, Prins van Oranje*, 513–17.

5. Jongepier, *Toegang tot het orgel*, 47, 101–2.

6. S. A. is an abbreviation for *Son Altesse*, "His Highness," a reference to Frederik Hendrik.

7. "... *Ce matin S. A. environnée de grand monde, est allée au presche de la grande Eglise et y a entendu, aveq beaucoup de satisfaction, la belle orgue, qui y est, accompagner*

Huygens also wrote the princess that the prince promised to install an organ in the Court Chapel of The Hague.[8] Incidentally, one magistrate with them was the Count of Oost-Friesland, and he must have been equally moved by this experience because the organ in his home church of Emden was used for the first time the following month.[9]

But the construction of a princely organ was not the most important result of that church service. Only a few weeks later, on Friday, December 16, 1639, Huygens finished work on a manuscript that would stir up controversy within the Dutch Reformed churches for a century and ultimately alter worship practice in the Low Countries. By February 1640 Huygens's first draft of *Orgel Gebruyck* was finished; he had it published anonymously and dedicated it to the municipal authorities of his hometown, The Hague.

This lengthy essay is clearly the work of a poet, politician, and scholar. *Orgel Gebruyck* is carefully organized according to the patterns of classical rhetoric: Huygens began by discussing three "uses" of the organ in the church after the Reformation. The first "use," referred (paradoxically) to those churches that did not use the organ in church at all, such as French and Swiss churches that "follow the precepts of Calvin." The second "use" referred to groups such as Anglicans and German Lutherans who did use the organ in worship. Then came the Dutch. Huygens called the practice in the Netherlands of playing the organ as a concert instrument before and after but not during worship as the third "use." "This use," said Huygens, was ". . . the most unedifying."[10]

Huygens narrated the positions of his opponents with quite salty language. The contemporary practice of treating the organ as some kind of musical entertainment he called unequivocally unedifying; as proof he listed one congregation's officially approved list of secular music that could be played on its church organ! He openly mocked the argument

---

le chant de peuple, aveq tant de gravité et majesté, que c'est une merveille combien tout le monde s'en trouve edifié. Cela m'anime davantage à faire imprimer cest hiver ce que j'ay escrit sur ceste matiere, ne pouvant plus souffrir, que noz florissantes eglises demeurent frustrées d'une si belle ayde à leur ordre et devotion. Et S. A. asseure, cela s'introduisant, elle seroit contente, de faire remettre une orgue dans la chapelle de la cour." Worp, Briefwisseling, 3:125.

8. Worp, *Briefwisseling,* 3:124.

9. Kaufmann, *Orgeln Ostfrieslands,* 29.

10. "Mijn voornemen is eerstelijck, te bewijsen, dat wy op den voorsz. Dry-sprong niet alleen den min stichtelicken, maer zelf den onstichtelicxten wegh gekoren hebben." Huygens, *Orgel Gebruyck,* 4.

made by city officials that playing such music after the sermon would cause congregants to remember the sermon longer and more accurately, thereby making them become better Christians. As far as Huygens was concerned, the organ prelude was nothing more than "the master's fancy: in which he [the organist] performed that which he had to play"[11] or ". . . a man's dream, blown out through the pipes."[12] One postlude that Huygens endured went on so long that by the end of it hardly a soul remained in the church, "except for the sexton and a few cripples."[13] While these organists were certainly gifted in their craft, Huygens was openly irritated by the fact that organists improvised on the tune for the day according to the current musical fad. In his opinion using popular, secular musical idioms in church was simply a misuse of the church organ and of worshipers' attention, even if the theme of the postludes were a psalm tune.

Huygens described in colorful detail the reactions of the congregation to such organ playing. He claimed that whoever was not in a hurry to leave after the worship service strolled around the church listening to the organ and seeking social contacts, inquiring about a friend's health or strutting the latest fashions. Huygens reasoned that after two hours—apparently was the standard length of these Reformed worship services—congregants would naturally want to chat with their neighbors and friends rather than sit silently and listen piously to the organ postlude as a way to reinforce the words of the sermon, as the city fathers had suggested. Indeed, Huygens said, it was certainly confusing and very likely sacrilegious to have an instrument that was used as public entertainment or background music share space inside the church with the pulpit and other liturgical fixtures. Huygens claimed that such a scandalous misuse of the organ was akin to washing one's hands in the baptismal font or eating Sunday dinner from the Communion table.

Huygens accepted without argument the notion that no building was inherently sacred or holy, not even a church; using a space for a holy purpose sanctified it, not incense and incantations. Still, he pleaded, the church was a "House of Prayer" and therefore "worldly luxury and

11. "*. . . naer 's Meesters welgevallen: daermede hy sich ten Toon bereide van 't ghene hem te spelen staet.*" Huygens, *Orgel Gebruyck*, 5.

12. "*Dat daer yemand stichtinge uyt dat voor-spel trecke, eens menschen droom, door pijpen uytgeblasen, en gelooff ick niet datmen staende houde.*" Huygens, *Orgel Gebruyck*, 5.

13. "*. . . daer de Koster ende weinighe kreupelen alleen in deelen.*" Huygens, *Orgel Gebruyck*, 10.

pleasure can never find a proper place there."[14] Finally, exasperated with the idea of popular tunes filling worshipers' heads before the service and ringing in their ears on the way home from church, Huygens called that practice "offensive, because it is indeed ridiculous to begin part of the religious exercises of the church when one is going home."[15] He continued his commentary by judging that the recitals performed before and after worship (when "common ditties"[16] were played) was worse than having no organ music in church at all, as was the practice in French Reformed churches. Of course, this suggestion was merely rhetorical, also; shutting down all the pipe organs in Holland would only pander to the most fervent anti-Catholic wing of the Reformed churches. He wondered if there might not be a more satisfying, albeit complicated solution, since, as he said, "the organ is in all respects the most perfect structure created by man to produce sound,"[17] especially the *Vox Humana* organ stop.[18]

In summary, Huygens argued, based on firsthand observations, that the practice of playing the organ only before and after worship did not produce a deeper appreciation for the sermon, as authorities intended, nor were Dutch worshipers built up in their Christian faith by the use of secular musical vocabulary to embellish psalm tunes.

Huygens next suggested not only that organs should be kept in the churches but also that new organs should be built so they could better accompany congregational singing.[19] After making this blatantly nonconformist suggestion, he reinforced the distance he had already placed between himself and the fiercest iconoclasts; he anticipated that this

---

14. "*Op 't eerste segg ick, dat alle wereldsche ydelheid die ἐν οἴκῳ προσευχῆς, in 't huys des Ghebeds, oft opentlick als sulx, oft onder schijn van geestelickheid gepleeght werdt, onbehoorlick, aenstootelick, ende onstichtigh is . . . . Maer de Wereldsche weelde en wel-lust kander noyt in voeghen.*" Huygens, *Orgel Gebruyck*, 11, 19.

15. "*. . . argerlick noem ick het nu, om dat het inder daed belacchelick is, een stuck vanden Gods-dienst te beginnen in de Kerck, alsmen t' huys gaet . . . .*" Huygens, *Orgel Gebruyck*, 25.

16. "*lichter deunen.*" Huygens, *Orgel Gebruyck*, 29.

17. "*. . . ende, voor soo verre mijn' geringhe kennisse streckt, het Orgel is in allen deelen het volmaeckste maecksel van all het ghene by menschen in 't uytspreken van Toonen te weghe is gebracht.*" Huygens, *Orgel Gebruyck*, 39.

18. Huygens's mention of the Vox Humana (*Menschenstemme*, lit. "Voice of a Human") is a reference to an organ stop, a thinly scaled reed used with tremulant to mimic the human voice.

19. "*. . . dat is, de Orgelen niet alleen behouden, maer oock niewe te maken, tot het dagelicksche gebruyck onser Kercken.*" Huygens, *Orgel Gebruyck*, 42.

suggestion would be interpreted as an attempt to reintroduce "popish frills"[20] into the Reformed churches, so he armed himself with a reference to the Old Testament that was sure to appeal to even the most hardened Calvinist: "we have not borrowed the church music from New Rome, but, with New Rome, have obtained it from Old Jerusalem."[21] What is more, he said, the objection was specious, since the Reformed Church continued to share many things with the Catholics, such as prayer and thanksgiving, fasting, the sermon, baptism, singing, pulpits, the use of godfathers and godmothers, and even "waffle cakes"[22] at baptism, to which none of the Dutch Reformed believers questioned in the slightest.

In fact, Huygens was clearly concerned that the Reformation was teaching untruths about the Roman Catholic Church, one of which was that the organ was a "damnable frivolity." Huygens wanted his readers to distinguish carefully between which features of the Roman Catholic Church were universally Christian and which were the results of human invention to which Calvinists could not subscribe. Huygens said that all worshipers—Reformed and Catholic alike—must praise God with all their faculties (intellect, heart, and mouth) acknowledging that praise flows first from the heart.

Then Huygens took a bold leap. He proposed that it was possible, contrary to orthodox Calvinist practice, to augment worship with reverent physical gestures such as kneeling.[23] Since we owe God all praise within our power, it was not possible to honor God too much with such gestures. If we address God in song or word, reasoned Huygens, it is also fully proper to raise our hands to heaven or lower our knees to the earth as well. Such a combination of physical and spiritual praise, he concluded, reached its apex in the church organist who praised God with heart, mind, mouth, foot, and hand all at the same time whenever he led the congregation in singing psalms of praise to the Lord God.

---

20. "... aenstootelicke ydelheden van 't Pausdom...." Huygens, *Orgel Gebruyck*, 44.

21. "... dat wy het Kerckspel niet van niew Roomen, maer, met niew Roomen, van Oud Hierusalem geleent hebben...." Huygens, *Orgel Gebruyck*, 45.

22. "Sy hebben Predick-stoelen ende wat daertoe behoort, ende wy oock; gebruycken Peters en Meters, en voor desen Wafel-koecken: ende de Kercke van Geneve oock." Huygens, *Orgel Gebruyck*, 46.

23. "het handen-vouwen, het bucken, het knielen...." Huygens, *Orgel Gebruyck*, 52–53.

Again Huygens quoted the Bible to support this position by referencing "the man after God's heart"[24] (King David) who used tongue and hand to praise God when he played upon his harp. Nowhere in Holy Scripture could Huygens find a command forbidding the playing of music to God's glory, so, how could the church not follow the example set by King David?

In this section of *Orgel Gebruyck*, Huygens referenced John Calvin's commentary on Psalm 33 where Calvin wrote against the "immature" use of instruments in worship. Huygens noticed that Calvin placed the organ in this discussion along with other typically Roman Catholic items such as incense and lamps. Though Huygens agreed with Calvin that the organ, incense, and lamps are all "lifeless," he contended that the organ distinguished itself because it could potentially assist humans in singing their praise. With that, Huygens brought the argument to an abrupt close:

> But I fight for the living organ. That is beyond discussion, and it makes, according to Chrysostom (Page 1, No. 20), "Man as a well-tuned lute, bringing forth unto God a perfect and spiritual song." Other statements, from papist as well as our own teachers, one could interpret in a like way, after giving them due consideration, even the vehement assault of Erasmus on the first epistle to the Corinthians, chapter 14 and in the *Lingua*. But I would linger too long on one point, which according to my insight does not need that much discussion.[25]

Even though he was not a clergyman, Huygens wrote like a theologian, using Scripture to support his claim that an organist who rightly accompanied a congregation singing a psalm praised God with heart, hands, and tongue.

Huygens then presented his solution:

> My opinion would then be that we, in part, cast our eyes on some of our neighboring cities, and that we, according to their usual practice of some years, accompany the daily singing of the

---

24. "den Man na 's Heeren Hert . . . ." Huygens, *Orgel Gebruyck*, 58.

25. "Maer ick strijde voor 't levendige: Dat 's boven op-spraeck; makende, soo wel als Chrysostomus, κίθάράν εμμελή τόν ανθρωπον, παναρμονιόν τινά μελώδιάν τόν πνευματικήν άνάφέροντά τώ θεώ, den Mensche tot een' wel-getoonde Luyt, die Gode een volkomen ende Geestelick Gesangh voorbrenghe. Andere, soo Paepsche als onser Leeraren voorgebrachte woorden soudemen, wel insiende, gelijck beduydsel konnen ende moeten geven, selfs de heftighe uytvaringhe van Erasmus op het 14. Cap. vande I. tot de Corinthen, ende in Lingua; maer waere hier te lang op een punt gestaen, dat, mijns bedunckens, soo veel beweerings niet en vereischt." Huygens, *Orgel Gebruyck*, 70.

congregation with the organ; that is, both before and after the sermon, beginning with the psalm and ending with it.[26]

In other words, Huygens wanted to discontinue the organ postlude and add an organ introduction before the singing of the psalm. Playing a dignified organ introduction (*statighe inleidinghe*) to the singing of the psalm, about ten to twenty measures in length, could

> ... prepare not only the voices of the congregation but even their hearts to that modest and devoted attention that is required for the pronouncement of the holy words which are to follow.[27]

Since music has the power to influence our inner life, Huygens warned that these introductions were to avoid all "artful frolicking"[28] and that the psalm accompaniment itself be of "dignified simplicity."[29] Once again, Huygens appealed to Scripture for support; the apostle Paul required that the Corinthian church conduct its Sunday worship in ways that were "fitting and orderly"[30] (1 Cor 14:40). Those ancient words certainly did not describe any Dutch church that Huygens knew; rather, during the service congregants sang out of tune and out of rhythm with each other, and before and after the service the organs played pop tunes. So, Huygens again exhorted that the proper use of the organ during the worship service itself could promote "increasing devoutness" (*stijgende Godvruchtigheid*) by focusing worshipers' attention on the words and meaning of the psalms while they were sung and by leading the congregation in singing them well. Huygens's promise to those who were

---

26. "*Mijne meeninghe dan soude wesen, dat wy, voor een gedeelte, het ooghe sloeghen op sommige onse naburighe Steden, ende dat wy, volgens haere nu eenighe jaeren gewoonlicke Wijze, den dagelixen Kerk-sang der Gemeente met het Orgel vergeselchapten: dat is, soo voor als nae de Predike, met den Psalm beginnende ende daermede eindigende.*" Huygens, *Orgel Gebruyck*, 71–72.

27 "*... ende niet de Stemmen der Gemeente alleen maer selfs hare herten holp bereiden tot die zedighe ende eerbiedighe aendacht, die in 't uytspreken van d'aenstaende heilighe woorden werdt vereischt....*" Huygens, *Orgel Gebruyck*, 72–73.

28. "*... konstighe dertelheden vanden Orgelist....*" Huygens, *Orgel Gebruyck*, 90.

29. "*Het orgel dan, even als vande uytsprake geseght is, het zij het God helpe aenspreken, oft my, God in Gebede ende Lofsang, my in beroering van Gemoede tot dat Gebed ende dien Lofsang, vereisch ick in alle statelicke eenvoudicheid gehandelt te werden....*" "Thus I require of the organ, as has been said about the speaking, whether helping me to address God or helping me to hear God during prayer and psalm by moving my soul, that it [the organ] be used in all stately simplicity." Huygens, *Orgel Gebruyck*, 97.

30. "*Dat alles betamelick ende ordentlick geschiede....*" Huygens, *Orgel Gebruyck*, 108.

still skeptical about the potential for increased devoutness that came with singing the psalms well: "they will tangibly experience that their well-shaped minds shall be lifted up from the earth, by the proper accompaniment of the organ between psalms that are sung, and they shall feel a certain rapture."[31]

Then Huygens described how the organ could function best. He criticized one attempted remedy for poor congregational psalmody, that of a *voorzanger* (cantor) who stood in front of the congregation and sang each psalm phrase in turn, which was then parroted by the congregation. However, Huygens reported that often the *voorzangers* could not be heard over the pitiful singing of the congregation; as the gathered worshipers dragged out the end of each line and sang at different tempi, the *voorzangers* sometimes had to "scream themselves to bursting"[32] just to be heard over the noise from the pews so they could belt out the next line of the psalm. What is worse, many congregants simply did not follow the *voorzanger*'s lead at all and sang some other tune entirely.

Huygens suggested what today seems like an obvious solution: use the organ to lead and improve congregational singing:

> Now the organ, being a strong and unwavering instrument, is powerful, and as I started to say, highly necessary to defend against and prevent all these above-mentioned absurdities [*ongherijmtheden*]. When the psalm is announced, let an organ pipe be sounded to indicate the best key for that particular psalm (in which often many blunders are made) and let the organ play along with the voices of the congregation, toned down to use such registration which is appropriate for the smaller or greater number of people present.[33]

31. "... *dat sy tastelick bevinden sullen haere welgestelde gemoederen door het schickelicke mede-luyden van 't Orgel, tusschen de gesonghene Lofsangen, vander aerde opwaerts getoghen, ende eenigher maten vervoert te sullen werden.*" Huygens, *Orgel Gebruyck*, 101–2.

32. "... *te bersten souden schreeuwen, eer sy het te boven quamē* ...." Huygens, *Orgel Gebruyck*, 113.

33. "*Het Orgel nu, een sterck ende onwanckelbaer Instrument zijnde, is machtigh, ende, als ick begonde te seggen, ten hoogsten noodigh, om alle voorgenoemde ongherijmtheden te weeren ende voor te komen. Laet, op het verkondigen vanden Psalm een' pijpe gheroert werden, tot aenwijsinge van de bequaemste hooghde tot soodanighen Psalm: (daer in mede veeltijds leelick mis-getast werdt) laet het gansche Orgel gesamenlick met de stemme der Gemeente roeren, getempert in soodanighen Register, als naer het meer oft minder getal der Menschen betamelick sal werden bevonden* ...." Huygens, *Orgel Gebruyck*, 114.

Since many worshipers would not have been used to singing with the organ, Huygens asked that organists avoid adornments and play with "steady medium measure that is neither too fast nor too slow"[34] (in which many organists "fail grossly")[35] and play temperately using such registers as were suitable for a small or large number of people.[36] The result would be Huygens's ideal of a steady, dignified, pleasing song amid even the largest congregation.

Next Huygens affirmed the Reformed principle that churches should sing only psalms in worship. Though he personally saw little danger in singing devotional songs "of our own creation" to God, he nevertheless chided the Provincial Synod of Utrecht which allowed the publication of a small book of hymns in 1610.[37] While Huygens agreed with this synod and Paul's instruction to the Ephesians to sing hymns in church, and while he was sure it was desirable for everyone to improvise prayers and songs of praise at home, he warned that it was better not to use these songs in corporate worship lest the psalms be forgotten.

Huygens also expressed his displeasure with singing the Ten Commandments during worship. Even though he had earlier approved of singing the Lord's Prayer, as was the practice in the "Greek Churches," he distinguished between the Decalogue and the Lord's Prayer for the Lord's Prayer and most of the psalms were human words meant to be addressed

---

34. "*Laet sulx ten uyt-einde toe vervolgen, met een' eenparighe, middelmatighe, dat is, een' onverhaeste ende onvertraeghde maet* . . . ." Huygens, *Orgel Gebruyck*, 116.

35. ". . . . (*waerin mede veeltijds groffelick werdt gefeilt*) . . . ." Huygens, *Orgel Gebruyck*, 116.

36. Huygens mentions that in London they went so far as to hang a curtain in front of the organ in order to deaden the sound. Huygens, *Orgel Gebruyck*, 115. During the seventeenth and eighteenth century in the Netherlands there were also examples of curtains placed in front of organs: Sint Jan in 's-Hertogenbosch received money on August 2, 1691 for the making of new "drapes for the great organ." Harst, *Grote orgel in de kathedrale*, 22.

37. *Hymni ofte Loffsangen op de Christelijcke feestdagen, ende andersins* ('s–Gravenhage, 1615). The preface states: "*De ghewoonte van de lof-sangen te singhen in onse en andere Gereformeerde Kercken gebruyckelijck, sal men onderhouden, ende ten selven eynde tot Godts lof ende prijs, mitsgaders stichtinge der Ghemeynte singhen: de hondert vijftich Psalmen ghenaemt: de Psalmen Davids . . . mits gaders soo vele andere Schrift-uyrlijcke lof-sanghen en Christelijcke Liedekens, handelende van Christi gheeboorte etc.*" "The custom to sing songs of praise in our and other Reformed Churches, shall be continued, and to that end sing to the Praise and Glory of God and also for the edification of the congregation: the hundred and fifty psalms, known as David's . . . as well as many other songs based on scripture, and Christian songs, concerning the birth of Christ etc." Hooijer, *Oude kerkordeningen*, 384.

to God, but the Ten Commandments were words that God had spoken to the Israelites. In Huygens's opinion, for Christians to take these words into their own mouths and sing them to God or to each other was both presumptuous and patently ridiculous: he asked his readers to imagine a group of citizens singing a list of civil laws to the city council.[38]

Huygens next wandered into an aside, and asked if the Reformed should not worship more often. "Is there any harm in one of these three things?" he questioned, "or would this seem too Roman Catholic?"[39] He answered his own questions by noting that the reduced worship frequency excluded, for example, "the tolerable if not commendable custom to present as an offering to God the Lord special hymns in thankfulness for the great general blessings that have come on the land."[40] After Huygens summarized his position, he reviewed once again his proposed solution. Then Huygens concluded by committing not to debate his work with any opponent, and bestowed upon his reader a trinitarian doxology.[41]

It took a year for the manuscript to be published, and while it was in preparation at the printer Huygens sent proofs to seventeen acquaintances asking for their reactions. Among those who received proof copies were theologians around the country and two ministers working in The Hague, Elezear Lotius (1591–1668) and Caspar Streso (1603–1664).

38. Huygens, *Orgel Gebruyck*, 128–31.

39. *"Is in een van dryen quaed? . . . . of rieckt het Roomsch . . . ."* Huygens, *Orgel Gebruyck*, 133.

40. *". . . soo niet loffelicke gebruyck, van Godt dē Heere bysondere Lofsangē op te offeren, in erkenteniss van groote allgemeene Weldadē den Lande overkomen . . . ."* Huygens, *Orgel Gebruyck*, 135. Huygens did not hide his irritation at the Dutch government, which he still served, and the way it encouraged its citizens to celebrate the recently-won freedom from Spanish rule. The country celebrated in "greedy taverns which seem to be going full swing, beyond the criticism of the church" "(. . . *verdrincken wyse niet in gulsighe gasterijen, die dan schijnen in vrijen swang, ende als buyten opspraecke vande Kerck te wesē . . . .*)," and with lighted barrels of tar, fireworks, and the "wildly ringing" bells. Huygens, *Orgel Gebruyck*, 136–137. Further, he found it unseemly that such celebratory practice was defended by some as a means to entertain the children. Huygens recounted a story of one child, not yet three years old, who was taken from his crib and made to watch the "fiery celebration" and "in baby talk" (*"op sijn' spraeck wist te seggen"* or "in his voice") said "It's very ice, but I must s'eep" (*"'T is heel faey, maer ick moet saepen"*). Huygens, *Orgel Gebruyck*, 137. Huygens thought it would be much more appropriate to celebrate Dutch independence in church, where one could give appropriate thanks to God. Huygens, *Orgel Gebruyck*, 139–40.

41. "Hem Gode, Vader, Sone ende H. Geest zij Lof en Lofsangh in eewigheid. AMEN." Huygens, *Orgel Gebruyck*, 141.

Lotius received the manuscript for review, not only because he was a personal friend of the Governor and of Huygens, but presumably also because he had served as delegate to the 1638 Provincial Synod of South Holland where organ use was declared a matter best left to the discretion of individual congregations. In fact, Lotius had preached a sermon in his own church in favor of using the church organ to accompany congregational singing. Thus, it should not be surprising that Lotius's reaction to Huygens's manuscript was exceptionally positive.

Streso was also an obvious choice to offer a public endorsement of Huygens's new work. Born in 1603 in Anhalt, Germany, son of a Reformed minister, Streso had a degree from the University of Leiden. Streso's Reformed credentials and education were impeccable, and he knew Huygens in his capacity as a Privy Councilor. While serving as the pastor of the church in Monster, Streso asked Huygens to intercede with his request to the provincial governor that the secretary of the town council, who was appointed by the governor, would not be a Roman Catholic. When Streso accepted a call to serve the Reformed congregation in The Hague, he then became Huygens's pastor.

Streso's response to *Orgel Gebruyck* was not as effusive as that of Lotius and was probably not what Huygens was expecting. Streso accepted the book's main thesis, "by properly wanting to fight misuse and wanting to promote proper use and this by way of solid arguments" but "where theology is concerned and in particular the doctrine of *adiaphoris* matters, it (*Orgel Gebruyck*) appears to be at odds with a few fundamentals of the Reformation."[42]

Huygens circulated the manuscript among select acquaintances of the "Muiderkring," a group of leading Dutch thinkers who regularly met at the Castle of Muiden near Amsterdam. The central figures in this erudite society were Huygens, the poet Pieter Cornelis Hooft, and Jan Pieterzoon Sweelinck, famous organist of the Wester Kerk of Amsterdam, among others. Four of these colleagues—Joachim Wickevoort, Caspar Barlaeus, David Mostart and Pieter Cornelis Hooft—met on July 2, 1640 at the Muider Castle for a joint reading day of Huygens's *Orgel Gebruyck*.

42. "*Perlegi scriptum de Organo. Ipsemet retulissem et judicium dixissem, nisi me valetudo laesa hac tempestate arceret a plateis. Dignum est istud thema consideratione doctorum, et synodos quoque nostras aliquoties habuit occupatas. Tractatio methodum habet elegantem, quosdam abusus recte perstringens, quosdam usus recte exigens, et argumentis solidis singula suadens. Quà parte theologiam et doctrinam de rebus adiaphoris propius concernit, videbatur impetere quaedam Reformationis essentialia.*" Worp, *Briefwisseling van Const. Huygens*, No. 2344, 3:21.

Afterwards, on September 3, 1640, Hooft expressed his opinion of Huygens's work to Wickevoort:

> My feelings about the writing of the Earl of Zuilichem is that the honorable gentleman asserts his intelligence in this piece with judgment-rich and indisputable proofs; and attacks and conquers the intelligence of his opponents with wonderful and careful humility.[43]

Hooft even wrote a threshold poem for the book; he sent it with a letter, which included this high praise:

> The thoughts which you, honorable gentleman, have about the use of the organ, I consider drawn from indisputable reasons, both pro and con: but this is tempered with a modesty that is so careful and considerate, that it will take away from the opponents not only the power but also the will to argue.[44]

Hooft's poem, published in the second and third editions of *Orgel Gebruyck* (published in 1559 and 1560, respectively), offers florid approval:

> Whoever diligently casts his eye on the book of the world
> In every type of creature finds spelled
> Praise be to the Creator. The bees and the ants
> Testify with their spirit. The dumb beasts
> From small to large—even the lowly worm—
> Declare it, each in its own form.
> The fixed parts, the inanimate things,
> Do not only speak it, but teach to sing it.
> The dry bone, the barren wood, the tin
> Raises its voice, and turns the human spirit
> To gentility, to humility, to worship
> Toward his God, with amazing power to stop
> Lack of civilization:[45] and preaches in language understood

---

43. "*Mijn gevoelen op 't schrift des Heeren van Zuilichems is dat zijn 'Ed. Gestra. Haer verstandt in dit stuck beweert met oordeelrijke ende onwederleggelijke bewijsredenen; ende 't verstandt der wedersprekeren aenvecht en overwint met wonderlijke en wel zorghvuldighe bescheidenheit.*" Hooft and Tricht, *Briefwisseling van Pieter Corneliszoon Hooft*, 1:292–300.

44. "*De Bedenking van U Ed. Gestr. op het gebruik der Orghelen, vind ik 't eenemael opgeleidt van onverwrikkelijke redenen, zoo in 't beweeren als in wederleggen: maer dit getempert met een' bescheidenhiet, zoo omzightigh ende ontziende, dat het der tegenparthye niet alleen de maght, maer ook den wil tot strijden beneemen moet.*" Hooft, *Brieven*, 3:372.

45. Literally "to weed the wasteland" = cultivate.

> By Norwegian and Moor, Eastern and Western Indian.
> Thanks be to the ingenuity, the inventor of the throats
> Of the Organs, that knows how to placate the souls
> And molds them, with pleasure, to the utmost
> Of its salvation. The dispute has been settled, moved by its
> artful use
> From which in the past much controversy had arisen
> Huygens has now determined, shown the correct way.[46]

Huygens thanked Hooft for his effort "in reading my dreams, in putting to rhyme my errant thoughts."[47]

David Mostart, present at the reading day at the Muider Castle, also wrote a threshold poem.[48] In it Mostart decries all desecrating actions done both in the church building proper and during worship:

To the Earl of Zuijlichem, about his honor's proper use and mis-use of the ORGANS

> He, who does not live in a house made with human hands
> But the Heavenly Forgiver, who receives the best of our offerings,
> Desires that in his house, made by human hands
> Where we bring worthy tributes to his divinity,
> Proper order and dignity be maintained.
> That is why, when the Jews misused the house of prayer
> As a market place, CHRIST did not tolerate this,
> But threw all the tables and benches that were there
> to the ground with all the merchandise on them,

---

46. "Wie vlijtigh 't oogh op 't boek der werelt velt, / In elke sort van schepsels vint gespelt / Des Scheppers lof. De bijen en de mieren / Getuighen 's met haer' geest. De domme dieren / Van groot tot kleen, jae d' alderminste worm, / Verklaeren 't, met geschiktheit hunner form. / 'T ontroerend tuigh, de leevenlooze dingen, / Die zeggen 't niet alleen, maer leeren 't zingen. / Het drooghe been, het dorre hout, het tin, / Verheft zijn' stem, en zwaeit des menschen zin / Tot deftigheit, tot ootmoedt, tot eerbieding / Aen zijnen God: met wonderlijk' uitwieding / Der woestigheit: een preekt in tael, verstaen / Van Noor en Moor, Oost- en Westindiaen. / Danck heb 't vernuft, uitvinder van de keelen / Des Orghels, dat de Zielen weet te streelen, / En ment ze met geneughte, tot het puick / Haers heils. Het pleit, gevoert om 't slim gebruick, / Waeruit voorheen veel aenstoots was gereezen, / Heeft Huighens nu beslecht; en 't Recht geweezen."

47. "... met eerbiedighe danckseghingh voor de moeijte in 't lesen mijner droomen, en 't berijmen mijner ongerijmtheden genomen." Worp, *Briefwisseling van Const. Huygens*, No. 2551, 3:113.

48. Noske, *Pathodia*, 293. The poem is made up of stanzas with a rhyming pattern in the Dutch of aabbcddeec.

And sent the merchants with a whip
From the sanctuary, and taught us, by his example,
Not to be slack in cleaning God's temple
Of all obscenity, and unacceptable mores,
And not to tolerate any unedifying things,
nor any irregularities within it.
That is why no love song should distract our thoughts there:
We should not hear any playing of frivolous ditties
No matter how artistic it is, no madrigal
Ballet or passamezzi, or no matter what it is called
any other way in our language.
Do away with the frivolities, this space demands other things:
Here one has to sing God's praise and of His miracles:
Decent and suitable, with a proper tone and measure.
But because most people cannot hold the tune,
We teach how to avoid these things,
In these learned pages, how to mold the human voice
Properly, and bend it with the organ;
In the Lord's house, where everything should be done properly,
Everyone should, with the sounds that foot and finger produce,
Mold their voice.[49]

The reaction of Caspar Barlaeus, another friend invited to the reading day at Muider Castle, was exceptionally enthusiastic, so much so that he urged Huygens to publish the manuscript immediately.

49. "*Aanden Heere van Zuijlichem, op zijner Ed: Gestr: / rechtgebruijck en misbruijck des ORGELS. / Hij, die geen huys bewoont gemaekt van menschen handen, / Maer d'opperste opperkwijts [Opperkwijts in this context appears to have the meaning of "to forgive a debt] doet onser offeranden, / Wil, dat men in zijn huys, door menschen vuyst gesticht, / Waer in onz' dienstplicht tot zijn Godtheit wordt ge*[richt.] / *Goede orde houw en regel. / Hierom, wanneer de Joôn dees huijzing der gebeeden / Misbruyckten tot een markt, heeft CHRISTUS 't niet gelee*[den,] / *Maer al' haer taefelen en banken daer gestelt / Met al de koopmanschap ter aerde neergevelt, / En 't koopvolk met een vlegel / Ter Kerken uytgejaeght, en ons, door zijn exempel, / Geleert niet slof te zijn in 't zuijv'ren van Gods temple / Van alle vuijligheid en ongeschickte zeên, / En geen' ontstichtlijckheit, nocht ongeregeltheên / Daer binnen te gedooghen. / Dies moet geen minnezang aldaer onz' aendacht stooren; / Men moet daer ook geen spel van lichte deuntjes hooren; / Hoe konstigh dat het is, noch eenigh madrigael, / Ballet oft passemez, oft hoe men z'in ons tael, / Zouw anders noemen moogen. / Wegh met die dartelheên, deez plaets eijscht and're dingen: / Hier moet men Godes lof en wonderdaden zingen; / Betamelijk en geschikt, op goede toon en maet. / Maer, om dat 't meeste volk de wijz' te buijten gaet: / Leert gij om dat te mijen, / In deez' geleerde blaên, hoe dat men 'smenschen gorgel / Bequam'lijk buijgen zal, en dwingen door het orgel; / Om in des Heeren huys, daer 't al naer peijl moet gaen, / Een yeder, naer 't geluijt, dat voet en vingers slaen, / Te doen zijn stemme vlijen* [shape as clay]."

Huygens asked René Descartes to read the manuscript and offer his opinion, even though Descartes was a French Catholic living in the Netherlands at the time, barely fluent in the Dutch language and hardly sympathetic to the Protestant movement; for his part, Huygens was clearly no Roman Catholic. Nonetheless, Descartes generously read *Orgel Gebruyck*. He was not converted to Protestantism by it (he even returned a few friendly theological barbs in his written response), but he praised the work's intellectual quality without commenting on the issue of Reformed church music, a topic which was beyond his expertise.

Another reaction bears special mention, that of the eighty-five-year-old Remonstrant theologian Johannes Uyttenbogaert. In 1640, a small and very new Remonstrant[50] congregation in Rotterdam wrote the venerable professor Uyttenbogaert asking him whether they should purchase a new church organ.[51] This congregation had just applied for acceptance into the Remonstrant communion, and the church council wondered if having an organ would risk its candidacy for full membership. Uyttenbogaert took a pastoral tone in his response by quoting Jas 5:13: "Is any one of you in trouble? He should pray. Is anyone happy? Let him sing songs of praise." But, he continued, the congregation should definitely not purchase an organ lest they seem too experimental in their approach to church music and worship. However, a year later when Huygens asked for Uyttenbogaert's endorsement of *Orgel Gebruyck*, Uyttenbogaert declared:

> Concerning the principal point, my feeling has long been and is still, that if the organ can be used in an edifying way in the meeting of Christians—which I think is the case—then the manner which Your Honor proposes, on proper grounds—in my humble opinion—proved and founded, is the most edifying, yes even the only edifying way, that therefore it can be and is properly practiced. I am one of those who love music—even *ipse sim αμουσοσ*—and find myself frequently in church in the evening and hear an organist play a psalm—which is usually done, for each verse, with several registers and melodies frequently ornamented—while I sing silently to the Lord during the playing, while my sad spirit raises its praise to God.[52]

50. A Reformed congregation who objected chiefly to the doctrine of predestination.

51. Milligen, *Kerkzang*, 116–17.

52. "'T principael aengaende, mijn gevoelen is lang geweest en is noch, indien 't orgel in de vergaderinge der christenen stichtelick gebruyckt kan worden—'t welck ick houde—dat de maniere bij U Ed. voorgestelt, oock met goeden grondt—mijns geringen

On February 9, 1640 the manuscript of *Orgel Gebruyck* was published in book form in The Hague, but anonymously and without the inclusion of the laudatory poems that had been written by the author's friends and supporters. The secretary of the magistracy, Philips Doublet, presented it to the magistrates on Huygens's behalf. The initial reaction from the magistrates was not positive, but not because of Huygens's recommendation that the organ be reintroduced into worship as musical accompaniment for psalmody. Rather, they were snubbed that the author called The Hague, this most elegant Dutch municipality, a "village" (*dorp*), when the authorities felt certain it deserved to be called a "town" (*stadt*) or at the very least a "community" (*gemeente*). Doublet attempted to reach Huygens at his home and at court in order to warn him of the brewing storm. He could not find him, so he wrote a panicked letter to Huygens asking him to change the offending word. Huygens indeed found out about the outcry, and two days later tried to defend himself by suggesting that the nomenclature of *dorp* was intended as a title of honor, one he had used in a poem years earlier in which he had listed The Hague amongst "some important villages." But this argument was unconvincing, and in the end Huygens offered to change the offensive reference:

> If it would satisfy, I shall scratch out the words *this* and *village* and substitute *this* and *place, town* if they wish, *market town* if they wish, *princely residence* if they so desire. But if it were my choice, it would say "this beautiful hamlet" as that would give more luster.[53]

The city authorities agreed to accept published references as either "this pleasant place," or "this pleasant place called The Hague." Since the

---

oordeels—aengewesen en bewesen, de stichtelickste, jae genoech alleen stichtelick is, bijaldien die wel gepractiseert kan werden ende wordt. Onder dieghene, die de musyck beminnen, ben ick een—howel ipse sim ἀμουσοσ—ende vinde mij altemet des avonds in de kercke, om den meester een psalm—dat doorgaens geschiet, op elck veers, met verscheyden registeren ende melodien verscheydelick zwierende—te hooren spelen, onder 't spel stillekens in mijn selven den Heer singende, ende mijnen bedroefden gheest in God tot sijnen loff vermakende." Worp, *briefwisseling van Const. Huygens*, No. 2653, 3:150. In fact, Uyttenbogaert would go on to confess that even as a minister he had attended an organ concert or two in the evenings purely for enjoyment.

53. *"Vindtmen 't goed, ick sal de woorden dit ende dorp doen doorhalen, ende daervoor stellen dese ende plaets. Stadt, soomen will, Coopstad, soomen will, Hoofdstad soomen will, Hof-stad, soomen will. Maer als 't mij te kiesen stonde, daer soude staen, dit schoone gehucht, ende soude meer luysters geuen."* Worp, *Briefwisseling van Const. Huygens*, No. 2629, 3:141.

printer already had the pages printed, unfolded, and cut, the change was implemented by cutting the sheet where the offending word was present and re-typesetting these pages. The finished book was ready on February 15, 1641.[54]

Huygens sent a presentation copy of the book to twenty-three *Reverendis & Clariβimis Viris* colleagues; each one praised his scholarly accomplishment and his generous friendship.

In retrospect, Huygens must certainly have preferred haggling with the city leaders of The Hague about whether to call his home town *dorp* or *stadt* to fending off the attacks that followed from other readers.

The first attack came from Reformed ministers, who felt that Reformed worship practices, their reputations, and their pastoral authority were all under attack in *Orgel Gebruyck*. They stated emphatically that civil magistrates such as Huygens would not dictate to them in ecclesiastical or theological matters. Despite this irritation, Huygens was by and large much more interested in the reactions of politicians and professors than the ministers. Consequently, Huygens sent a second round of complimentary books to non-clerical intelligentsia outside of the Netherlands, notably to Albert Joachimi of London, Ambassador Willem van Lyere of Paris, and Jean Ludovicq Calandrini of Geneva. Nearly all praised him; Calandrini seemed relieved to read Huygens's solution to a musical problem he admitted also existed in the Genevan Reformed churches.

However, one of these recipients was not favorably impressed. Gisbertus Voetius, a professor in Utrecht, received a copy with a letter from Huygens in which he requests Voetius's reaction: "At an earlier time you have already thought this matter worthy of your attention, but it would be even more valuable if you would let me know your opinion about this subject and about this book in a few words."[55] Voetius did reply, on March 18, 1641, but only to say that he had forwarded the copy of *Orgel Gebruyck* to a mutual acquaintance, Anna Maria van Schurman. At the close of the note, Voetius offers this brief comment about the work itself:

> I pray that God will support you with his Spirit so that you can continue with your rare and admirable example of study of pure

---

54. Zwaan, *Constantijn Huygens*, Appendix 1, 183–84.

55. "*Studeo unius horae molestiam adferre tibi, vir reveende, quam si dignaberis impendere lectioni dissertatiunculæ, ante annum et quod excurrit a me scriptæ, nun cut amicis ac typographis satisfacerem luci expositæ . . . .*" Worp, *Briefwisseling van Const. Huygens*, No. 2661, 3:153–54.

learning and piety, even though time and place allow for little opportunity for it.[56]

Acclaim also eluded Huygens from Catholic clergy. Huygens sent the book to a priest at Haarlem, Joan Albert Ban, and asked, "If it is worth it to you to read it, you will discover that I have written much that would earn me the death penalty in Rome. But your freedom of thought is such that you will tolerate the speaker."[57] Huygens asked Ban if he would discuss the *Orgel Gebruyck* with Leonardus Marius, priest at the Amsterdam *Begijnhof* (convent) in Amsterdam and report back to him. Apparently Ban did not reply; naturally, the anti-Catholic presumptions behind the topic of Reformed worship made it difficult for these priests to offer their public support.

The influence of *Orgel Gebruyck* in changing aural iconoclastic worship practices in the Netherlands can be seen in the next landmark event in the organ controversy. In Haarlem, the congregation sang with the organ for the first time during the celebration of Holy Communion on January 15, 1641, nearly coinciding with the initial publication and release of *Orgel Gebruyck*. But this event did not necessarily advance the use of the church organ in the way Huygens had hoped. The organist Pieter de Voys [Vois] and the *voorzanger* practiced tirelessly so that the service would progress in an orderly manner. There was no commotion during the service, but with all the musical preparation, it appears that no one thought to inform the church council that the organ would accompany the psalm. When the organ sounded, the council was surprised and so greatly offended (whether by the use of the organ itself or by the audacity of not having been asked for prior consent is not clear) that some "became ill, had to go home, have a drink (*candeeltgen*) and lie down to rest."[58] Here's how the incident was recorded:

---

56. "*Deum precor, te spiritu suo gubernet; ut raro atque admirando exemplo verae sapientiae et pietatis studia loco ac saeculo tam importuno pro viribus porro ornare ac promovere pergas.*" Duker, *Voetius*, 125.

57. "*Addo item dissertatiunculae meae exemplar de organo. Si tanti est ut perlegas, occurrent passim quae capitis discrimine Romae scripserim. Verum ea tua est humanitas et candor, ut in sede nativâ patriae libertatis disserentem feras pro* τῆς συνειδήσεως *instinctu.*" Worp, *Briefwisseling van Const. Huygens*, No. 2663, 3:154–155.

58. "*. . . als wanneer het orgel d' eerst mael alhier onder de psalmen speelden door schrick daer van de koorts op haer hals cregen ende naer huijs gaen mosten een candeeltgen innemen ende gaen leggen rusten.*" Acta 15 Januari 1641, Haarlem, Kerkeraadsarchief No. 106, as cited by Luth, "*Daer wert . . . ,*" 224.

As on this past Sunday during the serving of the holy communion when we sang the psalm, the organ has played without the knowledge or approval of any member of the church council and as this has created a great commotion, it was approved that when people think that the church masters have ordered this on their own, that we should first speak to the gentlemen church masters and inquire whether this was indeed the case; and if yes, that we shall ask them not to do such a thing again. And in case it had been done by order of the Lord City Councilors, that then they will be asked the same thing. And at the same time let them know that the church council would appreciate it very much if the Lords Councilors would not allow any further changes in the regular playing of the organ during the psalms before and after the preaching, without first having heard the views of the consistory about it.[59]

The council decided that the civil authorities would be made aware of their displeasure. The date of confrontation with the magistrates was left open, pending the compilation of the reactions of members of the congregation.[60]

Another surprise attack against Huygens's work came from his own pastor, Caspar Streso of The Hague, who had read the manuscript version of *Orgel Gebruyck* and had initially praised it. While Huygens was absent from The Hague with the army, Streso preached on the ninety-sixth question and answer of *The Heidelberg Catechism*.[61] Streso used the Catechism's commentary on making no graven images as the inspiration

---

59. "*Alsoo op sondagh voorleden onder de bedieninge des H. Avontmaels als men den Psalm sangh, het orgel heeft gespeelt, sonder kennisse ofte voorweten van eenigh lit des kercken-raeds ende tzelvige grote alteratie heeft gemaeckt, is goetgevonden als men verstaet dat de heeren Krkmrs. dit souden bestelt hebben by haer selven, dat men daerover eerst de heeren kerckmrs. sal aanspreken ende vernemen of het alsoe is, indien ja, dat men versoecke dat sulxc nyet meer en geschyet. ende in gevalle het met ordre van de H. heeren Burgemr. is geschiet, dat men hen alsdan by deselfde sal versoecken. En met een te kennen geven, dat het der kerckenraed seer lief soude wesen dat de Heeren Burgemr. geen verdere veranderinghe en maeckten in het ordinair orgel spelen onder de Psalmen voor en na de predicatie sonder alvorens de grieven des kerckenraets daer op gehoort hebben.*" Acta 15 Januari 1641, Haarlem, Kerkeraadsarchief No. 106, as cited by Luth, "Daer wert . . . ," 224.

60. The churches of Leiden and Delft also began using the organ to accompany their psalm singing, but the magistrates there first wisely consulted extensively with the church councils.

61. "What is God's will for us in the second commandment? That we in no way make any image of God nor worship him in any other way than he has commanded in his Word."

to preach against the use of the organ that he defined as a graven image in Reformed worship. Huygens had been informed by messenger about the content of the sermon while he was still out of the country, but when he returned he demanded a written copy of the sermon from Streso, who complied.

The sermon consisted of two main points: Christians should worship nothing man-made in place of God, and they should only worship God in ways prescribed in the Bible. Streso spent the largest part of the sermon on that second point, insisting that it was forbidden to use anything in worship, however useful it might be from a human viewpoint, that God himself had not ordained in Holy Scripture. It was easy for Streso to condemn Catholic practices such as praying to images and statues because this was a fundamental feature of Protestant theology that his parishioners would accept without debate.

But then Streso stretched that condemnation onto the use of the pipe organ. He knew full well that Huygens and other *orgelists* argued that Psalm 150, "Praise the Lord . . . with pipe," proved that God wanted organs to be played in church. Streso read the same text but reached a completely opposite interpretation: if the Reformed should play the instruments listed in Psalm 150, then they must also play trumpets, timbrels, and harps in church. This thought was so ludicrous that it could be dismissed without further discussion. No, said Streso, with the coming of Jesus Christ and the establishment of the Christian Church, all Old Testament forms of worship along with their tools and instruments had been permanently superseded. Biblical instructions for Christian worship could properly be taken only from the New Testament.

Thus Streso concluded by asking: "Can the organ bring about conversion and create spiritual joy in us?" "No," he responded, "for the Spirit does not speak with inanimate sound, but through the Word and the sacraments." Streso conceded that the organ could do much to elevate our mood, but if that were the criterion for using the organ, then anything else that made one happy, no matter how base, must also be employed by the church. Such a situation would surely turn worship into a festival of carnal satisfaction but not produce Christian piety. Even if the organ were a great work of art, in principle it must be used only outside the worship service.

Streso's sermon elicited quite a few reactions in The Hague. Many welcomed his pronouncements as clear criticism of the use of the organ. A group of like-minded congregants in Streso's flock who desired to return to the "old way" approached the church council on May 22, 1641 and stated their desire that organ use cease. The church council discussed the matter but did not come to a definite decision due to the lack of a quorum. The council members who were there did nevertheless ask the authorities to do away with organ accompaniment in the service.

The relationship between Huygens and his pastor grew strained, and came to a boiling point when, curiously, Streso wanted to dedicate a collection of sermons, including the offensive one about the organ, to Huygens. Streso went so far as to request that Huygens write the preface to the collection—even as Huygens was considering legal action at the time against Streso for having harmed his reputation. Perhaps Streso was simply extending an olive branch to Huygens in order to avoid this legal action. In the end, the offending organ sermon was excised from the collection and published separately, but Huygens's relationship with his pastor was understandably and irreparably harmed.

If Huygens thought that ignoring Streso would put an end to his problems, he was sorely mistaken, for he had still to meet his fiercest opponent. In The Hague, Aert van Meurs published at the beginning of November 1641 a book entitled "Antidotum: Antidote to the use and nonuse of the Organ in the Churches of the United Netherlands."[62] The author was Jan Jansz. Calckman, who dedicated the work to the "worthy brothers and sisters of the congregation of Jesus Christ in The Hague."[63]

Jan Jansz. Calckman was born in Amsterdam, and at the age of twenty joined a Reformed Church and counted himself among the first generation of the Reformed. This layman had an intense love for the Reformed faith and an extraordinary sense of justice and civic duty. After working first as a shipbuilder and then as the collector of beer taxes in The Hague,[64] he retired at the age of fifty-eight to Alphen aan de Rijn because he wanted to distance himself from a scandal unfolding around other tax collectors who had illegally pocketed some of the taxes. These scruples no doubt made him a model citizen, but, combined with his fierce loyalty to the Reformed movement, they also turned him into Huygens's nemesis in the organ controversy.

---

62. Calckman, *Antidotum*.

63. "*Eerwaerdige Broeders ende Susters der Ghemeynte Iesu Christi in 's Gravenhaghe....*" Calckman, *Antidotum*, 4.

64. Kalkman, "Constantijn Huygens," 176. On this same page, Kalkman stresses that there is no familial connection between he (Kalkman) and his subject (Calckman)!

In 1629 Calckman had published a sermon by Johannes Placius of Emden, a sermon that he had memorized in the pew and later rewrote from memory.[65] He dedicated this publication to his "kind friends who labor there in the harvest of the Lord, the Earl Gerrit Beunen van Wender, Theodorus Wijckenburg, and the church council at Alphen aan de Rijn." In the foreword, Calckman wrote an extensive description of the task of Reformed office bearers; in this writing one sees a fascinating glimpse of a punctilious Reformed layman who saw the Dutch Republic as a new Canaan.[66] As "eternal life consists of the true and sincere knowledge of Jesus Christ," argued Calckman, "the devil, an enemy of man's salvation, works to tempt the people with false teachings."[67] God himself had ordained for the church "such persons as defenders for his church so that the real true word of God that is taught here in the public church will be protected as a legitimate proclamation of God."[68]

Coincidentally, in this publication, which was printed years before Huygens's *Orgel Gebruyck*, Calckman wrote about the use of the pipe organ in the church. It appears that there were plans to use organ accompaniment in the church of Emden. Calckman cites Placius who was fiercely opposed to this for the same reasons that Streso had used in his sermon against organ playing in church; according to Placius, instrumental music belonged clearly "to the sacrifices and ceremonies of the old Law, of which the persecuted and martyred Justinus also asks: while these songs have been used by the unbelievers for the sake of deceit and temptation, and therefore have been introduced under the Law because of their lack

65. Calckman, *Christelijcke*.

66. "*De goede God, die wil met den geest sijner ghenade wercken in uwer aller harten, opdat een yeghelijck van u sijnen schuldigen plicht mach bewaren, met een goede conscientie voor God ende de menschen, soo sal oock onghetwijfelt Godt sorgh dragen, om een alsulcken Republijck, ende welstant sijner kercke, als voor sijn oochappel, ende het gheluck sal wesen over Zyon, en het welvaren over Ierusalem.*" "The great God who wishes to work in everyone's heart with the spirit of his grace, so that everyone of you may keep his obligatory task, with a good conscience before God and the people, this God will undoubtedly take care to keep such a Republic and the welfare of his church, like the apple of his eye, and blessing will be over Zion and welfare on Jerusalem." Calckman, *Christelijcke*, preface.

67. "*... het eeuwige leven bestaet in de waerachtige ende oprechte kenisse Jesu Christi... werkt de duivel, een vijand van de menselijke zaligheid, om de mensen te verleiden met zijn valse leer.*" Calckman, *Christelijcke*, preface.

68. "*... soodanighe personen als voetsters derselve opdat het ware onvervalste woort Gods dat alhier in de publiecke kercke wort geleert, worde beschermt, al seen wettelijke ordinatie Godes.*" Calckman, *Christelijcke*, preface.

of knowledge, then why is it that we use these hymns in our church, as we have received grace and more complete understanding?"[69]

It would seem that a retired tax collector residing in rural Alphen aan den Rijn would have no interest in, or be any threat to, an aristocrat such as Huygens who worked for the highest echelons of government. But after Calckman's first wife died, he remarried and returned to The Hague at his new bride's request. There he read Huygens's *Orgel Gebruyck*, and the effect on Calckman was incendiary. He published his invective response, *Antidotum*, in November 1641. In it, Calckman hurled accusations of heresy at Reformed clergy[70] and civil authorities alike, promising that anyone who did not reject Huygens's argument and prohibit organ playing during church service would suffer eternal damnation. Needless to say, Calckman was equally generous in his attacks on Huygens himself.

It should be mentioned that Calckman misquoted Huygens and even misrepresented that man's arguments. Nonetheless, Calckman was a master of rhetoric, although his rhetoric by no means approached the lofty, poetic, crafted language of Huygens. Instead, he filled *Antidotum* with colorful, pedestrian Dutch expressions that could be understood by Dutch readers even if they lacked a university education. Calckman used expressions like "put your feet in your shoes," "a saw that does not cut wood," "what good is a candle or glasses if I do not want to see," and "give the congregation sugar pills under the pretense of truth while they are yet laced with poison."[71] The most curious: "he would slobber, even if

---

69. "*Tot den offer ende ceremonien des ouden Wets. Daer van de verhaelde leerier ende martelaer Justinus also vraecht: dewijl die gesangen van den onghelovige om des bedrochs ende verleydinge wille zijn ghevonden geworden ende derhalven die onder de Wet waren inghevoert om haer onverstants wille, hoe komt dat wij in onse kercke ons des gesanghs ghebruycken, die wy doch meer ghenade ende volcomender onderwysinge ontfanghen hebben.*" Calckman, *Christelijcke*, 6.

70. Particularly any minister who allowed his hair to grow long, curled it, and then preached while wearing a hat decorated with "a bouquet of feathers" ("*Hoedt vol pluymen steke*"), Calckman, *Antidotum*, 176. This audacious move, along with reintroducing the organ and any and all other such "innovations," caused Calckman to scold sarcastically those supporters: "Like some ministers who don a hat with feathers, so you should not forget to put on a dunce cap" ("*Daerom zommige Predicanten een hoet met pluymen op setten / soo en vergeet u selven niet een Sotten-kap op te sette*"), Calckman, *Antidotum*, 177.

71. "*Om uwen voet te steecken in onse schoenen . . . . en een sage die geen hout en snijt . . . . wat baet kaers of bril / als ick niet sien en wil . . . . and onder schijn van waerheydt de ghemeynte suyckerde Pillen in te geven / die nochtans met vergif gemengt zijn.*" Calckman, *Antidotum*, 18, 67, 109, 131.

he ate no hazelnuts,"[72] which was apparently an adage for someone who was accident prone. The most vulgar: "When the cow has shit herself, she likes to hit herself (wag) with her tail,"[73] which Calckman explained to mean that the church ("the cow") continued on ("wagging her tail") as if nothing foul had happened (the "shit" of adding organ music to Reformed worship).

Calckman's main objection to the use of the organ in Reformed worship was undeniably and purely fundamentalist: "Reject all novelties no matter how good they appear, measure them against the touchstone of the scriptures."[74] This fundamentalism influenced his arguments throughout the rest of *Antidotum*, in which Calckman challenged whom he referred to as the self-proclaimed "philosopher of the organ."[75] Calckman organized the first section of *Antidotum* into four principle questions. The first:

> Question 1:
> Whether one can introduce into a well-established and settled congregation some new things which are not fundamental to the service of God, nor fundamental to the customs of the Apostolic Congregation and for a long time after, but are injurious to the continuing use of the old customs of the true religion?
>
> And furthermore, whether this does not contribute to unrest, when they attempt to introduce into a well-established and settled congregation such innovations that are not fundamentally one with God's word, nor agree with the customs of the original Apostolic church?[76]

---

72. "*Siet hoe ghy u selven alhier beüapt / al en eet ghy geen Hasenoten.*" Calckman, *Antidotum*, 73.

73. "*Als de Koe bescheten is / soo üaetse garen met de staert om.*" Calckman, *Antidotum*, 165–66.

74. "*. . . verwerpt alle nieuwicheden hoe lieffelick datse toonen, strijckt het aen den Toetsteen van Godts Woort. . . .*" Calckman, *Antidotum*, 5.

75. "*Laet ons nu eens gaen besien wat desen Philosophist van't Orgel ons wil diets maken, soo wy 't wilden gelooven.*" "Let us now consider what this philosopher of the organ wants us to believe, if we were to believe it." Calckman, *Antidotum*, 36.

76. "*Vraag I. Of men in een wel-gestelde ende geruste Gemeynte / mach invoeren eenighe nieuwicheden / de welcke niet fondamenteel en zijn tot den Godesdienst? noch met het gebruyck der Apostolische Ghemeynte / en langhe daer nae / niet nadeelich zijn het oude ghebruyck vanden oprechten Godes-dienst te volgen? En of het dan niet en streckt tot onrust / daermen in een wel gestelde en geruste Gemeynte soeckt in te voeren sodanighe nieuwicheden / die niet fondamenteel en zijn met Godes Woordt? noch over*

He answered: No. If one discovered that introduced novelties were not in accordance with God's Word, then they were an abuse, being introduced into the church by "eager and carnal people."⁷⁷ Although singing in the church was a practice already known among the Levites, it was never commanded by God. Besides, Old Testament singing was more a recitation-like pronouncement of the words. In fact, the apostle Paul condoned the psalm singing of the Corinthians since he saw that there was not much difference between their singing and the practice of the old Israelite congregation. But, Calckman argued, such singing was merely permitted by God, not commanded by him. Moreover, this proper recitation-like singing has, since the coming of "the antichrist" (the Roman Catholic Church), been superseded by all kinds of music and songs, without which the congregation would not lose anything because such chanting of hymns and formulae were of the flesh and not of the mind. "And the same can be said of those who publish books nowadays to introduce the novelty of the organ in the congregation, to remove totally the simplicity of the singing in an established congregation, and to deafen it [the congregation] by rattling the ears with the sound of dumb idols, namely the organ pipes."⁷⁸

Calckman's second question:

> Is the playing of the organ an old custom, or a new habit introduced by human ingenuity into the congregation neither by God's command nor by the judgment of the old church? And whether it is not better, then, to consider proper that which agrees with the word of God [and] with the concurring opinion of many true witnesses to the peacefulness of the congregation, or to follow the innovations introduced by carnal people that would fool the congregation into thinking that they can serve God with the same voice as is used for idols?⁷⁹

---

een en comen met het ghebruyck der eerster Apostolische Kercke?" Calckman, *Antidotum*, 7.

77. "*... nieusgierighe vleeschelijcke menschen.*" Calckman, *Antidotum*, 8.

78. "*Ende dit selve machmen nu mede wel segghen van sulcke / die heden ten daeghe Boecken derven uytgeven / om de nieuwicheydt met het Orgel inde Gemeynte in te voeren / om de eenvoudicheyt vant singhen inde welghestelde Ghemeynte / gantsch wech te nemen/ en te verdooven / door het gherammel inde ooren vant gheluydt der stomme Afgoden: namelijck de Orgel-pijpen.*" Calckman, *Antidotum*, 13.

79. "*Voor de II. Vrage is: Of het Orgel-spel zy een out gebruyck / ofte een nieu gebruyck / door menschen vindinge inde gemeynte ingebrocht / en niet door Godts bevel /*

His answer: the use of the organ was a new practice not validated by Scripture. Calckman traced the history of the organ beginning with the year 757 when an organ was brought to France as a gift to King Pepin of France.[80] What was certain to Calckman was that the organ was not introduced by Christ or the apostles, nor was it part of the apostolic tradition. Thus, reasoned Calckman, if the Reformed were to be called "Reformers and not Refuters,"[81] they should abstain from introducing such a papist practice into church. Use of the organ in churches since the time of 757 was not validation either. Proper religious practices should always conform to the truth of God's word, wrote Calckman, and in the case of the organ, God will not be pleased with the organ voice, which cannot even speak on its own accord:

> Tell me, how is it possible that the sound of the wind blowing through the organ pipes is necessary for worship, without [leading to] idolatry? For then there could be images created by men that have gained the ability to speak, and could continue to do so, as each pipe in the organ could be made into the image of an idol, and each could create as much sound as is now sounded by each pipe. Would there then be any difference whether it comes from the organ pipes or from idol images? And is someone would force such new things onto the congregation, would that not lead to idolatry? And in any city where this would be introduced, idolatry would be committed. So many cities, so many idols, says the prophet.[82]

---

noch door het oordeel der oude gemeynte? en of het dan niet beter is voor goet te houden het gene dat met Gods Woort over een comt / met het goede oordeel van veel ware getuygen / tot gerusticheydt der gemeynte; dan te volghen nieuwe vonden van vleeschelijcke menschen / die de gemeynte wel soude willen diets maecken / datmen door de Afgoden / Godt met de selve gelijcke stemme soude connen dienen." Calckman, *Antidotum*, 15–16.

80. He notes that this information is from a chronicle of Marinus Scotus: "*ghelijck MARINUS SCOTUS in zijn Chronijck te kennen gheest.*" Calckman, *Antidotum*, 16.

81. "*Refuteerders / dan Reformeerders.*" Calckman, *Antidotum*, 18.

82. "*Seght my nu hoe ist moghelijck dat het gheluyt vande wint door de Orgel-pijpen gedreven / nodelijck is tot den Godesdienst / sonder Afgoderye? want kan door konst der menschen beelden ghemaeckt worden / die geluyt van spraeck hebben ghemaeckt / en noch souden konnen doen / datse elcken Pijp inden Orgel tot een Afgodes beelt souden konnen maecken / en door elck even veel geluyt / als nu door elcken Pijp uytroepen / soude daer dan eenich ondertscheyt connen wesen / of het door de Orgel-pijpen gheschiet/ of door Afgodische Beelden? Ende ofmen dan soodanighe nieuwicheden de gemeynte wilde opdringē / niet soude drijven tot Afgoderye / ende soo menige Stadt daer het selve wordt inghevoert / afgoderye begaen? SOO MENIGE STADT, SOO MENIGEN AFGODT, SEYT DEN PROPHEET.*" Calckman, *Antidotum*, 21.

Calkman's third question defined the pipe organ as an idol:

> Since we in this country have been content since the year 1571, with peace in agreement with the truth according to God's word, until this day without the introduction of new things which cause dissatisfaction, whether it is then necessary to create unrest in the church in this country which has known peace as long as its worship of God has been according to the truth, through a new service of God which is against the truth and is contrary to its order, and thus not in agreement with it?[83]

His answer: No. Although those in support of the organ's use loved to introduce novelties, it must be remembered that ever since the Reformation the organ had always been considered an idolatrous thing. This was the reason why so many organs had been destroyed:

> The church has always considered the organ to be idolatry, and this is why it was torn out in many places. It is wrong, then, if we reinstate them [the organs], for it would be brought in as idolatry, would it not be like food that we had spit out earlier? How shall we account for that to the Roman Catholic Church? Shall we say to them, "We are going to use the organ in a proper way"? And they would say, "Did you not know that earlier when you tore down organs, considering them to be idols? You copied the use of the organ from us, therefore you have falsely accused us of committing idolatry with the organ." ... Who will counter that reasoning?[84]

---

83. "De III. Vrage. Daermen vanden Jare 71. en lange hier te lande inde ghemeynte heeft mede te vreden geweest met rust / conform de waerheyt / nae den woorde Godts / tot op desen dach toe / sonder invoeringe van nieuwichheden tot onvrede / of het dan nodich is de gemeynte hier te lande / die in vrede is gheweest / soo lange met haren Godesdienst die conform de waerheyt is/ onrustich te maecken? door eenen nieuwen Godsdienst die teghen de waerheyt / met de ordere van dien strijt / derhalven niet conform met de selve." Calckman, *Antidotum*, 21.

84. "De gemeynte heeft het Orgel altijt gehouden voor Afgoderye / en daerom isset tot veel plaesen om veer gesmeten: Wat schorter dan aen / als wy het selve weder soecken op te rechten / als Afgodery in te voeren / en op 't eeten dat wy uytgespogen hebben? hoe sal dat voor de Roomsche Kercke verantwoort worden / sullen wy seggen / wy rechtent op tot een recht gebruyck: sy sullen seggen / wist ghy dat te vooren niet / doen ghyse ter neder smeet / en voor Afgoderye hielt? so moet ghy dat van ons gheleert hebben / derhalven so beschuldicht ghy ons valschelick dat wy Afgodery bedrijven met het Orgel. ... Wie sal haer dese redden ontnemen?" Calckman, *Antidotum*, 27–28.

Calckman completed his answer to his third question by concluding that it would be better to retain the *status quo,* conforming to the truth, than to live in unrest after introducing novelties.

Calckman's fourth question focused on the origin of organ use in Christian worship:

> Who was the inventor of the organ? Secondly, when and by whom were the abuses introduced into the church? Thirdly, what of its [the organ's] progression?[85]

His answer: "It concerns us very little who the author of it [the organ] was, and since it is a fact that even the historians are not sure about who the inventor was, I want to just leave it at that."[86] Despite his own dismissal of the question, Calckman went on to produce a detailed history of the organ, and he told the story as a centuries-long pollution of church music by the Roman Catholics. First, a certain Vitalian, born in Sygnia or Campania, accompanied the voices of men with an organ around the year 660;[87] since Vitalian was a pope, this abuse was a papal introduction. Further, he described papal books that reported the introduction of the organ in the French churches around 828 by a priest Joris of Venice.[88] In addition, Abbot Gregorius had an organ in the chapel of his monastery with pipes of such circumference that they "exceeded all bounds."[89] Such pride about the pipes' size amounted to "nothing except idolatry."[90] To support his anti-organ stance, Calckman cited Erasmus's commentary on Corinthians 14 before concluding: "And what honor do such people gain, who by great learnedness, want to assert that the congregation needs the use of the organ to thank and praise God . . . . Even if he [an *orgelist*]

---

85. "*De IV. Vrage is: Je (Wie) de Autheur geweest is vant Orgel: Ten anderen / wanneer / ende door wien / dat het misbruyck is begonnen inde Kercken. Ten derden / van zijnen voortganck.*" Calckman, *Antidotum*, 29.

86. "*Dewijl ons weynich is gelegen wien den Autheur daer van is / en seecker zijn dattet is / nademael de Historyschrijvers daer selfs onseecker in zijn / soo wil ickt daer by laten* . . . ." Calckman, *Antidotum*, 29.

87. Here Calckman cites no source other than "a writing of Mantuanus": "*ghelijck MANTUANAS daer van seyt.*" Calckman, *Antidotum*, 29.

88. Here Calckman cites no source other than "a writing of Amonius": "*gelijck AMONIUS verhaelt.*" Calckman, *Antidotum*, 30.

89. ". . . *wiens Pijpen van een sulcken dickte waeren / die alle mate te buyten gingen.* For this information, Calckman cites no source other than "a writing of Sabellius": *ghelijck SABELLIUS te kennen geeft.*" Calckman, *Antidotum*, 30.

90. ". . . *en alles tot dienst vande afgoderye.* . . ." Calckman, *Antidotum*, 30.

brought forward a hundred thousand examples and as many sayings . . . if they are not commanded by Christ or the apostles, they are refutable."[91]

In the next section of his *Antidotum*, Calckman repeated Huygens's arguments in favor of the organ and one by one rebutted them with plentiful quotations from the Bible. Huygens had stated that the religious use of the organ was never expressly forbidden by Scripture, but Calckman answered that anything that was not commanded was forbidden,[92] and quoted the Bible to prove his point: "You shall not add unto the Word which I command you."[93] Whereas Huygens suggested the incorporation of good practices from other forms of Christianity into the Dutch Reformed Church, Calckman called him a "libertine" and concluded that these actions were sinful for a Reformed Christian: "You cannot drink the cup of the Lord, and the cup of devils."[94] Huygens quoted the apostle Paul, "Prove all things; hold fast to that which is good"[95] when justifying organ use in worship, but Calckman called this principle into question, saying that the Libertines who used the organ in worship put worshipers on "slippery ground, [and] mock all religions while not having one themselves."[96]

Finally, when Huygens suggested that churches be allowed to use discretion when deciding if practices from other expressions of Christianity could be incorporated into Reformed worship, Calckman warned:

> Please note, my dear fellow believers, that here he [the *orgelist*] has thrown a spanner (*spaeck*) into the wheel, and has cut the throat of the pig and leaves it there bleeding. His argument does not suffer from that, it is just the same to him, the matter is of no

---

91. "*Ey wat eere leggen dan sulcke lieden in / die door groote geleertheyt willen staende houden / dat het een werck is de gemeynte noodich / om Godt daer door te dancken en te loven. . . . Maer ick geve soodanige hinckers op beyde zijden . . . alst niet op een vast fundament ghestelt is / namelijck op het fundament Christi / ende zijner Apostlen / dat most het eerst wesen.*" Calckman, *Antidotum*, 31–32.

92. "*. . . want al dat tot gebruyck van dien niet en is gheboden / dat is verboden.*" Calckman, *Antidotum*, 56.

93. "*Ghy en sult daer niet toedoen dat ick u gebiede, ende ghy en sulter oock niet afdoen. Deut. 4. vers. 2.*" Calckman, *Antidotum*, 56.

94. "*Dat zy den Drinckbeker des Heeren niet en conden drincken, ende den Drinckbeecker der Duyvelen.*" Calckman, *Antidotum*, 64, quoting 1 Cor 10:21.

95. "*Proeft alle dingh, ende behout het goede.*" Calckman, *Antiodotum*, 73, quoting 1 Thess 5:21.

96. "*. . . om de menschen op het glat ys te setten / en alle Religien te bespotten / en selfs gheen te hebben.*" Calckman, *Antidotum*, 73.

importance, it is a matter on which salvation does not depend. See, my beloved, if this type of people take the helm of the ship of the church order, are they not pretty helmsmen that will sail the ship aground on Roman Catholic cliffs?[97]

Calckman was not impressed by Huygens's citations of classical writers and theologians:

> ... you and these men about which you boast do not have any reasoning power. Whatever you say, does it not belong to those people about which the Lord God says in Isaiah 6:9 and Ezekiel 12:2 and Christ in Matthew 13:14–15: "By hearing ye shall hear, and shall not understand; and seeing ye shall see, and shall not perceive. For this people's heart has grown fat, and their ears are dull of hearing, and their eyes they have closed; lest at any time they should see with their eyes, nor hear with their ears, nor understand with their hearts."[98]

Huygens described the atrocious quality of singing in the church without the use of instruments. In response to this musical deterioration, Calckman retorted:

> God has not measured the congregation according to the measure of worldly musicians and singers, but with the measure of the mind (spirit, *geestes*), which each one owes to God in simplicity in as much as he has received from God. If the measures then fight with worldly music, they do not struggle against the measure of the spirit, which they seek to learn better. Thus, "orgelist," in this way you try to eliminate simple singing from the congregation, introducing the use of the organ, about which

---

97. "*Siet seer lieve hier heeft hy het spaeck int Wiel gesteecken / en het Varcken de keel afgesteecken / en hy latet leggen bloeden / sijn besteck en leyt daer niet aen, het is hem even veel, de saecke is van geen gewichte, het is een sake daer geen salicheyt aen en kleeft. Siet seer geliefde / soo sulcke lieden het Schip vande Kercken-ordere inde hande wort gegeven: zijn dat niet fraeye Stier-lieden / om het Schip aen de Roomsche klippen inde gront te seylen?*" Calckman, *Antidotum*, 75.

98. "... *die ghy en dese Mannen daer ghy van roemt / die noch met gheen redenen en zijn overstemt / maer of ghy / en zy / niet en zijt van't volck daer Godt de Heere van seyt Esai 6. vers. 9. en Ezech. 12. vers. 2. en Christus Matth. 13. vers. 14. 15.* "*Met ooren sult ghy hooren en niet verstaen: ende met den oogen sult ghy sien, ende niet bemercken. Want het harte deses volcx is vet geworden, ende hebben swaerlijck gehoort met hare ooren, ende hare oogen hebben zy toegesloten: op dat zy niet en sien met de oogen, ende met de ooren hooren, ende met de harten verstaen.*" Calckman, *Antidotum*, 115–16.

the majority of the members of the congregation knows as much as a cow in Flanders.[99]

Besides criticizing Huygens directly, Calckman proceeded to call the delegates of the Provincial Synod of South Holland of 1638, which left the use or nonuse of the organ to each congregation's discretion, false prophets who did not observe God's Word:

> At the synod of Delft, what the religious teachers did there, when they tried to stop that damned use of the organ, in order to use it in the congregation as a religious service. They have, therefore, put their trust on external help and not on God's word, and have uttered a great deal of platitudes (the pious beyond these are few) just like the false prophets did during the time of the Kings.[100]

Huygens complained to the church authorities in The Hague about Calckman's scathing attack in the *Antidotum,* and in response the council decided on November 22, 1641 to have some representatives speak with Calckman to ascertain "whether he was not aware that he went too far in the aforementioned writing."[101] Further, the council was intent on investigating the involvement of the publisher, Aert van Meurs. Two weeks later the elders reported that Calckman had expressed his regrets, and "had confessed roundly and with tears, having been overtaken by his fervor, and having said a number of things which he regretted, and wished he had not said."[102]

---

99. "*Godt heeft de gemeynte geen mate gestelt / na het gebruyck vande Wereltsche Musise, singhers / maer na de mate des geestes / die elck Godt toebrenght in eenvoudicheyt / voor soo veel hy van God ontvangen heeft. Strijden dan de mate tegen het Wereltsch Musijck / soo en strijden sy niet teghen de mate des Geests / datse gaen beter soecken te leeren. Siet Orghelist aldus soecht ghy het eenvoudich singen uyt de gemeynte wech te nemen / en het Orgelspel in te voeren / daer het meestendeel vande gemeynte so veel verstants van heeft / als de Koe van Vlaenderlant.*" Calckman, *Antidotum*, 194.

100. "*. . . in de synode tot Delft / wat de Godts-geleerde aldaer deden; doemen dat vervloeckte orgelspel sochte te arresteren / om inde gemeynte als eenen Godtsdienst te ghebruycken. Doen hebben zy haer verlaeten op de uyterlijcke hulpe / en niet op Godts woort: En hebben gheseyt als een deel lichte plivieren: (de vroomen hier buyten die weynich zijn) ghelijck alle de valsche Propheten deden ten tijden des Conincx . . . .*" Calckman, *Antidotum*, 92–93.

101. "*Of hy zig niet bewust en vind, van sich te ver in dat genoemde schrift vergeten te hebben.*" Roodenburg, *Onder censuur*, 124.

102. "*Rondelyck en met tranen bekend, dat hij door iever wechgeruckt sijnde, verscheydene dingen heeft gesteld die hem leet waren, en wenschte niet gesteld te hebben.*" Roodenburg, *Onder censuur*, 131.

Notwithstanding Calckman's apparent remorse, the council drew up a declaration of guilt for him to sign as a signal that it could not accept the harsh tone of the *Antidotum* against Huygens or the church. Specifically, the council objected to Calckman's use of the label "idol worshippers" to describe anyone who supported organ playing. The council even declared that Calckman was promoting schism in the denomination by pitting proponents and opponents of the organ against each other. Thus the council resolved on December 20, 1641:

> ... that he [Calckman], especially having undertaken to refute the books of the Earl of Zuilichem, recently published about this matter, he not just intellectually misquotes and distorts his [Huygens'] opinion in a number of passages, but also often slanders and judges the Earl bitterly, contrary to all Christian and brotherly love, and that [Calckman did so] not only in regard to his [Huygens'] public life and behavior, but also (to which only the Lord has the right) with regard to his heart and inner Godly worship of the Lord.[103]

The council sentenced Calckman to make an apology to Huygens, express himself more gently in the future, and sign the declaration of guilt. Further, Calckman was prohibited from the Lord's Table, a suspension that was lifted about a year later. It was a light sentence given in consideration of Calckman's advanced age.

Calckman was reprimanded not only by the council of the St. Jacob's church in The Hague but also by a certain "W. S.," who in 1641 released his own pamphlet entitled "Short rejoinder, that the anti-dote by the organ iconoclast is unhealthy"[104] In this essay, W. S. postulated that God instituted worship "for edification, attention, and that God wanted to be served by way of these externalities."[105] Since the Bible did not give explicit rules for how to do this, he suggested that it is a matter of human choice to find the most appropriate type of worship. W. S. specifically

---

103. "*Dat hy in 't besonder voorgenomen hebbende te wederleggen, het Boexken van den Ed. Heere van Zuylechem, onlangs te voren over deze materie uytgegeven, niet alleenlick desselfs meyninghe in verscheide passagien, onverstandelijck misduyt en verdraeyt; maer oock denselven Heere doorgaens seer bitterlijck tegen alle Christelicke ende Broederlicke liefde lastert ende veroordeelt; ende sulkx niet alleenlick ten aensien van desselfs uyterlijck leven ende comportement, maer oock (dat alleen Gode toekomt) ten aensien van desselfs herte ende inwendigen Gods-dienst voor den Heere.*" Roodenburg, *Onder censuur*, 131.

104. W. S., *Korte aen-wijsinge*.

105. W. S., *Korte aen-wijsing*, 7.

chided anyone who claimed biblical support for prohibiting accompanied singing in church: "Observing these stated distinctions, it will be easy to refute the rude invectives of the organ-attacker [Calckman]; allowing himself to be used as a coarse organ pipe."[106] W. S. concluded by reminding his readers that not every aspect of worship ceremonies was specifically mandated in the Bible; thus, it did not follow that what Calckman called "novelties" were necessarily unbiblical. What was paramount was that all things in worship—new and old—were done "fittingly and in good order."

Huygens had no formal response to either Calckman's *Antidotum* or W. S.'s *Korte Aen-wijsinge* following the publication of *Orgel Gebruyck*, but he did collate the opinions of his acquaintances who read his initial draft and published them under the title *Responsa prudentum ad autorem dissertationis de organo in ecclesiis Confoed. Belgii*. This time, Huygens wrote in Latin, probably as a way to ensure that only the well-educated could read this work.[107] It was a collection of responses from various acquaintances which praised the publication of *Orgel Gebruyck* and the disciplinary resolution against Calckman issued by the church council in The Hague.

Though Huygens may have not formally reacted to Calckman, Calckman's *Antidotum* did stir up more opposition to the organ's use, especially in The Hague where Calckman and Huygens lived and worshiped together. A group calling themselves the "Alliance of the Concerned"[108] appeared before the church council on January 3, 1642 and objected not so much to the letters in Huygens's *Responsa* but to the published resolution by the church council of the Jacob Church of The Hague. They presented a written (but unsigned) objection against Huygens's *Orgel Gebruyck*. After they departed, the clerk of council read the Alliance's statement aloud. The church officers heard the petition rattle off objections against Huygen's *Orgel Gebruyck*: the book gave opportunity for outsiders to slander the Reformed public worship service; the book mocked the good name of

---

106. "*Dese aen-ghetogene Distinctien waer-ghenomen, sal seer licht te beantwoorden zijn des Orghel-bestormers plompet invectiven: latende sich ghebruycken als een seer grof Orghelpijp.*" W. S., *Korte aen-wijsing*, 11.

107. Only three written replies to *Responsa* are known: from René Descartes, Willem de Groot, and Johannes Polyander van Kerckhoven. What is clear is that *Responsa* received much less notice than *Orgel Gebruyck*.

108. Known members: Melchior Arents, Servaes van der Wielen, Andries Jacobsen, Coenraet Gerritsen, Jan Caron, and Jan van Steenwyck.

the Reformers; the book lightly judged sin; the book libeled the congregation; the book gave unworthy arguments; the book introduced a disputable matter between the church and the authorities, between teachers and teachers, between teachers and church members; the book allowed a private individual to prescribe rules that the church should follow.

After the objection was read, the church council decided that each member of the council would read the *Orgel Gebruyck* for himself so he could make an informed decision on the matter, and they told the members of the alliance that, if they were so displeased with the spiritual health of the church, they should refrain from Holy Communion until the matter was resolved and Christian brotherhood was restored within the congregation. The council also agreed to try and discover the meeting time and location of the Alliance, for they were displeased that a group such as the Alliance had formed within the church without their prior knowledge or consent.

After these actions by the church council, there is no record of any more activity of the Alliance on this matter, save a brief mention of the Van der Wielen family who had left the congregation over the disputes and was encouraged to return. However, another group within the church was formed to oppose the Alliance and submitted a subsequent petition to the council. It is possible that Huygens himself was the author of this petition, but the truth will never be known. To be sure, the literary style is quite unlike Huygens's characteristically erudite Dutch; on the other hand, only someone with a university education and the mind of a poet could so masterfully parody the clumsy, strained syntax and overblown sentences of the Alliance's petition.[109]

As a matter of fact, neither being denied Holy Communion for a year nor tearfully signing a statement of guilt silenced the irascible Calckman. In 1642 he published an overwrought "lament," entitled "Sad complaints of the repressed congregation of Jesus Christ, in these times of persecution by all of Christendom and comforting words by her redeemer Jesus Christ, to the encouragement of the repressed and weak souls in this type of trial. Everything put together simply from the Word of God by a lover of the truth, Jan Jansz. Calckman."[110] The motto was taken from James 1:2 and 12, and dedicated to "all people of this age, both the elite and the

---

109. For the complete text see *Sound Theology: A Reader*.
110. Calckman, *Droevighe*.

common that love the truth and cherish religion."[111] Calckman's entire text, which continues in this same flavor, clearly suggests that he himself is a martyr for the sake of righteousness at the hands of merciless *orgelists*.

Not Calckman but a Henricus Bruno (1617–1664) sent Huygens a copy of *Lament*,[112] and with that the matter between these two men seems to have been dropped.

Huygens published two more editions of *Orgel Gebruyck*, in 1659 and 1660, and had them printed in Amsterdam by Arent Gerretsz. van den Heuvel. The first edition of *Orgel Gebruyck* was anonymous, but these editions bore the name of Constantijn Huygens boldly and in full, and the title was expanded. These editions added laudatory poems by Pieter Cornelisz. Hooft and Hendrik Frederiksz. Waterloos, the song leader of the Nieuwe (New) Church in Amsterdam. One example of Waterloos' work reads:

> Correctly Huygens has connected the place and the times
> of Heavenly music, and the stately organ tones,
> To the holy place, and time, and substance and style,
> And to the songs on the harp by the King of Israel.
> Away with Orlandoos spirit. The frolicking madrigals
> And worldly songs, they must be banned from God's Church,
> The spirit of Huygens hovers above all pillars.[113]

After these editions, Huygens did once more briefly write about church music in a 1658 letter to Anna Schurman.[114] He lamented that the

---

111. "*Alle persoonen deses tijdts, hooge en leeghe, die de waerheyt beminnen en den Godsdienst liefhebben.*" Calckman, *Droevighe*, preface.

112. "*Ik zal u het boekje zenden, dat tegen u geschreven is.*" Worp, *Briefwisseling van Const. Huygens*, No. 3081, 3:321.

113. "*Met recht heeft Huighens dan de plaatzen, en de stonden, Van 't Goddelijk Muzijk, en 't staatlijk orgelspel, Aan heilige plaats, en tijt, en stoff, en stijl gebonden, En aan den harpzangh van den vorst van Israël, Wegh met Orlandoos gheest. De dart'le magdrigaalen, En lichte liederen, die moeten uit Godts kerk, De gheest van Huyghens zweefft hier boven alle paalen*" Huygens, *Orgel Gebruyck*.

114. This letter, *Kerk-gebruyck der Psalmen*, was published in 1876 in Moll and Scheffer's *Studiën en bijdragen*, 3:111. In brief, Huygens raises questions about psalm use in the Dutch Reformed Church: should they best use metrical psalms set to rhyme after the French example, or should they employ a prose version? And should the church continue to use the imported Genevan melodies, or compose new ones for their use? Huygens favored a prose version, following the example of the Greek, English and Roman Catholic churches. Since the Dutch had been using the metrical version of the Psalms, he felt it best that this use continue, but he offered suggestions for improvement, such as dropping the rhyming pattern and using free verse instead. Huygens

singing was "unorderly" (*onordentelicke*) and "mis-tuned" (*mistooning*) because "as among us they do not wish to accept the aid of the organ, contrary to most of our neighbors who use it, not without pleasure."[115] Huygens then seems to no longer involve himself with the subject, or with further developments concerning the organ in his home church, the Jacob Church of The Hague.

Though Huygens could turn aside from the organ question at this time, the council of his home church continued to deal with the question of appropriate organ use during worship, resulting in a flurry of letters exchanged during 1648–1649. First, in 1648, the magistrates of The Hague decided to abolish organ accompaniment outright,[116] but the very next year rescinded this decision themselves when they decreed "to continue with the organ accompaniment which the consistory would have liked to see done differently, in accordance with previous resolutions passed here."[117] Apparently their quick change of opinion was due to the fact that organ accompaniment had begun on December 1, 1648 without any directive from the consistory—nor with the approval of the magistrates. Now blaming each other for the change in the use of the organ, the church consistory accused the city magistrates of condoning the action, but the magistrates recused themselves, writing the very next week that no one had appeared before them to speak of "the test of the organ playing."[118] These contradictory decisions and confusing communiqués heightened the tension between church consistory and the city magistrates, both of whom saw themselves as the representatives of the

suggested new tunes be composed that fit the character of each Psalm and that had a limited vocal range so that worshipers with little musical experience could sing them well. Huygens also criticized *The Genevan Psalter*, thinking the Dutch translation by Datheen did not match the music well and distorted the original French rhythms.

115. "... ende niet dan al te seer is blijckende uyt de onordentelicke mistooning onser Psalmen, dat vrome lieden in onse kercken dagelix met leed- wesen moeten verdraghen, dewijle men bij ons niet en wil verstaen tot de hulpe van 't orgel, die onse meeste naburen daertegens, niet souder genoeghen, sijn gebruijckende." Moll and Scheffer, *Studiën en bijdragen*, 119.

116. *Acta 8 december 1648*, Haarlem, Kerkeraadarchief No. 107, as cited by Luth, "Daer wert ...," 224.

117. "... met het orgelspelen onder het singen te vaeren t'welck de E. Kerckenraet geerne anders hadden gesien tegens voorgaende resolution hier opgenomen." *Acta 12 januari 1649*, Haarlem, Kerkeraadarchief No. 107, as cited by Luth, "Daer wert ...," 224.

118. *Acta 13 december 1648*, Haarlem, Kerkeraadsarchief No. 107, as cited by Luth, "Daer wert ...," 224.

Christian people, yet held contradictory opinions as they asserted leadership in the organ controversy.

Huygens's long political, theological, and musical struggle culminated in a quiet but magnificent symbolic victory nearly thirty years later. On May 1, 1671 the magistrates in The Hague gave Steven Hermansz. van Eyk permission to play the organ of the Jacob Church during the singing of the congregation for the "greater harmony in the worship services."[119] This does not mean that the church services instantly became immune from worldly concerns; records show that the church continued to pay the local bailiff (sheriff) to keep disturbances out of the church building, particularly during the concerts on Saturday, and they even had to pay the dog-beaters in the area to desist from their "work" during services.[120] Still, a most important church in the most powerful city in the land had reinstated the church organ as a tool for worship without producing a schism.

Huygens edited some of his poems for the last time in 1672, one of which referenced the Calckman ordeal,[121] and died in his ninety-first year, on March 28, 1687.

In conclusion, this chapter revealed that Constantijn Huygens became a fervent, public proponent of using the existing organs to improve congregational singing for the greater glory of God. Accordingly, Huygens wrote *Orgel Gebruyck* to lay out a line of theological reasoning

---

119. "*Meerder harmonie in de godsdiensten.*"

120. Kler and Eck, *Zeven eeuwen orgels*, 32–33.

121. The poem was actually directed against Jan Zoet, who had challenged Huygens's work "Holy Days" (*Heilige Dagen*). But Calckman is present in the poem as a past tormentor:
"OP EEN DOLL GEDICHT VAN IAN SOET TEGENS MIJNE HEILIGE DAGHEN
De snaer van een' ontsteldë veel / Bestaet weerom mijn oor t'ontstellen. / Wat komt mij dese Calckman quellen / Het zijn een-galghighe gesellen, / Het zijn doctoren sonder scheel. / Een touw, een touw voor keel en keel. / Sij konnen beid' haer naem niet spellen, / Sy schrijven L. of E. te veel."
"ABOUT A FOOLISH POEM BY JAN SOET CONTRA MY 'HOLY DAYS'
The string of an out-of-tune violin / Again manages to disturb my ear / How does this Calckman come to annoy me / With his mates who think the same / They are doctors without a degree / a rope, a rope for throat and voice. / Neither one was able to spell his name / They write L. or E. too much."
Huygens's suggestion that his opponents cannot spell correctly is actually a masked *ad hominem* attack on Calckman and Soet. First, removing the letter "l" from Calckman's name leaves *Cack-man*, the first syllable clearly is scatological, as is much of Dutch humor of this period. To take away an "e" from Soet's name leaves the archaic Dutch word *sot*, or "idiot."

that could redeem the church organ in the eyes—and ears—of aural iconoclasts. The compromise of using the organ before and after but not during worship had seemingly stilled the conflict over the organ's use in the Dutch Reformed churches. But *Orgel Gebruyck* proved that this compromise was indeed brittle, both because its thesis was bitterly contested by Reformed clergy and laymen and because it was heartily endorsed by influential cultural and ecclesiastical leaders who, like Huygens, realized that the *status quo* was based on hasty and poorly reasoned decisions. Huygens dared question the veracity of one key feature of doctrinaire Reformed theology and to doubt its applicability to the specific situation in the Low Countries.

But in the end, the organ controversy did not die with Huygens or Calckman. Indeed, as this chapter shows, the historical reality is that Huygens's work ignited negative reactions in the pew, pulpit, and church council room, and, as the next chapter illustrates, now also even from the podium of the university.

6

VOETIUS OUTSCORED

Teaching from his post at Utrecht's then newly founded university, Gisbertus Voetius,[1] who had earlier corresponded with Huygens about *Orgel Gebruyck*, rose to lead an *anti-orgelist* campaign from the academy. As professor at the newly founded academy of Utrecht, Voetius wrote on the subject no less than four times, and included two essays in his *Politicæ Ecclesiasticæ*.[2] This *anti-orgelist* essay is invaluable for its scope and bibliographical references as well as its theological architecture that built the *anti-orgelist* position after Calvin's death, giving us insight into the mind of second generation Reformers such as Dr. Voet. In addition, Voetius's influence extended far beyond Utrecht once the city's young university began graduating Reformed ministers who served churches across the Dutch republic.

Prior to his arrival in Utrecht, Voetius became a fervent Calvinist as a university student in Leiden during the time of the great Arminian controversy. After being graduated, Voetius pastored a Reformed church in Vlijmen in 1611 and subsequently served as an army chaplain. Six years later, in 1617, he returned to his hometown of Heusden to pastor that church, preaching there no less than eight times a week. Besides his homiletical duties, Voetius was also so musically inclined that he often led the congregational singing as *voorzanger*. As a result, he must have known full well the poor state of unaccompanied congregational singing

---

1. While there were several Dutch variants of his name, such as Gys Voet, Gijs Voet, or even Voët (though the diaresis makes no sense), I will use the Latinized version of his name *Gisbertus Voetius*.

2. Both essays are included in *Sound Theology: A Reader*.

and, given his intellectual stature, one must assume that Voetius was tempted at least once to use the organ to remedy the painful results of banning church organs well documented by his contemporaries.

While pastoring the church at Heusden, Voetius continued his disciplined scholarship and castigated vehemently the Remonstrants, the Cartesians, Johannes Coccejus (1603–1669) and followers,[3] the Federalists, the Labadists,[4] and Copernicus[5]—to say nothing of the Roman Catholic Church, Judaism, or anyone who deviated in any way from his own rigid interpretation of Calvinism, which he defended with the greatest theological fervor. In 1634 he was appointed professor of theology and languages at the new *illustere school* ("Illustrious School") of Utrecht; a few years later the school was granted the higher status of a university.

In addition to teaching at the newly founded Utrecht University, Voetius held disputations each Saturday afternoon. At these events, theologians, students, and colleagues debated the questions of the day in public. It is clear that these debates in turn informed Voetius's writing and inspired publication. The Voetian corpus is, therefore, extremely valuable; in addition to revealing the theological concerns of his day, the disputations are supplemented with valuable bibliographical references such that, as Christiaan Sepp notes, "the wealth of knowledge contained in Voetius's work is almost limitless."[6]

A disputation on the organ question was held in 1634, the inaugural year of the *illustere school* of Utrecht. Voetius himself recalls that:

> In August of 1634, in the school in Utrecht, at my first disputation, the first of my career, I proposed, amongst other questions to be discussed, the question which is discussed in *Musicam organicam, nec partem, nec appendicem esse Cultus publici*.[7]

In other words, Voetius's first disputation was on the subject of the use of the pipe organ in services of Reformed worship. In that debate and

---

3. Coccejus was a theology professor at Franecker and Leiden whose covenant theology, in Voetius's opinion, overemphasized the historical and contextual character of specific ages. See McCoy, "Covenant Theology of Johannes Cocceius."

4. Though Jean de Labadie (1610–1674) helped the Protestant movement in Switzerland, Voetius alleged that Labadie promoted mystical subjectivism. See Graafland, "Nadere Reformatie en het Labadisme."

5. On the Dutch reactions to Copernicus, see Vermij, *Calvinist Copernicans*.

6. Beeke, *Gisbertus Voetius*, 9.

7. Voetius, PE, 1:592. Schoock identified two such disputations, but placed them not during August, but on July 3 and July 10, 1634. Schoock, *Exercitationes variæ*, 516.

consistently for the rest of his life he was an *anti-orgelist*; that is to say, he insisted that the organ should never be played during any part of a public worship service, nor even immediately before or after any service.

Initial Responses to Voetius

This oral disputation in 1634 and Voetius's initial, pejorative opinion of the organ might have gone unnoticed were it not for written refutations by David van Boxtel (1614–1666), a minister living in Gouda, and Jacobus Johannes Batelier (1593–1672), a Remonstrant minister living in The Hague.[8] Batelier threw down the gauntlet with this invective: "If I should enumerate the empty inquiries put forward by Voetius, I would whole-heartedly say that it will be necessary to rethink the major part of the list of his arguments."[9] In specific regard to the organ issue, Batelier emphasized that the matter was not a matter of principle, in other words, it was *adiaphora*. Batelier reasoned that if Voetius elevated the organ question to the level of a doctrinal debate, then other trivial issues would have to be summarily addressed in the same way, such as the number of members on the church council, whether church buildings should have a designated room for the Consistory, or whether the collection should be taken during the worship service or after the service as the congregation exited the building. Batelier's concern was confirmed by Voetius's demand that should a church use an organist, then he should be required to sign the Form of Subscription or be removed from service. Batelier cautioned that this practice would essentially make the church organist into a new type of church office previously unknown to the church.

Voetius forcefully rebutted these perceived attacks by Boxtel and Batelier in a comprehensive work entitled *Thersites heautontimorumenos*, in which he stated his case anew that the sound of the organ could not be religious worship as the "less educated might easily imagine."[10] Voetius pleaded again that the "daily noise of the organs" in the churches cease:

---

8. Van Oudenhoven, *Beschryvinga der stadt Heusden*, 189. Van Boxtel, *De præjudiciis veræ religionis*, reprinted in Voetius, *Thersites heautontimorumenos*, 335–54; Voetius, *Selectæ disputationes theologicæ*, 539–51. Batelier, *Examen accuratum disputationis*.

9. Batelier, *Examen*, 60–61. See also Brandt, *Historie der reformatie*, 3:938.

10. Ἑαυτόν τιμωρούμενος is the title of a play by Menander, the "self-tormentor." Θερσίτης an Homeric name meaning "the audacious." Voetius's commentary on the organ is to be found in *Thersites heautontimorumenos*, 293–94.

> It is not useless vanity to discuss a controversy between us and the papists, particularly one of a kind that pertains to religious practice and worship. . . . For our "Reformers," as it were, of organs the issue was raised by Cudsemius (if I am not mistaken) in *Desperata causa Calvini*, and by Eckhardus in *Fasciculus controversiarum*, chapter 21, question 5. Now you see the usefulness of our question. The daily noise of organs in our churches also encourages us to diligently impress these cautions on the common people, lest they think that the organist is an ecclesiastical minister, or that the sound of organs is religious worship, as some of the less educated might easily imagine, along with the papists.[11]

He concluded by branding those who did not share his views on the organ as hostile to the Reformed cause. However, writing later in a small essay entitled *Appendix Apologetica*, Voetius did concede that in this early writing he was writing against organ music as solo music, and not as accompaniment for psalm singing. He stated that it was only after the 1634 disputations that he became aware of an "Ecclesiâ aliquâ Hollandicâ" that used the organ to accompany their psalm singing.[12]

With his closest critics refuted, Voetius picked up his pen to write more thoroughly on the subject of the church organ again in 1641, no doubt prompted by the publication that year of Constantijn Huygens's *Orgel Gebruyck*. Huygens even sent Voetius a complimentary copy of *Orgel Gebruyck*, thereby inviting Voetius to the debate the subject in print, while implicitly acknowledging that Voetius was a voice to be reckoned with. Voetius offered Huygens backhanded praise for the gift and the invitation to debate, simply stating that he (Voetius) was grateful for the gift but that he himself had thoughts on the subject which were soon to be published.[13]

---

11. Voetius, *Thersites heautontimorumenos*, 293–94. For the works mentioned by Voetius, see Petrus Cudsemius, *Desperata Calvini causa*, and Eckardi, *Fasciculus controversiarum theologicarum quæstiones*.

12. Voetius, PE, 1:593.

13. "Utrecht, 8 March, 1641. Most noble and magnificent sir, I have received two copies of your dissertation on the use and abuse of the organ, one of which I have passed on to our heroic lady Schuurman. She gives thanks for the literary gift, as do I, most profoundly. I would have wanted to write you my opinion right now, if I were not prevented from doing so by some meditations whose publication is pressing at the moment, and I were not reserving all of this, such as it is, for a more detailed future publication. I here display the image of our Schuurman, which she herself painted and engraved, if perhaps you have not yet seen it, together with some verses with which

Voetius's Pronouncement on the Pipe Organ in Worship

Around that same time, Voetius promised to closer colleagues, such as Martinus Schoock, a professor of philosophy at Utrecht and a theologian, a more thorough work on the subject predicting that the forthcoming work would be complete and authoritative.[14] Voetius began that major work in 1641. At nearly the same time as he received Huygen's letter, Voetius accepted Johannes Heimenberg (= Johannes van Heymenberg, 1621–1677) as a doctoral student (*promovendus*) who, according to Schoock, was present at the 1634 inaugural disputations.[15] In July 1641 Heimenberg submitted a thesis to Voetius entitled *De organis et canu organico in Sacro [sub præsidio Gisberti Voetii]*.[16] It is clear that Voetius published Heimenberg's 1641 thesis, save very minor edits, as his (Voetius's) 1663 chapter in *Politicæ ecclesiasticæ*. Voetius's resulting essay is consistently and clearly *anti-orgelist* and organized in classical rhetorical fashion. First Voetius rephrased his opponents' arguments in favor of using the organ, then refuted each one before finally presenting his own *anti-orgelist* position. The essay is expansive in length, and Voetius is prone to wander off subject, or to circle back and repeat what he had previously stated. In brief, Voetius's principal themes against the use of the organ in public worship are these:

---

she tried in vain to persuade the distinguished jurist Schotanus to delay his departure. I pray that God will govern you with his Spirit, in order that you may continue to the best of your abilities in such an unsuitable place and age to further grace and advance with your extraordinary and admirable example the study of true wisdom and godliness. The most obedient servant of your nobility and magnificence, Gisbertus Voetius." Quoted in Duker, *Voetius*, 2:cxxv.

14. "8th day before the Ides of March [March 8] 1641. Indeed I would have liked to write my judgment out now in full, if certain other works in preparation, whose publication now is pressing, did not hinder me. And I would reserve this entire matter, whatever it is, for a more precise discussion to be published some other time." Schoock, *Exercitationes variae*, 516.

15. Schoock identifies the student as "Ionnes Heimenbergio," or Heimenbergius (Schoock, *Exercitationes variae*, 516); Voetius himself never names the student, only saying "I turn now to those of less importance, and touch briefly on the ones which I put forward for discussion in my academic discourse in 1641" (Voetius, PE 1:584). Heimenberg was born in Utrecht and pastored churches at Bergambacht and Ammerstol (1644), Montfoort (1653) and Utrecht (1656); see van Lieburg, *Repertorium van Nederlandse hervormde predikanten tot 1816*, 1:97.

16. The only extant copy of his thesis is Ionnes Heimenbergius, "Organis et canu organico in Sacro [sub præsidio Gisberti Voetii] [1641]," MS KA 48, Koninklijke Bibliotheek, The Hague.

First, Voetius, like Calvin, affirmed music first as a gift of God to be enjoyed. In fact, in what is a quite astonishing concession of *De Organis*, as Voetius defended his position, he stated theoretically that the organ had the potential to be used in a God-glorifying manner. What is more, Voetius posited that had church synods ruled another way, he might be convinced otherwise.[17] But as quickly as Voetius offered these two hypothetical scenarios which could have made him an *orgelist*, he just as quickly dismissed them with the observation that such would never be possible. All this is to say that Voetius recognized the value and beauty of music, and even affirmed his personal skill of the art.[18] That music was intrinsically evil was never Voetius's point; rather, the issue was that in corporate worship the risk of misuse of the organ overshadowed any possible benefit.

The minister Joos van Laren (= Joducus van Larenus, 1565–1653)[19] who pastored the church in Vlissingen, reiterated a similar point in a 1647 sermon. Van Laren's overriding concern was that the instrument could potentially stir up sinful emotions:

> And indeed God is to be praised with songs; Jehovah is my psalm.[20] By his authority musical instruments may also be employed for the celebration of God's praises, which many irreverently misuse for the purpose of monotonously repeating frivolous—no, disgraceful[21]—things. But this raises the weighty question of whether it is appropriate in the time of the New Testament to use musical instruments in public worship. There are those for whom the soothing of their ears is more important than the edification of their souls, who will no doubt answer in the affirmative. The author of Stilts[22] faults the council of the Middelburg church, that a number of times it had advised the magistracy that it wanted to remove the playing of the organ from public worship. In order for that pleasing sound to be removed from the sanctuary, it reluctantly removed it.

17. Voetius, PE, 1:591.
18. Voetius, PE, 1:578.
19. Van Lieburg, *Repertorium van Nederlandse hervormde*, 145.
20. Isa 12:2.
21. Lewd, *turpis*.
22. The Walcheren clergymen Larenus and Van Lansbergin both took part in a heated and apparently often personal "stilts" (*grallæ*) controversy, the issue being whether or not the Dutch state could rightly impose rules on the clergy. Larenus, *Data pensa trahamus*, 8.

> But explain, priests: what good does gold do in the sacred rites?[23]
>
> And explain, priests: what purpose does the organ serve in the sacred places?
> ... If one or two should be aroused through harmony of an organ strongly toward spiritual joy and elevation of the mind to God; a hundred, on the other hand, through the same will be pulled away from heavenly matters and will be roused to fleshly pleasures at least. Music in public sacred worship should be more plain in order to less hinder the understanding of words, then it will be more powerful and more effective for encouraging a low-lying spirit and for transporting it to spiritual and heavenly matters. On the contrary, the more melodious and ringing music will be, the more easily it will also attract fleshly pleasure our mind to which much flesh still clings.[24]

With these kinds of concessions made to the beauty of music, *antiorgelists* were forced to reckon with another prolegomena issue as they made the case against organ use in Reformed worship. *Orgelists* like Huygens asserted that the organ made worship more beautiful: it aided the singing, added solemnity, and relieved boredom.[25] With witnesses such as Voetius and Laurenus both conceding, however slightly, that such might

---

23. A quotation from the Roman satirist Persius, *Satires*, 2:69, implying that gold does no good.

24. "*Etiam Canticis Deus laudandus est, Iehova est Psalmus meus. Quinomino* [= *quo nomine*] *et musica instrumenta adhiberi possunt ad celebrandum laudes Dei, quibus nunc multi impie abutuntur ad decantandum red ludicras imo turpes. Sed gravis hic quaestio movetur, num tempore Novi Test. ad publicum cultum divinum instrumenta musica adhiberi conveniat. quibuscunque aurium suarum delinimenta magis cordi sunt, quam animae suae aedificatio, citra dubium affirmativam tuebuntur. Grallarum author reprehendit Synedrium Ecclesiae Middelburgensis, quod aliquoties monuerit Magistratum, ut vellet organi concentum removere e templis, a publico cultu divino. suavitatem igitur illam e templis tolli, aegre ferret. sed,*
    Dicite Pontifices in sacris quid facit aurum? et
    Dicite Pontifices in sacris organa quorsum?
    . . . . *Si unus et alter per Organicum concentum forte ad spiritualem laetitiam, et elevationem mentis ad Deum excitetur; centum contra per eundem a caelestibus avellentur, et ad carnalem duntaxat voluptatem commovebuntur. quo cantus in publico cultu sacro erit simplicior, et quo verborum intelligentiam minus impediet, eo erit potentior efficaciorque ad erigendum animum jacentem, et ad spiritualia caelestiaque subvehendum: et contra, quo erit modulatior et resonantior, eo facilius quoque mentem nostram cui multum adhuc carnis adhaeret, in carnalem voluptatem illiciet.*" Larenus, *Epinicium Ecclesiæ*, 47–48.

25. Voetius, PE, 1:570, 572, 580.

be true, then could it not be that the organ could just as well be used for good? The answer sounded from *anti-orgelists* was that beauty was in the ears of the hearer; the human voice, a God-made instrument, singing freely of the joy within, was the most ideal form of worship. Wind-blown pipes of a man-made contraption such as the organ could never equal this beauty. Thus the issue at hand for *anti-orgelists* was the addition of instruments to the voice; while the organ could indeed improve congregational singing and thereby focus the attention of Reformed worshipers more strongly on God Almighty, more certain was the threat to Christian purity that came from melodious organ music.

Anti-orgelists were not even convinced that organ accompaniment necessarily enabled a more glorious song of praise sung by the congregants. Larenus even claimed that organ accompaniment was counterproductive in leading decent congregational singing:

> We say that in those sanctuaries where organs are heard, no less frequent flaws of psalmody and foul dissonances are committed than in those sanctuaries where no usage of organs exists. Certainly, in this Church of ours, with so large a throng of worshippers, in no way for us is there a need for organs for the purpose of correcting dissonances.[26]

For Voetius and his followers, however, organ nonuse was not only automatically conferred by antiquity nor by the validity of formal ecclesiastical pronouncements, as we shall see below.

Second, Voetius, in good Calvinist fashion, continues with arguments from Scripture. He examines the etymology of the word [pipe] *organ*. Though several Scripture passages cite the *organ*,[27] Voetius pointed out that the actual Hebrew word is *ugab* [עגב]. In the Septuagint, the term used is ὀργάνω, which Jerome translated into Latin as *organo*. But neither *ugab*, ὀργάνω, nor *organo* was the complicated instrument known as the contemporary pipe organ known to the seventeenth-century Dutch. As Voetius saw it, the pipe organ was clearly a postbiblical, pagan invention that had been introduced by the Roman church. Thus, there was no biblical support for any sacred use of the pipe organ. If there were, then

---

26. "*In illis templis, ubi audiuntur organa, non minus crebra psalmodiae vitia et discentus turpes committie, si non plura, quam in illis templis, ubi nullus organorum usus est. Certe in hac nostra Ecclesia, in tanta audito rum frequentia, organis neutiquam nobis opus est, ad discentus turpes corrigendos.*" Larenus, *Epinicium Ecclesiæ*, 50–51.

27. Voetius cites Gen 4:21; Job 21:12, 30, 31; Ezek 33:32; Ps 150:4. Voetius, PE, 1:545.

all instruments and not just the organ would have to be used in worship: "Once the organ is allowed, all other instruments, such as horns, trumpets, flutes . . . would also have to be sanctioned."[28] Further, even if there were Old Testament evidence of the use of the pipe organ (which Voetius emphatically denied), the church established by Christ was not supposed to return to Jewish customs.[29]

Third, Voetius also denied that New Testament citations of music and instruments provided any valid scriptural precedent to use the organ. For example, Voetius lists the arguments that Christians sang at the agape meals and used instrumental music in heaven.[30] But he counters that none of these passages actually refers to the pipe organ, and that the agape meals were simply social gatherings, not acts of corporate worship. He relied on apostolic writers who rejected the use of instruments in worship by arguing that those instruments and other "ceremonies" were traits of an infant church (i.e., the first-generation church of the Jewish age), but could not be features of the mature church (i.e., the Christian age). Therefore the use of instruments was limited to use in the Old Testament church.[31]

Voetius correctly showed that the apostolic writers rejected the use of instruments in worship. Patristics argued that those instruments and other "ceremonies" were traits of a puerile church (i.e., of the Jewish era), but could not be features of the mature church (i.e., the Christian era). Therefore the use of instruments was limited to use in the Old Testament church.[32] What is more, the early fathers taught that instruments and their sound held pagan connotations. For instance, trumpets brought to mind the advance of the Roman army; bells and cymbals invoked the Eastern mystery religions. Sometimes certain sounds of instruments were even associated with immoral practice, such as the circus, funereal rites, and the Roman Coliseum—the place of many Christian martyrdoms.[33] Voetius cited Tertullian[34] to confirm the horrific, secular past of the organ:

28. Voetius, PE, 1:585.
29. Voetius, PE, 1:562.
30. Voetius, PE, 1:570.
31. Voetius, PE, 1:553.
32. Voetius, PE, 1:553.
33. Williams, *Story of the Organ*, 4–5; Bittermann, "Organ in the Early Middle Ages," 390–91.
34. Voetius, PE, 1:549.

> Let us pass on now to theatrical exhibitions, which we have already shown have a common origin with the circus, and bear like idolatrous designations—even as from the first they have borne the name of "Ludi," and equally minister to idols. They resemble each other also in their pomp, having the same procession to the scene of their display from temples and altars, and that mournful profusion of incense and blood, with music of pipes and trumpets, all under the direction of the soothsayer and the undertaker, those two foul masters of funeral rites and sacrifices.[35]

Thus, Voetius argued that the church should reject entirely the use of these instruments on fundamental moral grounds, not merely for theological or artistic reasons. It would be easier to destroy "the bad tree completely from root to branches than it is to remove its top or to prune it."[36] Further, even if its past could be pruned and discarded, what was left of the organ would still have the potential power to arouse "unholy" feeling during worship. It would seem best to Voetius not to risk misuse.[37]

Finally, to fortify these arguments, Voetius referred even to works of Catholic writers such as Cardinal Cajetano (1469–1534),[38] Molano (= Johannes van der Meulen 1533–1585),[39] and Raphael de la Torre (1509–1584),[40] who joined him in condemning the organ—Martin Aspilcueta (1492?–1586) known as Navarrus, a Spanish professor at Toulouse, is cited no less than twelve times.[41] Surely this was because Navarrus's work *De horis canonicis* described organ playing as it was practiced within the Roman Catholic church as profane, vain, and leading to evil song.[42] Voetius

---

35. "*Transeamus ad scaenicas res, quarum et originem communem et titulos pares secundum ipsam ab initio ludorum appellationem et administrationem coniunctam cum re equestri iam ostendimus. Apparatus etiam ex ea parte consortes, qua ad scaenam a templis et aris et illa infelicitate turis et sanguinis inter tibias et tubas itur duobus inquinatissimis arbitris funerum et sacrorum, dissignatore et haruspice.*" Tertullian, *Spectaculis*, 10:1–2.

36. "*Praestat ergo arborum radicitus succidere, & non tantum defrondare aut decorticare.*" Voetius, PE, 1:586.

37. Voetius, PE, 1:566–67.

38. Voetius, PE, 1:550, 552, 553, 554, 557, 558, 560, 578, 579, 562, 580, 582, 585, 585.

39. Mollerus or Malderus; Voetius, PE, 1:557, 556, 561, 562, 572, 579, 582, 588.

40. Voetius, PE, 1:551, 564.

41. Voetius, PE, 1:550, 554, 557, 558, 560, 567, 578, 579, 580, 582, 583, 588.

42. "Many organists frequently play profane, and even vain and sometimes evil songs in the church on the organ; of this sort are the ones they call 'baxas,' [a type of

thus used Roman Catholic theologians to bolster his thesis that the organ would automatically cause Calvinists to become insincere worshipers.

Voetius's arguments consistently reference the fourteenth chapter of Paul's epistle to the church of Corinth. There Paul insisted that whatever was done in worship should contribute to the edification (οἰκοδομήν, building up) of the body. Whatever is spoken, then, must be intelligible, meaning it must be spoken in the vernacular, or at least interpreted in the vernacular so that all may understand and benefit. In verse seven, Paul referred specifically to music in worship:

> Even in the case of lifeless things that make sounds, such as the flute (αὐλός, *tibia*) or harp (κιθάρα, *cithara*), how will anyone know what tune is being played (αὐλούμενον, lit: what is being piped) unless there is a distinction in the notes?

With Paul's specific reference to αὐλός Voetius and many others used this text to prohibit instrumental music in general, and the pipe organ in specific. As Paul linked the instrument "without life-giving sound" directly to the flute, so Voetius reasoned that the organ was a "dead" instrument (its sound produced mechanically through lifeless pipes or flutes) as opposed to a "living" instrument (its sound produced by the human body).

Voetius was not the first to use this Pauline text as support for a proscription of the organ. As reviewed in chapter 2, this chapter and verse of

---

show on the comic stage in ancient times, possibly also referring to comic song] and 'Atlas' [the classical demigod doomed to support the world on his shoulders], and other songs that the people know to be filthy, obscene, and wanton. This is clearly sin, especially when they do this during the divine offices, because of the occasion it may present for diverting the mind's attention from divine and spiritual things and bending it to the temporal, vain and evil. For this reason, in many places the *Credo* and *Gloria* are neither sung nor heard by the people at festivals; these are ordered not to be sung so that the pipes and harmonies may be heard. Instead of this, we should confess the holy catholic faith through heart and prayer, directing thanks to the Lord for his advent. Moreover, many organists, who display their skill so that they may be heard more fully, beat the keys so long (though this beating is no more than what one has called empty sound) that the Mass is protracted an hour too long. Such hearing so tires the people that it often introduces a great disdain for the assembly, the contemplation of the Redeemer's passion, and the redemption of humankind which is presented in that most holy consecration; thus, they think more about getting out of church than about its mysteries. Moreover, while the organs play, occasion is given for those in the choir to converse, joke, laugh, and carry on business; whenever they may think a little more on what the organs are playing, they thing rather of the pipes than of what they themselves are doing or saying." Azpilcueta, *Enchiridion*, 186.

Paul were the biblical basis for many a church organ ban imposed by the early Reformed gatherings. The premise was that the pipes of an organ only served to blow noise into the nave, confusing and distracting worshipers who were trying to worship God in spirit and in inward reflection. Thus, Voetius would rather the church speak "five intelligible words to instruct others than ten thousand words in a tongue" (1 Cor 14:19). The pipe organ's many voices only introduced more sound into worship, sound that was not needed; the resultant noise was just as confusing as those who spoke in unknown and garbled tongues.

Voetius reminded his readers that this use of 1 Corinthians 14 to stave off organ music goes even further back than the recent Dutch provisional and national synods. Erasmus's notorious lament on contemporary church music, which is found in his *Annotations* to 1 Corinthians printed in 1519 and which was cited by Voetius and his contemporaries,[43] offered a vivid description of the situation of the time. Erasmus's opinion left little doubt about the use of the organ in worship—or any instruments— and he used a commentary on 1 Corinthians 14 as the forum to do so:

> [*In margin*: Music in today's churches] What do they think of Christ, I ask you, those who think that they are pleasing Him with such a din of sounds? Not content even with these things, we have brought into the churches some kind of laborious and theatrical music, an uproarious chattering of varied voices, which I doubt was ever heard in the theaters of the Greeks and Romans. The whole thing is a noisy racket of trumpets, crumhorns, shawms, and sackbuts, and the human voices are vying with them. Obscene love songs are heard, such as harlots and minstrels dance to. One flocks together in church as if it were a theater, for the gratification of the ears. And for this custom, organ builders are maintained at large stipends, and crowds of children, whose entire youth is wasted in arduously learning such yelpings, meanwhile studying nothing of value.[44]

---

43. Voetius, PE, 1:550, 555, 560, 561, 592. See Sowards, "Two Lost Years of Erasmus," 161–186; Schoeck, *Erasmus of Europe*, 109–25. Voetius also mentioned the diplomat Alberto Pio (*Pium*, or *Pii*, "the pious"), Prince of Carpi (1475–1531) who took Erasmus to task for his views on church music. Voetius, PE, 1:550, 555, 556, 558, 560.

44. [In margin: *Musia quae hodie in templis*] "*Obsecro quid sentient de Christo, qui credunt illum huiusmodi uocum strepitu delectari? Nec his contenti, operosam quondam ac theatricam musicam, in sacras aedes induximus, tumultuosum diuersarum uocum garritum, qualem non opinor in Graecorum aut Romanorum theatris unquam auditum fuisee. Omnia tubis, liutuis, fistulis, ac sambusic perstrepunt, cumque his certant hominum uoces. Audiantur amatoriae foedaeque cantilenae, ad quas scrota mimique*

Though Erasmus's observations are helpful as a descriptor of the worship of his time, he did not expound upon the Scripture text as thoroughly as Voetius. As mentioned previously, Voetius was drawn to Paul's proscription of "inanimate sound," and reasoned with him that if something could not be understood or used profitably then it best be not used, particularly in public worship where only the mature fruit of faith should be modeled.

Guilelmus Zepperus (= Wilhelm Zepper, 1550–1607), cited by Voetius,[45] Reformed theologian, *anti-orgelist*, minister, court chaplain, and professor of practical theology at Herborn, explained:

> Instrumental music, in the religious worship of the Jews, belonged to the ceremonial law which is now abolished. . . . It is evident that it is contrary to the precept of St. Paul, I Corinthians 14 who wills that in Christian assemblies everything should be done for edification, that others may understand and be Reformed, so even that of speaking in unknown tongues should be banished from the church, much less should that jarring organic music which produces a garbling of many voices, be allowed with its pipes and trumpets and whistles making our church resound, nay, bellow and roar.[46]

In addition to invoking the teaching of 1 Corinthians 14 as authorative, Zepper also lamented the fact that some Reformed churches retained or even returned to organ use in direct contradiction to the ideals of the Reformation:

> In some of the Reformed churches, these musical instruments are retained, but they are not played until the congregation is dismissed, all the parts of divine worship being finished. And

---

saltitant. In sacram aedem uelut in theatrum concurritur, ad deliniendas aures. Et in hunc usum, magnis salarijs aluntur organorum opifices, puerorum greges, quorum omnis aetas in perdiscendis huiusmodi gannitibus consumitur, nihil interim bonae rei discentium." Erasmus, *Annotations*, 508–9.

45. Voetius, PE, 1:551, 592, 597.

46. "*Instrumentalis musica in sacris & cultu divino populi Judaici ad ceremonialia Mosaica pertinuit quæ nunc abolita sunt* . . . . *Utut sit contra præceptum et regulam Pauli factum est, qui I Cor. Xix. 26. vult, ut in conventibus ecclesiasticis ad edificationem omnia fiant, atque alii intelligent & informentur, quo quidem nominee linguas etiam in ecclesia ibidem rejicit, nedum confragosa illa Organa musica quæ varium vocum garritum efficient & templa lituis, tubis et fistulis personare, imo perboare et remugire faciunt.*" Zepperus, *Legum*, 4.

they are then used for a political purpose, to gratify those who seek pleasure from sound and harmony.⁴⁷

Such interpretations of Paul's exhortation were not limited to the Netherlands; even the German theologian David Pareus⁴⁸ (1548–1622) shared the same opinion regarding the organ:

> In the Christian church the mind must be incited to spiritual joy, not by pipes, and trumpets, and timbrels, with which God formerly indulged his ancient people on account of the hardness of their hearts, but by spiritual songs, psalms, and hymns.⁴⁹

Not all of Voetius's contemporaries used 1 Corinthians 14 similarly, nor with the specific application that the organ's use cease and desist. One such theologian was the Roman Catholic Cornelius á Lapide,⁵⁰ (1567–1637, hereafter Lapide), the very one Voetius challenged for the idea that the heavenly music evidenced in Revelation set precedent for instrumental music in the present. When commenting on 1 Cor 14:7, not only did Lapide suggest that the Latin tongue be used in worship because it ensured universal understanding amongst worshipers of differing dialects, but he also argued that the organ could be an aid to remove garbled singing, and thereby enable more intelligible worship. Lapide's stated his three assertions, with a requisite caution, as such:

> First, as we join in praising God, not only in spirit but also in body, so we should praise Him, not only with the best music of the voice, but also of instruments; for every spirit, every creature, every instrument ought to praise Him whose due never can be reached.

---

47. "*In quibusdame ecclesiis Reformatis Organa illa musica retinentur, non autem nisi omnibus cultus divini partibus peractis et demisso cœtu ecclesiastico pulsantur. Ad finem politicum propter illos qui ex sono et numeris oblectationem quondam quærunt quibusque huix instrumentali musica interesse libet.*" Zepperus, *Politica ecclesiastica*, 175–76.

48. Voetius, PE, 1:561, 592.

49. "*In ecclesia enim excitandus est animus ad Deum & lætitiam spiritualem non tibiis, tubis, tympanis: quod veteri duræ ceruicis & stupidæ mentis populo Deus olim indulsit: sed sacris concionibus, psalmodiis & hymnis.*" Pareus, *Davidis Parei In divinam*, 770.

50. Voetius, PE, 1:550, 1:562, 1:569, 1:570, 1:572, 1:573, 1:577, 1:580, 1:581, 1:582, 1:584, 1:592, 1:597.

Second, to arouse the listeners, and especially the uneducated, to religious fervor, as David and Elisha were enkindled by psalms and harps, and as Saul was stirred up by music to give God praise.

Third, that the beauty, solemnity, and majesty of Divine service may be the greater. Prudentius, in his *Apotheosis*, written against the Jews, and the Faculty of Paris, in its decree (chapter 14, proposition 6), explains this verse this way: *When St. Paul says that in the church he would rather speak five words with his understanding than ten thousand words in an unknown tongue, he is speaking of sermons addressed to the people, in which a flow of words void of thought is useless. He says nothing about Church canticles, which are governed by another law.*

Nevertheless, we must in these matters guard against lightness, as the Council of Trent asks. Hence Saint Augustine (*Homily on Psalm 33*) says that pipes and organs used in theaters had been rejected by the Church, because the heathen used them then for lust in the theatres, and for banquets, and at their sacrifices. But, following the example of injunctions of David, we may use organs and other musical instruments, if it be done with piety, soberness, and gravity (see Psalm 150: 3, 4, 5, 6). Saint John also (Rev. 5:8 and 14:2) heard in heaven, where all are perfected, harps, though of course more solemn and Divine than ours on earth.[51]

---

51. "*Primo, ut sicut non tantum spiritu, sed et corpore constamus, Deumque Iaudamus: sic non tantum voce, eaque concordi et pulcherrima, qualis est musica, sed et instrumentis Deum laudemus. Omnis enim spiritus, omnis creatura, omne instrumentum laudare debet Deum, quem omnis laus decet. Secundo, ut audientes, præsertim plebeii, ad devotionem excitentur, sicut David et Eliseus per psaltes et psalteria excitabantur, et sicut excitabant Saulem et alios per musicam ad Dei laudem. Tertio, ut major sit sacrorum décor, solemnitas et majestas. Ita Prudentius in Apotheosi contra Judæos; et Facultas Pariensis in sua censura tit, 19. propos. Ita hunc Pauli locum explicat: Scibens Paulus, in Ecclesia volo quinque verba sensu meo loqui, quam decem millia verborum in lingua; de concionibus, seu sermonibus, qui habentur ad populum, tractat, in quibus inutilis est copia verborum non intellectorum; non de cantibus Ecclesiasticis, quorum alia est ratio. Cavenda tamen est in hisce levitas, ut jubet Concil. Trident. Unde S. August. In psal. 32, conc. 1. dicit repulsas ab Ecclesia citharas et organa theatrica: quia scilicet Gentiles iis ad luxum et libinem ut theatris, conviviis et sacrificiis utebantur eo tempore. Uti ergo organis in Ecclesia, et subinde aliis instrumentis musicis, si fiat sobrie, pie, modeste et graviter, Davidis exemplo et exhortatione, Psalm 159* [sic] *v. 3,4,5,6, patet esse pium: unde et S. Joannes in Apocal. C. 5. v. 8. et c. 14. v. 2. in cœlo ubi omnes sunt perfecti; audivit citharas, licet nostris graviores et diviniores*." Lapide, *Commentarii in Scripturam*, 9:329–30.

With this sort of teaching put forth, made all the worse because of its writer's Catholic loyalties, there is little wonder that Voetius streamed forth commentary such as that on 1 Cor 14:7; he used it first to apply its teaching to the organ question in worship, and then again to ward off misapplication of the passage such as Lapide's.

As one would inevitably expect, *anti-orgelists* such as Voetius layered the above-mentioned arguments with clear and consistent references to the abuses of Rome. They pleaded for an uncomplicated style of worship free from ceremony and ostentatiousness that, to the Reformed mind, characterized the Catholic church. Voetius's criticism of those who wanted to retrieve these aspects of Catholic liturgy was, frankly, uncouth:

> ... the organ, like all new novelties, is dangerous and suspicious, especially as the churches would appear to return to that which they had just discarded like a sick dog to its vomit.[52]

Though not as graphic as his teacher, Voetius's student, the pietist preacher Theodorus Jacobus Frelinghuysen (1691–1747), called Catholic worship "God-dishonoring and dead formalism."[53] The assumption was that the organ was needed by the Catholic church to carry out said "dead formalism;" and with dead formalism brushed out of the church by the Reformation, the organ was no longer needed.

With this principle invoked, that is, that the organ was a Catholic tool, it also became clear that other "superstitious" and Catholic utensils such as bells, salt, candles, oil, holy water, and the like summarily be disregarded if not entirely discarded. His "Commentary on the Heidelberg Catechism,"[54] in the context of his explication of the Second Commandment, Voetius insisted on the elimination of any and all vestiges of Roman Catholic practice. Here he not only cataloged all such

---

52. "*Quia omnis novitas periculosa, & meritò suspecta; imprimis si aliquâ ex parte per eam Ecclesiae nostrae viderentur redire ad vomitum aut palinodiam canere* . . . ." Voetius, PE, 1:585, no doubt recalling 2 Pet 2:22.

53. Hastings, *Ecclesiastical Records*, 4:2354, as cited by Meeter in *"Bless the Lord, O My Soul,"* 35. As late as 1656 the consistory of Amsterdam still viewed organ playing as "Catholic," and even included organ playing in their list of "popish abuses." Apparently, the hidden Catholic churches in Amsterdam played the organs so loudly that people on the streets could even hear them: "[the Catholics are] . . . singing and playing on them [positive] organs, violins and other instruments so that people could hear it on the street and in the houses of the neighbors." ". . . *singhende en spelende dij beselve op positive orlighen fyolen en andere instrementen dat men het buiten op de straat en in de buiren huisen kan horen.*" *Archief Nederlands Hervormde Gemeente*, 9:184–85.

54. Voetius and Poudroyen, *Voetius' catechisatie*.

"superstitious" items, but also clearly linked them to the Catholic church as he emphatically called for their elimination:

> Q. Which are the ceremonies that are in common use with the papism etc. these days?
>
> A. Some ceremonies are such that they are openly and directly, yes even in themselves, abominable and lead to evil; some are of such a nature, however, that they are not inherently evil, nor lead to evil, but are dangerous just the same because the smell and sound like evil, and give an appearance of evil.
>
> Q. Please name the ceremonies which are really and directly evil and lead to evil?
>
> A. The consecration of the churches, the consecration of the altars, Ember Days, the forty days of fasting, the festivals, crosses, pilgrimages, processions, consecrated garments, anointing oil, incantations [exorcism] and readings of Satan, the consecration of bells, cemeteries, and particularly of water, the lighting of wax candles and lights, the relics of Christ and other saints, the *Agnus Dei*, the rosary, the tidings, the litanies, self-flagellation, etc.
>
> Q. Name the ceremonies that are dangerous because they sound and have the appearance of evil?
>
> A. The genuflection when receiving the Lord's supper, the making of a cross in the air after baptism, the white cloth, the bowing and doffing of one's hat when speaking the name of Jesus, the doffing of the hat when walking through the church, or past the table on which communion is served, turning oneself to the east in the church when praying, the kiss of peace, such as by the Roman Catholics, and other similar things of that kind and nature.[55]

---

55. "*V: Welck zijn de ceremonien die heden ten dage by die van 't Pausdom, &c. in swangh gaen?*
A: Sommige ceremonien zijn soodanigh datse opentlick en directelick, ja in haer selven quaet zijn, ende tot het quaet stricken: sommige daerentegen zijn soodanigh datse in haer selven ende innerlick niet quaet zijn, noch tot het quaet stricken, maer nochtans periculeus om datse na het quaet riecken of luyden, ende een schijn des quaets zijn.
V: Noemt eens die ceremonien die eygentlick ende directelick quaet zijn, ende tot het quaet stricken?
A: De wyinge der Kercken, de wyinge des Altaers, het quatertemper, het vasten van veertigh dagen, de feesten, kruycen, pelgimagien of bedevaerden, ommegangen, gewijdde

Clearing the church of anything with such connotations could only be a positive step, instructed Voetius.

So far in this analysis, *anti-orgelists* such as Voetius and his peers have built their case upon foundational arguments already laid down in the organ controversy. But it is also important to see how the *anti-orgelists* went further in making their case against the organ's use than their forbears. First, they rejected the categorization of the organ as *adiaphora*. That church music fell into this category was generally assumed, indeed, affirmed by the Provincial Synod of Delft 1638 when it attempted to put the organ controversy to rest for the churches in its classis. But to the *anti-orgelists*, freedom to use the organ was a misapplication of the principle, for if it were decided that Reformed worship was completed by both the organ and the voice—that the organ was to be part of worship—then this matter was foundational, i.e., not adiaphora.[56]

In the context of his discussion of adiaphora, Voetius referenced the Colloquy of Montebéliard, and thus it is important to examine, however briefly, this insightful reference. The Colloquy of Montebéliard, a theological debate in 1586, was held between Jacob Andreæ, provost of the Lutheran University in Tübingen, and Théodore Beza, Reformed professor in Geneva.[57] Count Frederick of Montebéliard convened the colloquy hoping to resolve the conflicts troubling this French-speaking territory which was ruled by the dukes of Württemberg. Count Frederick was aware that local church traditions stemming from Geneva clashed with

---

kleederen, roockingen, salvingen, besweeringen ende beleesingen des Satans, de wyinge van klocken, cerckhoven, ende insonderheyt des waters, het aensteken van wassekeerssen ende lampen, de reliquien Christi ende andere Heyligen, het Agnus Dei, het rose-kransken, de getijden, de litanien, hemselvent te geesselen, &c.

V: Noemt eens de ceremonien die periculeus zijn om datse na het quaet luyden ende een schijn van quaet zijn?

A: Het knie-buygen in de ontfanginge des Avontmaels, het maken van een kruys in de lucht na de bedieninge des Doops, het witte kleet, het buygen ende afdoen van den hoet op het spreken van de naam Jesus, het afdoen van den hoet als men door de kerck gaet, ofte voorby de tafel daer op het Nachtmael bedient wort, sich in de kercken te keeren na het Oosten als men bidt, de kus des vredes, als by die van 't Pausdom, ende andere meer van diergelijcke aert ende natuur." Kuyper, *Voetius' catechisatie,* 798–99.

56. Voetius, PE, 1:585.

57. Adiaphora: Voetius, PE, 1:547, 1:554, 1:583, 1:584, 1:597; Colloquy: Voetius, PE, 1:552, 1:561, 1:592, 1:597; Beza: Voetius, PE, 1:552, 1:561, 1:592, 1:597; Andreæ: Voetius, PE, 1:552, 1:593. About the Colloquy, see Schoock, *Exercitationes variae,* 517; Herl, *Worship Wars in Early Lutheranism,* 109 and Appendix E where a small portion of the debate transcript is translated into English; Irwin, "Music and the Doctrine," 157–72.

pressures for adherence to Lutheran orthodoxy emanating from Stuttgart and Tübingen. Beza and Andreæ argued so bitterly over the Eucharist, the nature of Christ, and predestination that they would not shake hands when it was all over.

The discussion of church organs at this august meeting was no less fractious. Having heard incidents in which horses were brought into Reformed churches in order to tear down the organs, Beza interpreted such actions as reflecting a belief that organs were expressly forbidden by God; therefore, organ music was out of the realm of adiaphora and should not be used in worship. Andreæ agreed with Beza but only insofar as condemning the destructive, iconoclastic nature of such incidents. Music, Andreæ argued, while it had been abused under the papacy when it served only to delight the ears, still retained a positive power to move the human spirit in devotion and true worship. Therefore, concluded Andreæ, music is inherently neither good nor evil; music established its value in the manner (*genus*) by which it was used in worship.[58] Yet Beza would not agree:

> If the Apostle justly prohibits the use of unknown tongues in the church, much less would he have tolerated these artificial musical performances, which are addressed to the ear alone, and seldom strike the understanding, even of the performers themselves.[59]

Voetius clearly follows Beza, and did not agree with the position Andreæ put forward here.[60] Though Andreæ attempted to make the case that the organ had the potential to be used profitably in worship, Voetius, as Beza, claimed that anything that was not unequivocally edifying to the congregation—no matter how worthy in its own right—must be rejected:

> Whatever in the public worship service neither edifies nor is apt to edify the Church should not be used, even though in itself it might be an excellent thing . . . .[61]

---

58. Andreæ et al., *Colloquium Mompelgartense*, 730–32. This Colloquy did not end the debate. Ten years later the issue was brought up again by the theologians of Zerbst-Anhalt. See Irwin, *Music and the Doctrine*, 163–72 and Herl, *Worship Wars in Early Lutheranism*.

59. "*Si Apostolus merito peregrinarum linguarum usum in caetu Ecclesiastico prohibuit, multo minus sonos illos Musices Harmonicos, quibus aures solae, iis quae cantantur nullo modo, ne ab iis quidem.*" Schoock, *Exercitationes variae*, 517.

60. Voetius, PE, 1:552, 1:561, 1:592, 1:597.

61. Voetius, PE, 1:553–554.

In specific regard to organ use within the Reformed churches of the Netherlands, while the Provincial Synod of Delft had declared the organ's use adiaphora, Voetius argued that the organ cannot be of medium importance if its use had a negative impact. In fact, the organ "does not stir, fortify nor confirm the spirituality and rationality of the soul, nor the internal and external experience, but on the contrary restricts, traps, confuses, saps and enfeebles."[62]

Therefore, Voetius's prescription, so often repeated, was that the church return to article 77 of the National Synod of Dordrecht which demanded that organ use cease. It is also important here to notice Voetius's reminder that said rulings were decreed "in the presence of the magistrates"[63]—yet another plea to the magistrates that they follow ecclesiastical rulings in the buildings under their jurisdiction. While the issue could have been settled had it been a theological matter to be decided amongst the churches, the problem confounded itself because whatever ecclesiastical decisions were made, they had no effect over instruments that local church councils did not control. Voetius lamented:

> Whatever the ministers and their followers pleaded against vainly, against fear and major abuses, [they] obtained nothing but were forced to tolerate whatever seemed by certain elected lay officials whom, because the power of the music of the instrument, or because of the love of the ancient ways of doing things (sive ἠφων ἀρχάιων amore), or for some other reason, did it this way.[64]

Voetius further appealed to his readers that his objections were consistent with these previous Reformed teachings:

> We have decided with Reformed theologians cited below, that organ music is neither a convenient prop nor a part nor an appendage of divine worship, or of the church, whatever may be happening concerning the use or tolerance of this in various places which still have them.[65]

---

62. Voetius, PE, 1:553–554.

63. Voetius, PE, 1:561.

64. "*Quidquid monuerint & moliti fuerint Ministri metumque majoris abusus secuturi minimè vanum allegârint, nihil obtinuerunt: sed tolerare coacti sunt, quodcunque Aedili alicui; aut potentiori sive musicae instrumentalis, sive ἠφων ἀρχάιων amore, sive quocunque alio respectu hic agere visum fuit.*" Voetius, PE, 1:598.

65. "*Nos statuimus cum Reformatis Theologis infra citandis, Musicam organicam nec adminiculum conveniens, nec partem, nec appendicem esse cultus divini, seu*

It is crucial to see at this point that *anti-orgelists* categorically moved the organ out of adiaphora and into those things that were of the devil. It is not always clear how or why *anti-orgelists* directly associated the devil with the organ. Some have suggested it was because organ cases often had "wings," like the triptych paintings in the space above Catholic altars, which were actually case doors that could be closed when not in use, protecting the expensive metal pipes from exposure to the cold. Sometimes these case doors were used as a canvas, painted and gilded with images of saints or biblical scenes. *Anti-orgelists* feared that such images, now doubly destructive as they appeared *on* the diabolical organ, led all the more to false worship. Thus it was just one more step to finally label the organ demonic:

> ... if the organ were to be used, the workload of the minister would be substantially increase because they would have to then be vigilant to ward off other possible abuses and tricks of Satan.[66]

Other *anti-orgelists* were not bothered so much by the physical appearance of the organ as they were by the sound it produced, and, even more specifically, by the manner in which the pipe organ produced the sound. Pipe organs were wind instruments; they breathed and exhaled, using the bellows as "lungs" in order to blow music through its pipes. They were sibilant. The projected sound could too easily confuse a worshiper, tempt him with carnal thoughts because of the genre of music being played, or deceive him. With the pipe organ wheezing and hissing in its loft, only to produce unwanted and needless sound, *anti-orgelists* became convinced that the organ was the devil's voice (*duyvelschen fluytenkast*) in disguise. Calckman posed the question this bluntly:

> What is the difference between the organ and the idols through which the devils spoke? . . . Aren't the organ pipes hollow as well, do they have a might or knowledge from which to speak or to make sound by their own power? . . . Haven't the pipes themselves been fashioned from many different materials like the idols of the heathens?[67]

Ecclesiastici; quidquid sit de ejusdem usu aut tolerantia, variis in locis, quae ad huc obtinent." Voetius, PE, 1:553.

66. "*XI. Ratio; quia crescet labor noster, & cogemur semper ad vigilare, ne abusus irrepant; ne Satan & mundus obrepat, ne falsi fraters insidientur; haut aliter ac illi qui picturas, aut imagines, aut altaria retinent in Templis.*" Voetius, PE, 1:585–86.

67. "*Waer in bestaet nu het verschil? tusschen het Orgel / en haere Afgoden daer de*

If organ music were the sound of the devil, then clearly its use must cease and the issue no longer adiaphora.

Voetius was not done writing about the organ when he finished this essay for *Politicæ ecclesisticæ*, nor did his *anti-orgelist* position ever waver. As reviewed in the previous chapter, Voetius was joined by University of Utrecht colleagues Andreas Essenius (1618–1677) and Matthias Nethenus (1618–1686), he issued yet another condemnation of all organ use in public worship in 1655. This triumvirate of *anti-orgelisten* must have savored the opportunity to have a chance to silence Utrecht's church organs once and for all when the city council requested the professors' advice to answer the question "Whether the Christian Civic Authorities have the power, during this time of the New Testament, to institute the playing of the organ during the public singing of the psalms, all the more and principally since this had not been the custom previously."[68] The trio eagerly accepted "such an honest request." First, they stated that congregational singing should be regarded as a purely ecclesiastical matter. Although music was an "honorable practice" that could be freely practiced privately (*in 't privé*) for the accompaniment of psalms and hymns, such public use would disrupt public worship by diverting the attention of the worshiper toward worldly amusement. When that happened, worship in spirit and in truth suffered greatly, violating the warning of 1 Corinthians 14:

> But just the same, the playing of the organ in the public worship of the New Testament is a useless and unedifying practice, which draws the thoughts of the majority of the Christians from appropriate attention toward human entertainment, and thus prevents rather than promotes true worship, which must happen in spirit and in truth. Note then that the apostle teaches us in which way we should conduct the meetings of the believers and to which end all public acts and practices that are carried out there should be directed, when he writes this way in 1 Cor. 14:26 . . . .[69]

Duyvelen door spraken . . . . Sijn de Orgel-pijpen niet mede hol / isser eenighe macht of wetenschap in om te spreecken / of geluyt te maken uyt haer selven? . . . . sijn de Pijpen selve niet van veelderhande materien gemaeckt / gelijck de Afgoden der Heydenen?" Calckman, *Antidotum*, 157.

68. [Gilbertus Voetius, Andreas Essenius, and Matthias Nethenus], Theologisch Advys op 29 januari 1655, Afdeling Kerkeraad I (bijlage bij de notulen van de Kerkeraad d.d. 31 october 1683), Archief der Hervormde Gemeente, Utrecht.

69. [Voetius, Essenius, and Nethenus], Theologisch Advys, January 29, 1655.

The three professors continued and called organ playing not *adiaphora* but a "dumb and nonsensical" noise.[70] As Voetius had argued in his earlier essay, these three men pointed out that organ use in public worship was a practice that Christ, his apostles, the first congregations, and the later ancient churches had not known. Thus the authors concluded that a Christian government that did not wish to exceed the bounds of its duties could not and should not introduce organ playing during the public singing of the psalms.

Martin Schoock against Voetius

Alas, there is no evidence that this theological advice effected any change in the practice at Utrecht. To the contrary, much evidence suggests that Utrecht churches continued to use their pipe organs (if the church still had one) and that organ use possibly even increased.[71] Among the loudest voices leading Reformed churches away from Voetius's position and toward including pipe organ music in worship was Martin Schoock. Born a generation after Voetius, Schoock was first a student of Voetius in Utrecht, then a professor in Deventer, Groningen, and finally at Frankfurt upon Oder, where he died in 1665 at the age of fifty-one.[72] In 1663, Schoock published a telling—and daring—*orgelist* article that attacked his mentor Gisbertus Voetius. Claiming that Voetius is "pseudo-faithful" to his sources, Schoock proclaimed about Voetius's references:

> These [prooftexting errors] are measured out to the unsuspecting reader not just by the handful, but by the peck, indeed by the bushel. And in order that they may appear more formidable, he draws them up in a line of battle, distributed as it were into legions.[73]

In his attack on Voetius, and in building his own case for pipe organ inclusion in services of Reformed worship, Schoock follows typical rhetorical tactics of the era. Schoock recounts the history of the organ controversy before reminding readers that John Calvin was never opposed to organ use per se. That matter settled, Schoock deconstructs

---

70. [Voetius, Essenius, and Nethenus], Theologisch Advys, January 29, 1655.

71. See Vente, *Utrechtse orgelhistorische verkenningen*; *Rekest van de Gereformeerde Kerkeraad van Abcoude*, 25:313–14; Rijksarchief, Archief van de Staten van Utrecht.

72. Aa, *Biographisch woordenboek*, 396–98.

73. Schoock, *Exercitationes variae*, 531.

Voetius's *anti-orgel* stance point by point, relying on a veritable Who's Who of theologians as he does so. Schoock ends his article by constructing his own theological support for pipe organ use in worship. Frankly, Schoock uses many *orgelist* ideas already circulated by others: that organ accompaniment ensures a more dignified psalmody appropriate for worship, that organ use is a matter best left up to each individual church, that the Reformed provincial and national synods have already ruled on the subject, and so forth.

However, Schoock posits three new arguments not heard in the organ controversy to date that prove to be extremely valuable and insightful to the issue at hand. First, Schoock returns the reader to the writings of Paul and studies anew previously used proof texts against organ use. Specifically, Schoock points out that in Eph 5:20 Paul did say "Sing and make music in your heart to the Lord." But what is regrettable, Schoock points out, is that Paul's second verb choice in that clause, "make music" [ψάλλοντες], was not thoroughly studied. For, upon closer examination, according to *Etymologicus Magnus*, ψάλλοντες expressly connotes "gently touching, by playing, the strings of the lyre or of another musical instrument."[74] Schoock therefore concludes that here Paul sanctions the use of instruments to heighten devotion to God as he connects singing [ἄδοντες] with instrumentation [ψάλλοντες].

Schoock also re-examines Col 3:16 where Paul directs that one should "sing psalms, hymns and spiritual songs with gratitude [ἐν χάριτι] in your hearts to God." Schoock zeroes in on the Pauline descriptive to sing "with gratitude in the heart." He notes that many have used this verse to direct their singing toward giving thanks to God, just as Paul also said in Eph 5:19. But Schoock posits that "gratitude" used here is better rendered "grace and beauty" [*cum gratia et venustate*] just as Theophylactus first suggested.[75] This is justified, Schoock says, because Paul uses the very same construction in the very next chapter, Col 4:6, when he says that our speech must be "full of grace." Likewise, back to Col 3:16,

---

74. "Not only his Etymology but also in the Glossary, he explains and teach what ψάλλειν means. About that, the author of the *Etymologicus Magnus* says this: ψάλλειν, ἐπὶ τῶν χορδῶν τῆς λύρας παρὰ τὸ προσεγγίζω, ὁυ προσάγωγον ψάυω. There he expressly signifies that ψάλλειν is the same thing as gently touching, by playing, the strings of the lyre or of another musical instrument. Indeed, in the Glossary these words appear: φάλλω, nabizo, psalmizo; φαλτήριον, sambucum; ψάλτης: nablio, psalta. These abundantly serve to confirm my opinion." Schoock, *Exercitationes variae*, 523.

75. θεοφύλακτος = Theophylact of Ohrid, 1055–1107.

public singing in the church must be full of grace and beauty. According to Schoock, the early church followed this directive by establishing choirs to ensure that the public singing was beautiful and graceful.[76]

In the most obvious contradiction of Voetius's position, after establishing a biblical justification for the use of pipe organs in worship, Schoock suggests that other instruments can surely be employed in order to produce a more beautiful, holy, and—dare he suggest—biblical result. Because the church was guided by the Holy Spirit in this process of instrumental inclusion, first Roman and then Reformed, there is nothing to fear. Besides, how could first century biblical writers write against an instrument such as a pipe organ that was not yet even invented?

Schoock's third practical argument to justify the inclusion of the pipe organ in worship looks to the practice of the *voorzanger* to aid congregational singing. The *voorzanger*—most often the local school principal—was the song leader sanctioned by even the most extreme Calvinist churches. He would stand in front of a congregation and guide the singing of the psalmody phrase by phrase. Why did almost every Dutch Reformed church adopt and support the use of a *voorzanger*? Because his intonation and rhythm were full of both grace and beauty, and this singing was a model for the congregation to follow. If this principle was acceptable for using a *voorzanger*, Schoock asks, why should the pipe organ not be used in the very same way? He does concede that in smaller sanctuaries where the *voorzanger* approach is successful then, of course, the organ should not be added—why would it need to be? But in other situations, such as in larger sanctuaries where a lone *voorzanger* could not possibly be heard, is the organ in such a situation not a holy option?[77]

The Next Generations

Schoock was not the only contemporary of Voetius who publicly endorsed organ use. Though some of Voetius's protégés carried forward Voetius's *anti-orgelist* theology, Voetius's bellicosity against the organ appears to have died with him. Voetius's own students and successors increasingly turned a deaf ear to his organ proscription as time moved on. For example, Simon Ooms (1630–1706) first studied at Leiden and then later at Utrecht under Voetius himself before authoring an expansive,

---

76. Schoock, *Exercitationes variae*, 527.
77. Schoock, *Exercitationes variae*, 528.

though unfinished, *Institutiones theologiæ practicæ*. Tellingly, he dedicates an entire chapter to the issue of worship, but never once does he challenge organ use. It would have been easy and obvious to do so since Ooms's own church was using an organ to accompany its psalm singing.[78] Though Ooms cites his mentor explicitly on several key points to emphasize the biblical mandate of psalm singing, he rhetorically ignores Voetius's *anti-orgelist* writing and focuses instead on the proper internal disposition of worshipers.[79] According to Ooms, this inward disposition also had to alter outward conduct throughout the entire worship service. He rebukes blithe worshipers who blaspheme God with all manner of improper conduct at worship—the chatterers (*klappaerts*[80]), the quarrelers (*kijvers*[81]), the flaunters (*pronckers en praelders*[82]), the idle dawdlers (*beuselaers*[83]), the readers (*lesers*[84]), and the sleepers (*slaepers*[85]). He emphasizes that worshipers need to pay attention to all aspects of worship, singing and sermon alike, with both body and soul. But especially during

---

78. The church in Purmerland and the Broederkerk of Kampen, Ooms's career parishes, both had pipe organs. In fact, the former parish became a Protestant church around 1573 and the church had a pre-existing organ dating to the sixteenth century that was enlarged so that it could accompany congregational singing.

79. Oomius, *Institutiones*, 544–74.

80. "The chatterers who, during the sermon or also during any other part of the public worship service, sit talking, making noise, and clapping, telling stories, often to the distraction of many others and of the preacher, and particularly of others whose attention is drawn away; acting like the church is a house of gossip where people go to hear some news just as the Athenians went to the place called the Areopagus. Acts 17:21." Oomius, *Institutiones*, 679.

81. "The arguers who dispute about a handbreadth of space, who slander, curse and swear, and wish each other every bad thing, as if it were not in God's house, but on the market square, on the streets, yes indeed in the House of Babel." Oomius, *Institutiones*, 680.

82. "The flaunters and show-offs who appear before God's face with impudent faces, glittery eyes, curled and powdered hair, having spent more time on this vain and cursed labor than they ever did in prayer or improvement of the soul. They come with pasted and plastered countenances, like speckled birds, as if they want to outshine heaven and all its stars." Oomius, *Institutiones*, 680.

83. "The vain triflers, whom I will not name, who smile, nod and nudge one another when this or that sin is condemned in order to show that they think the preacher has hit the nail on the head, or they have someone who is also present in mind, then they are happy with that and think that is on his account." Oomius, *Institutiones*, 680.

84. "The readers who sit reading one tract or another, or even a chapter when they do not like the sermon." Oomius, *Institutiones*, 682.

85. Oomius, *Institutiones*, 682.

the sermon, that central event where God speaks to his people through the words of the preacher, worshipers should hang on the mouth of the preacher like babies hang on the breasts of their mother.[86]

It is striking to any reader of Ooms's prolix pages, which address numerous issues of the liturgy in picayune detail, that organ use is not mentioned once, much less challenged. Undoubtedly, that is because organ music was, by 1672—one short generation after Voetius's 1641 essay—simply no longer a matter of confessional purity for the Reformed, certainly not in comparison with weightier doctrinal matters facing the church. Heirs of Voetius, for all intents and purposes, dropped the subject—the presence and use of the organ now having been irreversibly established in most Dutch churches—and instead (re)focused liturgical discussions upon the inner piety of worshipers, the outward comportment during worship, and the proper observance of the Sabbath day.[87] And nearly all Reformed congregations who held out against organ use capitulated fully and finally in 1773 when the state sponsored a new Dutch edition of the *Genevan Psalter*.[88] This psalter, which included new music written for four voices, surely invited and nearly demanded instrumental accompaniment. As a result, by the late eighteenth century, the pipe organ had become firmly incorporated into Reformed worship across the Netherlands, all former Calvinist fervor to the contrary notwithstanding.

Of course, even in this post-Voetius era, just as we have seen throughout the entire organ controversy, there were exceptions to an *orgelist* majority. Some towns and cities were still resistant to yield to organ use. For example, as late as 1781, in Jelsum on October 7, the eighty-year-old preacher Johannes Cornelius Wiersma (1702–1795) agreed to dedicate his church's new organ, but he would not climb into the pulpit to preach a dedicatory sermon lest such action be read as a Roman Catholic-type consecration of an instrument. Rather, he spoke from the church floor and instructed his flock with "humble dependence on the Lord" how this new wind instrument could be used in a God-glorifying manner to sing psalms to the Lord.[89]

---

86. Oomius, *Institutiones*, 687.

87. Likewise Wilhelmus à Brakel, arguably the most prolific and well-known Voetian, never broaches the subject of organ use in his *Logikē latreia, dat is, Redelyke Godtsdienst*.

88. *Statenberijming*.

89. Schotel, *Openbare*, 79–80.

The case of Johann Capito (?–1624) summarizes the story well. Johann Capito was known as a zealous yet pious Christian man. When Capito began his pastorate at the St. Martin's Church of Bremen, the church did not have an organ and Capito is on record as railing against organ use almost daily. He even went to the point of labeling the pipes of the organ as "devil's pipes."[90] However, unfortunately for Capito, his church building properly belonged not to him, his council, or even his congregation. Like almost every Reformed building of the era, the church building was owned by the city. It came to pass that, despite Capito's protestations, the city magistrates commissioned a beautiful new pipe organ to be installed in the building. After that decision, suddenly and inexplicably, Capito could not find enough praises for the new church equipment! What Capito labeled at one time as the "devil's pipes" he now referred to as "the music of angels," and a "foretaste of the joys of heaven." It seems that Capito, like Schoock who followed him, came to believe that God-fearing Calvinists could indeed sing worshipfully before the Lord even with the aid of wind-blown organ pipes.[91] Instrumental music is defended for its own nonverbal eloquence, a properly musical eloquence, which is able to offer something that complements verbal intelligibility: sonorous beauty, ritual solemnity, emotional appeal, and its own unique means of shaping a disparate crowd of people into a worshiping assembly. Such a revelation, in fact, made Schoock conclude, "Thus do the judgments of men often change as the times change,"[92] the motto of the Dutch organ controversy if ever there was one.

Indeed, time passed for Voetius. He died in 1676 and was placed in his grave in Utrecht's Catharijnekerk, buried amongst the nobles in the church floor.[93] Little could anyone know on the day of his burial that in but a hundred years' time the building would be reconsecrated as a Roman Catholic cathedral church, which later installed a pipe organ that has played every day since. May Gisbertus Voetius rest in peace.

90. Schoock, *Exercitationes variae*, 539.

91. Capito was not the first nor the last Reformed minister to change his stance on the organ question. But for one other example see Ægeidus Francken, *Heilig gebruick des orgels*.

92. Schoock, *Exercitationes variae*, 539.

93. Asselt, *Voetius*, 38.

POSTLUDE

A historical fallacy concerning the newly birthed Dutch Republic is the assumption that the Dutch Reformed Church was comparable with the Anglican in England and the Lutheran in various states of Germany and Scandinavia: Calvinism was irrevocably declared and placed over the subordinate populace by rule of law. Moreover, it is assumed that almost every Dutch citizen was a dyed-in-the-wool Calvinist and that adherents of other religions formed only a negligible and silent section of the populace. If this were true, the early synodical declaration that the organ was unfit for Reformed worship would have been held unquestioned and unilaterally enforced to this day; perhaps relaxed somewhat a few generations later when, in 1773, a new four-part canon of psalmody needed musical (read *instrumental*) assistance in order to succeed.

But here are the facts: the Dutch Reformed Church was not a state church—this would have been inconsistent with Reformed principles. Rather, it was a privileged church insofar as the tenure of public functions and professions was open only to its members. As a result, an indefinite number of people likely adhered to the Genevan Confession for reasons that could hardly be called religious, and several "Calvinists" supported organ use regardless of official decree. Further, it is clear that organ use continued in spite of said decrees; apart from the a few Lutherans and a larger number of Mennonites, two cultures that, as shown, continued to use the organ, the vast majority of the non-Calvinists were, or remained, Roman Catholic, a church that also used the organ in its liturgy.

Analysis of the differing liturgical practices amongst the Reformed of this era show that the incongruity between theory and practice lies in understanding the political structures under which the church lived. The political situation in the Netherlands proved more complicated for the Calvinists trying to assert their opinion over the use of the organ. The

Netherlands of this time was unique in Europe: politically, it was a new republic led by citizens rather than an absolute monarch; financially, it boasted a booming economy in which hard work, lively trade with other countries, and entrepreneurship counted more than a noble title; and theologically, it was a country where religious diversity was tolerated lest any one religious practice dominate, as Roman Catholicism had only a few generations earlier.

As to the Dutch Reformed Church, its extremely sober liturgy called for unison and unaccompanied psalm singing—ironically and paradoxically, most probably very similar in sound to the chant of the Roman church. But that the faithful could participate in the music of the church was one of the crown jewels of the Reformation. Reformed Christians now sang with gusto the psalms in their native language.

But this came with a musical price tag, especially among the Calvinists. They stripped the liturgy of all florid music, banned church choirs, and with them, the rich tradition of polyphonic church music. Organ music was also (initially) formally forbidden. But many instruments survived because they were property of the civil government; these magnificent instruments loomed large and silent over worshipers below. Not surprisingly, unaccompanied psalm singing in seventeenth-century worship services was not a treat for musical ears. The congregation sang melodies that they often only half knew. Even though psalters were published, with musical notation, the assumption was that all worshipers were musically and linguistically literate. They were not. Even when organ playing returned midway through the seventeenth century and the congregation was again accompanied by the organ, psalm singing still had its problems.

Thus, despite the best efforts by church order, ministers, concerned members, conventicles, and even later by the strict (*preciese*) Calvinists "furthering" the Reformation to proscribe organ use in worship, organ proscriptions could not hold. Civic magistrates zealously resisted attempts by church—even though they were armed with biblical arguments—to either require or prohibit the use of organs throughout the entire nation. Still further, even within their own circles, the Reformed were awash with a variety of opinions on the subject. We have seen the importance of these factors that caused this variation of practice amongst Reformed groups, which were otherwise solidly united in matters of faith and practice.

The Netherlands, during and after independence from Catholic Spain, illustrates on a very small geographic scale the widely divergent application of Calvin's teaching regarding Reformed liturgy, as well as the constraints put on Reformed church authorities by the political powers in the young republic. As was shown, the Dutch wanted to assure that the strict, autocratic rule of the Spanish would not be replaced by a strict, theocratic rule of Dutch Calvinists ministers who hoped to emulate John Calvin's government in Geneva. The acrimony between the two sides of the organ question in the Netherlands, as exemplified by the vicious exchanges between Calckman and Huygens, Voetius and his peers, increased the longer synods dithered and offered ambiguous statements on the matter. Although these ardent anti-Catholics had every intention of being faithful to Calvin's teachings regarding pure, biblical worship, the permissibility of pipe organs in Calvinist localities and regions varied widely: while organs were torn out and burned or sold as scrap in some staunchly Calvinist cities or countries, other synods, which were equally theologically orthodox in every other way, gave permission to use organs (albeit judiciously) during worship.

That is not to suggest that all Reformed Christians immediately and fully accepted the organ; some remained convinced that it was the devil himself or his minions blowing through those evil ranks of pipes, others heard it as angels singing through golden, metallic throats. Whatever it was or was not, in the end the pipe organ did indeed help the Reformed worshipful congregation sing their beloved psalms more angelically and reverently. And that result was something, perhaps the only thing, on which the Reformed and the magistracy could all finally give a resounding "Amen."

BIBLIOGRAPHY

Aa, van der Abraham Jacob, et. al. *Biographisch Woordenboek der Nederlanden.* 21 vols. Haarlem: J. J. van Brederode, 1852-1878.

Andreæ, Jakob, et al. *Colloquium Mompelgartense: Gespräch, in gegenwart des Durchleuchtigen Hochgebornen Fürsten vnd Herrn, Herrn Friderichen, Grauen zu Würtemberg vnd Mümpelgart.* Tübingen: Georg Gruppenbach, 1587.

Archief Nederlands Hervormde Gemeente te Amsterdame; Kerkenraad, 1578-1899 (inv. 376), "Protocollen van den bizonderen kerkenraad," band I-XXXVI (1578-1843).

Archief voor de geschiedenis van het Aartsbisdom Utrecht. Utrecht: Van Rossum. Vol. 1, 1874-75. Vol. 11, 1883. Vol. 20, 1893. Vol. 49, 1929.

Archief voor Kerkelijke en Wereldsche Geschiedenissen, inzonderheid in Utrecht. Edited by Johannes J. Dodt van Flensburg. Utrecht: N. van der Monde, 1843.

Asselt, Willem J. van. *Gisbertus Voetius (1589-1676).* Kampen: De Groot Goudriaan, 2007.

Asselt, Willem J. van, and Eef Dekker, eds. *Reformation and Scholasticism: An Ecumenical Enterprise.* Grand Rapids: Eerdmans, 2001.

Azpilcueta, Martino de [Navarrus]. *Manuale sive Enchiridion confessariorum et paenitentium.* Rome: Iacobi Torne, 1588.

Balfoort, Dirk J. *Het muziekleven in Nederland in de 17de en 18de eeuw.* Amsterdam: P. N. van Kampen & Zoon, 1938.

Basler Beiträge zur vaterländischen Geschichte. Basel: Schweighauser, 1888.

Batelier, Jacobus Johannes. *Examen accuratum disputationis primae & quasi inauguralis D. Gisberti Voetii, quam proposuit in illustri gymnasio ultrajecti die 3. Sept. stylo vet. Anno 1634.* Utrecht, 1634.

Beck, Andreas J. *Gisbertus Voetius (1589-1676): Sein Theologieverständnis und seine Gotteslehre.* Göttingen: Vandenhoeck & Ruprecht, 2007.

Beeke, Joel. *Gisbertus Voetius: Towards a Reformed Marriage of Knowledge and Piety.* Grand Rapids: Reformation Heritage, 2000.

Benedict, Philip. *Christ's Churches Purely Reformed: A Social History of Calvinism.* New Haven: Yale University Press, 2002.

Bergsma, Wiebe. *Tussen Gideonsbende en publieke kerk: Een studie over gereformeerd protestantisme in Friesland, 1580-1650.* Verloren/Fryske Akademy: Hilversum/Leeuwarden, 1999.

Berkvens-Stevelinck, Christiane, et al. *The Emergence of Tolerance in the Dutch Republic.* Leiden: H. J. Brill, 1997.

Bernet Kempers, Karel Philippus. "Meerstemming psalmgezang in de hervormde kerk van Nederland." *Tijdschrift voor muziekwetenschap* 17 (1950) 167–80.

Besluiten van het algemeen christelijk synode der Hervormde Kerk in het Koningrijk der Nederlanden, te 's Gravenhage den 11 den julij 1817. Rotterdam: Mensing & Van Westreenen, 1817.

Biesterveld, Petrus, and Herman Huber Kuijper. *Kerkelijk handboekje bevattende de bepalingen der Nederlandsche synoden en andere stukken van beteekenis voor de regeering der kerken.* Kampen: J. H. Bos, 1905.

Bijdragen en mededeelingen van de Vereeniging Gelre. Vol. 28. Arnhem: S. Gouda Quint, 1925.

Bijdragen en mededeelingen van het Historisch Genootschap te Utrecht. Vol. 69. Utrecht: Kemink en Zoon, 1880.

Bijtelaar, Barendina. *De orgels van de Oude Kerk in Amsterdam.* Leiden: Stichting Orgelcentrum, 1975.

Bittermann, Helen Robbins. "The Organ in the Early Middle Ages." *Speculum* 4 (1929) 390–410.

Bleyswijck, Dirck van. *Beschryvinge der stadt Delft; betreffende des selfs situatie, oorsprong en ouderdom, opkomst en voortgangh. . . . Voor-af met een korte beschrijvinge van Delflandt.* Delft: Arnold Bon, 1667.

Blok, Dirk Peter, et al. *Algemene geschiedenis der Nederlanden.* Haarlem: Fibula-Van Dishoeck, 1979.

Blom, Johannes Cornelis Hendrik, and Emiel Lamberts, eds. *Geschiedenis van de Nederlanden.* Amsterdam: Agon, 1994.

Blom, Simon. *Geschiedenis van Maassluis.* Maassluis: De Maassluise Boekhandel, 1972.

Blume, Friedrich. *Geschichte der evangelischen Kirchenmusik.* Translated by Ludwig Finscher. New York: Norton, 1974.

Het boek der psalmen, nevens de gezangen bij de Hervormde Kerk in gebruik, door last van de Hoog Mogende Heeren Staaten Generaal der Vereenigde Nederlanden, uit drie berijmingen, in den jaare 1773, gekooren, met de noodige daarin gemaakte veranderingen. Den Haag: Isaac Scheltus, 1773.

Boersma, Owe. "Vluchtig voorbeeld: De Nederlandse, Franse en Italiaanse vluchtelingenkerken in Londen, 1568–1585." ThD diss., Kampen Theologische Academie, 1994.

Boge, Birgit, and Ralf Georg Bogner, eds. *Oratio funebris. Die katholische Leichenpredigt der frühen Neuzeit. Zwölf Studien.* Amsterdam: Rodopi, 1999.

Bol, Hans. "Hendrik Joosten Speuy, een tijdgenoot van Sweelinck." *Het Orgel* 54 (1958) 97–8, 129–32.

Bollmann, Anne, and Koen Goudriaan. *Vernieuwde innigheid: over de Moderne Devotie, Geert Grote en Deventer.* Nieuwegein: Arko, 2008.

Bolt, Klaas. "The Character and Function of the Dutch Organ in the Seventeenth and Eighteenth Centuries." Translated by Adrianus de Groot. Easthampton, MA: Westfield Center for Keyboard Studies, 1986.

Boogman, Johan Christiaan. "The Union of Utrecht, its Genesis and Consequences." *Bijdragen en mededelingen betreffende de geschiedenis der Nederlanden* 94 (1979) 377–407.

Boom, Hendrick ten. *De Reformatie in Rotterdam 1530–1588.* The Hague: Hollandse Historische Reeks, 1987.

Boom, Hendrik ten, et al. *Utrechters entre-deux: Stad en sticht in de eeuw van de reformatie, 1520–1620*. Delft: Eburon, 1992.

Booma, Jan Gerard Jakob van. "Acta van de Overijsselse synode van 1581." *Nederlands archief voor kerkgeschiedenis* 62 (1982) 166–179.

Booma, Jan Gerard Jakob van, and Jacobus Leonardus van der Gouw, eds. *Communio et mater Fidelium: Acta des Konsistoriums der niederländischen reformierten Flüchtlingsgemeinde in Wesel, 1573–1582*. Evangelische Kirchengemeinde Wesel Konsistorium. Köln: Rheinland-Verlag, 1991; Delft: Eburon, 1991.

Borren, Charles van den. *Les origines de la musique de clavier dans les Pays-Bas (nord et sud) jusque vers 1630*. Bruxelles, NY: Breitkopf et Haertel, 1914.

Bosma, Jelle. *Woorden van een gezond verstand. De invloed van de Verlichting op de in het Nederlands uitgegeven preken van 1750 tot 1800*. Nieuwkoop: De Graaf, 1997.

Bothof, Arnoldus, and C. Bothof. *Het leven in de zestiende tot twintigste eeuw op het platteland in westelijk Nederland*. Oegstgeest, 2003.

Bouwsteenen. Eerste jaarboek der vereeniging voor Nederlandsche muziekgeschiedenis 1869–1872. Amsterdam: Stoomdrukkerij Loman, Kirberger & van Kesteren.

Bouwsteenen. Derde jaarboek der vereeniging voor Nederlandsche muziekgeschiedenis 1874–1881. Amsterdam: Stoomdrukkerij Loman, Kirberger & van Kesteren.

Bovet, Félix. *Histoire du Psautier des Églises Réformées*. Paris: Neuchâtel, 1872.

Boyd, Andrew Kennedy Hutchison. *Lessons of Middle Age with Some Account of Various Cities and Men*. London: Longmans, 1868.

Brady, Thomas A. *Turning Swiss: Cities and Empire, 1450–1550*. Cambridge: Cambridge University Press, 1985.

Brandt, Geeraerdt. *Historie der reformatie en andre kerkelyke geschiedenissen in en ontrent de Nederlanden*. Amsterdam: J. Rieuwertsz. & H. en D. Boom, 1671–1704.

———. *In and About the Low Countries*. London: T. [& J.] Childe [& J. Nicks], 1720–23.

Bremmer, Rolf Hendrik. *Uit de geboortegeschiedenis van de Gereformeerde Kerken in Nederland*. 's-Gravenhage: Willem de Zwijgerstichting, 1977.

Brienen, Teunis, et al. *De Nadere Reformatie. Beschrijving van haar voornaamste vertegenwoordigers*. 's-Gravenhage: Uitgeverij Boekencentrum, 1986.

Broeyer, F. G. M. "Franciscus Burman, een collega met verdachte denkbeelden." In *Vier eeuwen theologie in Utrecht. Bijdragen tot de geschiedenis van de theologische faculteit aan de Universiteit Utrecht*, edited by A. de Groot and O. J. de Jong, 109–19. Zoetermeer: Meinema, 2001.

Brower, William Leverich, et al. *Collegiate Reformed Protestant Dutch Church of the City of New York, Her Organization and Development*. New York: Collegiate Reformed Dutch Church, 1928.

Brucherus, Heino Hermannus. *Geschiedenis van de opkomst der kerkhervorming in de provincie Groningen tot aan het jaar 1594: gevolgd door de geschiedenis van de vestiging der kerkhervorming in dezelfde provincie, tot aan de Nationale Synode van Dordrecht in 1618 en 1619; uit echte stukken zamengesteld*. Groningen: J. Oomkens, 1821.

Bruggeman, Marijke, et al. *Mensen van de Nieuwe Tijd. Een liber amicorum voor A. Th. van Deursen*. Amsterdam: Bakker, 1996.

Bruinsma, Henry A. "The Organ Controversy in the Netherlands Reformation to 1640." *Journal of the American Musicological Society* 7 (1954) 205–212.

Bucer, Martin. *Martin Bucers Deutsche Schriften*. Edited by Robert von Stupperich. Gütersloh: Mohn, 1960.

Bucsay, Mihány. *Geschichte des Protestantismus in Ungarn*. Stuttgart: Evangelisches Verlagswerk, 1959.
Bulletin van de Koninklijke Nederlandse Oudheidkundige Bond. Leiden: 1912.
Burgon, John William. *The Life and Times of Sir Thomas Gresham*. London: Robert Jennings, 1839.
Caecilia. Algemeen muzikaal tijdschrift van Nederland. Utrecht, Rotterdam: The Hague, 1844–1880.
Calckman, Jan Jansz. *Antidotum, tegen-gift vant gebruyck of on-gebruyck vant orgel inde kercken der Vereenighde Nederlanden*. 's-Gravenhage: Aert van Meurs, 1641.
———. *Christelijcke danckpredicatie wt den 126. psalm. Over de wonderbaerlijcke ghenadige verlossinge der stadt, ende kercke tot Wezel, gheschiet, den 9. augusti, anno 1629. Ghehouden door Johannem Placium, bediender des Woorts Godts tot Emden, den 16 augusti, anno 1629. Overghezet uyt het Hoochduyts door Jan Jansz. Calckman*. Leiden: D. J. van Ilpendam, 1629.
———. *Droevighe clachten der bedruckte gemeynte Iesu Christi, in dese tijden der vervolginge door gheheel christenheydt ende troostelijcke antwoorden hares verlossers Christi Iesu, tot versterckinge van de verslagene ende zwacke gemoederen in sodanige besoeckinge. Alles uyt de Woorden Godes eenvoudelijck te samengestelt door een liefhebber der waerheyt Ian Iansen Calckman*. 's-Gravenhage: Aert van Meurs, 1642.
Calderwood, David. *The pastor and the prelate, or, Reformation and conformity shortly compared by the word of God, by antiquity and the proceedings of the ancient church . . . with the answer of the common and chiefest objections against every part: shewing whether of the two is to be followed by the true Christian and countryman*. Edinburgh: Alexander Henderson, 16922.
Calkoen, Jan Frederick van Beeck. *Onderzoek naar den rechtstoestand der geestelijke en kerkelijke goederen in Holland na de reformatie*. Amsterdam: J. H. de Bussy, 1910.
Callegari, J. "Okólnik o muzyce kościelnej." *Muzyka Kościelna* 9 (1886).
Calvin, John. *Institutes of the Christian Religion*. Edited by John T. McNeill. Philadelphia: Westminster, 1960.
The Canons and Decrees of the Sacred and Oecumenical Council of Trent, Celebrated Under the Sovereign Pontiffs, Paul III, Julius III and Pius IV. Edited by James Waterworth. London: Burns and Oates, 1848.
Cardaux, Jean-Daniël. "Le psautier huguenot chez les imprimeurs néerlandais: Concurrence ou spécialisation?" In *Le magasin de l'univers*, edited by C. Berkvens-Stevelinck et al., 71-83. Leiden: Brill, 1992.
Classicale Acta 1573–1620 I: Particuliere Synode Zuid-Holland, Classis Dordrecht 1573–1600. Edited by J. P. van Dooren. The Hague: Instituut voor Nederlandse Geschiedenis, 1980.
Classicale Acta 1573–1620 II: Particuliere Synode Zuid-Holland, Classis Dordrecht 1601–1620, Classis Breda 1616–1620. Edited by J. Roelevink. The Hague: Instituut voor Nederlandse Geschiedenis, 1991.
Classicale Acta 1573–1620 III: Particuliere Synode Zuid-Holland, Classis Rotterdam en Schieland 1580–1620. Edited by J. Bouterse. The Hague: Instituut voor Nederlandse Geschiedenis, 1991.
Classicale Acta 1573–1620 IV: Provinciale Synode Zeeland, Classis Walcheren 1602–1620, Classis Zuid-Beveland 1579–1591. Edited by J. Bouterse. The Hague: Instituut voor Nederlandse Geschiedenis, 1995.

Classicale Acta 1573-1620 V: Provinciale Synode Zuid-Holland, Classis Leiden 1585-1620, Classis Woerden 1617-1620. Edited by M. Kok and J. Roelevink. The Hague: Instituut voor Nederlandse Geschiedenis, 1996.

Classicale Acta 1573-1620 VI: Provinciale synode Overijssel, Classis Deventer 1601-1620, Classis Kampen 1596-1602 en 1618-1620, Classis Steenwijk/Vollenhove 1601-1620. Edited by J. van Gelderen and C. Ravensbergen. The Hague: Instituut voor Nederlandse Geschiedenis, 2000.

Classicale Acta 1573-1620 VII: Provinciale Synode Zuid-Holland. Classis Delft en Delfland 1572-1620. Edited by P. H. A. M. Abels and A. Ph. F. Wouters. The Hague: Instituut voor Nederlandse Geschiedenis, 2001.

Concilii Tridentini Acta. Edited by Stephanus Ehses. Friburgi Brisgoniae: B. Herder, 1904-1922.

Concilium Tridentinum: Diariorum. Edited by J. Massarelli. Freiburg im Breisgau: Herder, 1901-1924.

Confessio Ecclesiae Debreciensis de praecipuis articulis, et quaestionibus quibusdam, necessariis ad consulendum turbatis conscientiis, exhibita ut sit testimonium doctrinae et fidei contra calumniatores sanae doctrinae. Edited by Petrus Melius Juhász. Debreceni, 1562.

Conradt, Nancy. "John Calvin, Theodore Beza and the Reformation in Poland." PhD diss., University of Wisconsin, 1974.

Contzen, Adam. *Politicorum Libri Decem*. Moguntiae: Joannis Kimckii, 1629.

Cottret, Bernard. *Calvin: A Biography*. Grand Rapids: Eerdmans, 2000.

Courvoisier, Jaques. *Zwingli: A Reformed Theologian*. Richmond, VA: John Knox, 1963.

Cramer, Samuel. "Bijdragen tot de geschiedenis van ons kerklied en ons kerkgezang." *Doopsgezinde bijdragen* 40 (1900) 71-124.

Crew, Phyllis Mack. *Calvinistic Preaching and Iconoclasm in the Netherlands 1544-1569*. Cambridge: Cambridge University Press, 1973.

Cudsemius, Petrus. *De desperata Caluini causa: tractatus breuis, lectu non minùs vtilis, atque iucundus, in quo sectae Calvinisticae non tam picta effigies, quam viuum corpus, cuiuis spectandum ad oculum exhibetur; adornatus in gratiam euangelicorum protestantium*. Moguntiæ: Ex officina Ioannis Albini, 1609.

Culmer, Richard. *Cathedrall newes from Canterbury shewing, the Canterburian Cathedrall to bee in an abbey-like, corrupt, and rotten condition, which cals for a speedy reformation, or dissolution: vvhich dissolution is already foreshowne, and begun there, by many remarkeable passages upon that place, and the prelats there: amongst which passages of wonder is, the Archbishop of Canterburies passing-bell, rung miraculously in that cathedrall*. London: Rich. Cotes for Fulk Clifton, 1644.

Curtis, Alan. "Henderick Speuy and the Earliest Printed Dutch Keyboard Music." *Tijdschrift van de Vereniging voor Nederlandse Muziekgeschiedenis* 19 (1962-63) 143-62.

Dalen, Jan Leendert van. *De Groote Kerk (Onze Lieve Vrouwenkerk) te Dordrecht*. Dordrecht: Dordrechtse Drukkerij en Uitgevers Maatschap-pij, 1927.

Dankbaar, Willem Frederick. *Hoogtepunten uit het Nederlandsche calvinism in de zestiende eeuw*. Haarlem: Tjeenk Willink, 1946.

Das, Gerrit. "De strijd over het orgelgebruik in de protestantse kerken." *Stemmen des Tijds* (1925) 57-85.

Davies, Norman. *God's Playground: A History of Poland in Two Volumes*. Oxford: Clarendon, 1981.

Davies, Sarah. *Destroying the Devil's Bagpipe: Iconoclasm and the Fate of the Organ in Reformation Switzerland.* Budapest: Institute for Musicology of the Hungarian Academy of Sciences, 2000.

De Jong, Otto Jan. *De reformatie in Culemborg.* Assen: Hak & Prakke, 1957.

De Jong, Peter Y., ed. *Crisis in the Reformed Churches, Essays in Commemoration of the Great Synod of Dordt, 1618–1619.* Grand Rapids: Eerdmans, 1968.

Decavele, Johan. *De dageraad van de reformatie in Vlaanderen (1520–1565).* Brussel: Paleis der Academiën, 1975.

Dreier, Johannes. "Reformatorische Frömmigkeit. Die Kirchenordnung des Dr. Johannes Dreier aus dem Jahre 1532." Herford: Kirchenkries Herford, 1982.

Deursen, Arie Theodorus van. *Bavianen en slijkgeuzen: Kerk en kerkvolk ten tijde van Maurits en Oldenbarneveldt.* Assen: Van Gorcum, 1974, reprint Franeker: Van Wijnen, 1991.

———. *Een dorp in de polder: Graft in de zeventiende eeuw.* Amsterdam: Bakker, 2006.

———. "Kerk of parochie? De kerkmeesters en de dood ten tijde van de Republiek." *Tijdschrift voor geschiedenis* 89 (1976) 531–537.

———. *Het kopergeld van de Gouden Eeuw.* Assen: Van Gorcum, 1978–1980.

———. *Plain Lives in a Golden Age. Popular Culture, Religion and Society in Seventeenth-Century Holland.* Translated by Maarten Ultee. Cambridge: Cambridge University Press, 1991.

Deursen, Arie Theodorus van, E. K. Grootes, and P. E. L. Verkuyl, eds. *Veelzijdigheid als levensvorm: Facetten van Constantijn Huygens' leven en werk: Een bundel studies t.g.v. zijn driehonderste sterfdag.* Deventer: Sub Rosa, 1987.

Dis, Leendert Meeuwis van. *Reformatorische rederijkersspelen uit de eerste helft van de 16e eeuw.* Haarlem: Vijlbrief, 1937.

Dixhoorn, Adriaan Cornelis van. "Lustige geesten: rederijkers en hun kamers in het publieke leven van de Noordelijke Nederlanden in de vijftiende, zestiende en zeventiende eeuw." PhD diss., Vrije Universiteit Amsterdam, 2004.

Doel, Huibrecht G. van den. *Daar moet veel strijds gestreden zijn: Dirk Rafael Camphuysen en de contraremonstranten: Een biografie.* Meppel: Boom, 1967.

Dooren, Jan Pieter van. "Leichenpredigten in den Niederlanden. Eine umstrittene Sache (1550–1751)" In *Leichenpredigten als Quelle historischer Wissenschaften*, Bd. 2, edited by Rudolph Lenz, 397–410. Marburg: Schwarz Verlag, 1979.

———. "Der Weseler Konvent 1568: Neue Forschungserbebnisse." *Monatshefte für Evanglische Kirchengeschichte des Rheinlandes* 31 (1982) 41–55.

Doove, Jan A .F. "Prestanten en fusten. De 17de-eeuwse organisten–familie De Vois." *Mens and Melodie* 24 (1969) 342–43.

Dordrecht Consistorie Boeck, no. 9, June 17, 1621.

Dordrecht Kerkelijke Rekeningen 1595–1596, fol. 108.

Douen, Orentin. *Clément Marot et le Psautier huguenot, étude historique.* Paris: Imprimerie nationale, 1860–1879.

Douglas, William. *Vindiciæ Psalmodiæ ecclesiastico-divinæ. In quibus corruptelæ & errores circa hunc sacrum cultum dereguntur & refelluntur, ipseque cultus hic sacer clarè afferitur. Authore Gulielmo Dowglasio S.S. Theologiæ Professore in Academia Regia Aberdonensi.* Aberdoniæ: Excudebat Jacobus Brunus urbis & Academiæ typographus, 1657.

Duisberg, Jan van, and Willem van Haagt. *De CL psalmen Davids, in Nederduytsche, oude en nieuwe rymen: Begrypende d'oude, alle d'in gebruyk zijnde psalmen, eertijds gerijmt door Willem van Haagt, ende de nieuwe, alle de buyten gebruyk geblevene psalmen, onlangs van hare onbekende, op bekende kerk-zangwijsen gestelt en gerijmt, door J. v. Duisburg. Aldus geheel op bekende zang-wijsen, beneffens alle de gewoone geestelijke liederen, ten dienste van de christelijke gemeynte van d'onveranderde Augsburgsche geloofs-belijdenis in't licht gegeven, en met eenige nieuw-geapprobeerde liederen vermeerdert.* Amsterdam, 1688.

Duisberg, Jan van. *LXXXV nieu-gerijmde psalmen des propheten Davids: Alle welcke psalmen, in haere oude rijmen, in de meeste Nederlantsche kerken van d'Augsburgsche belijdenis, om d'onkunde der sang-wijsen, niet gewoonelijck werden gesongen, ende derhalven nu van nieus op bekende en gevoeghelijcke sang-wijsen gestelt en gerijmt zijn.* Amsterdam, 1680.

Duke, Alastair, ed., with Rosemary Jones. "Toward a Reformed Polity in Holland, 1572-78." In *Reformation and Revolt*, edited by Alastair C. Duke, 199–226. London: Hambledon, 1990.

Duke, Alastair C. *Reformation and Revolt in the Low Countries*. London: Hambledon, 1990.

Duker, Arnoldus Cornelius. *Gisbertus Voetius*. Leiden: E. J. Brill, 1910.

Dunthorne, Hugh. "Dramatizing the Dutch Revolt. Romantic History and its Sixteenth-Century Antecedents." In *Public Opinion and Changing Identities in the Early Modern Netherlands: Essays in Honour of Alastair Duke*, edited by Judith Pollmann and Andrew Spicer, 11–32. Leiden: E. J. Brill, 2007.

Eckhardi, M. Heinrich. *Fasciculus controversiarum theologicarum quæstiones centum et triginta, de quibus inter Augustanæ Confessionis Theologos & Calvinianæ doctrinæ sectatores disputatio est, continens: et non tantum veræ sententiæ apodicticam confirmationem, sed prætereà contrariorum etiam argumentorum serè omnium, quæ in adversariorum libris occurrunt, & difficultatis aliquid habere videntur.* Lipsiæ: Grosius, 1607.

Eijnatten, Joris van. *God, Nederland en Oranje Dutch Calvanism and the Search for the Social Centre*. Kampen: Kok, 1993.

Eijnatten, Joris van, and Fred van Lieburg. *Nederlandse religiegeschiedenis*. Hilversum: Verloren, 2005.

Eire, Carlos M. N. *War Against the Idols: The Reformation of Worship from Erasmus to Calvin*. Cambridge: Cambridge University Press, 1986.

Eitner, Robert, and Hermann Wilhelm Springer. *Biographisch-bibliographisches quellenlexikon der musiker und musikgelehrten der christlichen zeitrechnung bis zur mitte des neunzehnten jahrhunderts*. Leipzig: Breitkopf & Haertel, 1900–1904.

Elliott, John Paul. "Protestantization in the Netherlands, A Case Study: The Classis of Dordrecht, 1572–1640." PhD diss., Columbia University, 1990.

Engen, John H. van. *Sisters and Brothers of the Common Life: The Devotio Moderna and the World of the Later Middle Ages*. Philadelphia: University of Pennsylvania Press, 2008.

Engle, Randall Dean. "A Devil's Siren or an Angel's Throat? The Pipe Organ Controversy among the Calvinists." In *John Calvin, Myth and Reality: Images and Impact of Geneva's Reformer*, edited by Amy Nelson Burnett, 107–25. Eugene, OR: Cascade, 2011.

———. "De duyvelsche fluytenkast. De orgelcontroverse in de Nederlanden." *Tijdschrift voor Nederlandse Kerkgeschiedenis* 13 (2010) 150–57.

———. "Song of the Synod." *Calvin Theological Journal* 54:2 (2019) 383–97.

———. "Voetius Outscored." In *Semper Refromanda: John Calvin, Worship and Reformed Traditions*, edited by Barbara Pitkin, 143–62. Göttingen: Vandenhoeck & Ruprecht, 2018.

Erasmus, Desiderius. *Erasmus' Annotations on the New Testament: Acts, Romans, I and II Corinthians: facsimile of the final Latin text with all earlier variants*. Edited and translated by Anne Reeve and M. A. Screech. Leiden: Brill, 1990.

Eubulus, Christophilus (Koelman, Jacobus). *De pointen van nodige reformatie, omtrent de kerk, en kerkelijke, en belijders der gereformeerde kerke van Nederlandt*. Vlissingen: Abraham van Laaren, 1678.

Evangelische liederen, uit het Hoogduits vertaalt. Amsterdam: J. ter Beek, 1738.

Evelyn, John. *The Diary of John Evelyn*, edited by Esmond de Beer. Oxford: Oxford University Press, 1955.

Evenhuis, Rudolf Barteld. *Ook dat was Amsterdam: De kerk der hervorming in de Gouden Eeuw*. Amsterdam: Ten Have, 1967.

Exalto, John. *Gereformeerde heiligen: De religieuze exempeltraditie in vroegmodern Nederland*. Nijmegen: Vantilt, 2005.

Faukeel, Hermannus. *Bruylofts-liet, ter eeren Jesu Christi gesonghen; inden 45. psalm, onder 't voorbeelt vanden coninck Juda, ende zijne bruyt: affbeeldende Christi gheestelijck houwelijck, met zijne heylighe kercke: Inhoudende de liefde, uyt welcke Christud zijne h. bruyt hem vertrouwt, ende de bruyt van hare schuldighe plicht t'hemwaerts, wort gheleert ende onderwesen*. Middelburgh: Symon Moulert, 1628.

Fekete, Csaba. "A debreceni Oratorium elsö orgonája [1830]." *Magyar Egyházzene* 3 (1995/1996) 462–66.

———. "Debrecen és az orgona [1838]." *Magyar Egyházzene* 6 (1998/1999) 355–74, 441–557.

Finney, Paul Corby, ed. *Seeing Beyond the Word: Visual Arts and the Calvinist Tradition*. Grand Rapids: Eerdmans, 1999.

Florijn, Henk, et al. *Het eigene van de Nederlandse Nadere Reformatie*. Houten: Den Hertog, 1992.

Fock, Gustav. *Hamburg's Role in Northern European Organ Building*. Edited and translated by Harald Vogel et al. Easthampton, MA: Westfield, 1997.

Forrester, Duncan, and Douglas Murray. *Studies in the History of Worship in Scotland*. Edinburgh: T. & T. Clark, 1984.

Francken, Ægidius. *Het Heilig gebruik des orgels, vertoont in een leer-reden over Psalm CL. vers III–VI. Gedaan op de inwyding van't Maassluische orgel. Met een toegift van een leer-reden over het verborgen manna en de witte keursteen*. Delft: Pieter van der Kloot, 1734.

Frenay, Joseph David. "Aanteekeningen betreffende de Leydsche pastoors sedert 'de Hervorming' tot aan 'de Herstelling' van 1557 tot 1857." National Library of the Netherlands (original from Universiteitsbibliotheek Utrecht), 1873.

Friccium, Christophorum M. *Music-buchlein, oder Nutzlicher bericht von dem uhrsprunge / gebrauche vnd erhaltung christlicher music vnd also von dem lobe Gottes / welches die Christẽ . . . verrichten sollen . . . Mit vorher gesetztem summarischem inhalt / vnd zu ende hinzu-gethanem register*. Luneburg: J. & H. Sternen, 1631.

Friesen, Stanley R. *Erasmus: Paradigm of Renaissance humanism. His influence on the arts and sciences in the intellectual revolution*. Padova: Piccin, 2001.

Frijhoff, Willem. "Religious toleration in the United Provinces: from 'case' to 'model.'" In *Calvinism and Religious Toleration in the Dutch Golden Age*, edited by R. Po-Chia Hsia and Henk van Nierop, 27–52. Cambridge: Cambridge University Press, 2002.

———. "Votive Boats or Secular Models? An Approach to the Question of the Figurative ships in the Dutch Protestant Churches." In *Embodied Belief: Ten Essays on Religious Culture in Dutch History*, edited by Joris van Eijnatten and Fred van Lieburg, 215–34. Hilversum: Uitgeverij Verloren, 2002.

Garside, Charles, Jr. *The Origins of Calvin's Theology of Music, 1536–1543*. Philadelphia: American Philosophical Society, 1979.

———. *Zwingli and the Arts*. New Haven: Yale University Press, 1966.

Gelder, Herman Arend Enno van. *Getemperde vrijheid. Een verhandeling over de verhouding van kerk en staat in de Republiek der Verenigde Nederlanden en de vrijheid van meningsuiting in zake godsdienst, drukpers en onderwijs, gedurende de 17e eeuw*. Groningen: Wolters-Noordhoff, 1972.

———. "Nederland geprotestantiseerd?" *Tijdschrift voor geschiedenis* 81 (1968) 445–64.

Gerbert, Martin. *De cantu et musica sacra a prima ecclesiae aetate usque ad praesens tempus*. [St. Blasien]: Typis San-Blasianis, 1774.

Gerding, Michiel Alexander Wilhelm, et al. *In alle onwetenschap, bijsterije unde wildicheyt: De reformatie in Drenthe in de zestiende en zeventiende eeuw*. Delft: Eburon, 1998.

Geyl, Pieter. *Noord en Zuid. Eenheid en tweeheid in de Lage Landen*. Utrecht/Antwerpen: Spectrum, 1960.

Gier, K. De. *De Dordtse kerkorde*. Houten: Den Hertog, 1989.

Girardeau, John. *Instrumental Music in the Public Worship of the Church*. Richmond: Whittet & Shepperson, 1888.

Goeman, Jaspar. "Das Emder Enchiridion aus dem Jahre 1630 in niedersächischer Sprache (Gesang und Orgelspiel im Reformationsjahrhundert)." In *Jahrbuch der Gesellschaft für bildende Kunst und vaterländische Altertümer zu Emden* 17 (1910) 73–196.

Goeters, Johann Friedrich Gerhard. *Die Akten der Synode der Niederländischen Kirchen zu Emden vom 4.–13. Oktober 1571. Im lateinischen Grundtext mitsamt den alten niederländischen, französischen und deutschen Übersetzungen. Beitrage zur Geschichte und Lehre der Reformierten Kirche*. Neukirchen: Neukirchener Verlag, 1971.

Goeters, Wilhelm. *Die Vorbereitung des Pietismus in der reformierten Kirche der Niederlande bis zur labadistischen Krisis 1670*. Utrecht: Oosthoek, 1911; Amsterdam: Bolland, 1974.

Gołos, Jerzy. *The Polish Organ: The Instrument and its History*. Translated by Barbara Dejlidko. Warsaw: Sutkowski, 1972.

Goovaerts, Alphonse Jean Marie André. *Histoire et bibliographie de la typographie musicale dans les Pays-Bas*. Antwerp: P. Kockx, 1880.

Gordon, Bruce, ed. *God's Armed Prophet, Zwingli*. New Haven: Yale University Press, 2021.

———. *Protestant History and Identity in Sixteenth-Century Europe*. Aldershot: Scolar, 1996.

Gordon, James. *History of Scots Affairs*. Aberdeen: Spalding Club, 1841.

Graafland, Cornelis, et al. "Nadere Reformatie: opnieuw een poging tot begripsbepaling." In *Documentatieblad Nadere Reformatie*, 105-84. Stichting Studie der Nadere Reformatie, 1995.

Groenveld, Simon. "'Speelstryt,' Constantijn Huygens en het orgelgebruik in zijn tijd (1640/41)." *Tijdschrift voor geschiedenis* 79 (1966) 260-78.

Groenveld, Simon, et al. *De kogel door de kerk? De Opstand in de Nederlanden en de rol van de Unie van Utrecht, 1559-1609*. Zutphen: Walburg, 1983.

Groot placaet-boeck, vervattende de placaten, ordonnantien ende edicten van de . . . Staten Generael der Vereenighde Nederlanden, ende van de . . . Staten van Hollandt en West-Vrieslandt, mitsgaders vande . . . Staten van Zeelandt. Edited by Cornelis Cau, et al. 's-Gravenhage: By de weduwe, ende erfgenamen van wylen Hillebrandt Iacobsz. van Wouw, 1658.

Haecht, Willem van, and Jan van Duisberg. *De CL psalmen Davids, in Nederduytsche zang-verssen, oude en nieuwe rymen: Begrypende d'oude, alle d'in gebruyk zijnde psalmen, eertijds gerijmt door Willem van Haagt, ende de nieuwe, alle de buyten gebruyk geblevene psalmen, onlangs van hare onbekende, op bekende kerk-zangwijsen gestelt en gerijmt, door J. v. Duisburg. Aldus geheel op bekende zangwijsen, beneffens alle de gewoone geestelijke liederen, ten dienste van de christelijke gemeynte van d'onveranderde Augsburgsche geloofs-belijdenis in't licht gegeven, en met eenige nieuw-geapprobeerde liederen vermeerdert*. Amsterdam: Bruyn, 1688.

Hageman, Martinus Johannes Maria. *Het kwade exempel van Gelre: De stad Nijmegen, de beeldenstorm en de raad van beroerten, 1566-1568*. Nijmegen: Vantilt, 2005.

Hales, John. *Golden remains of the ever memorable Mr. John Hales . . . with additions from the authours own copy, viz., sermons & miscellanies, also letters and expresses concerning the Synod of Dort (not before printed), from an authentick hand*. London: Tho. Newcomb for Robert Pawlet, 1673.

Hard, David Cameron. *The Origin and Development of John Frith's Doctrinal Adiaphora*. PhD diss., Westminster Theological Seminary, 1997.

Harst, Hans van der. *Het grote orgel in de kathedrale basiliek van St. Jan te 's-Hertogenbosch 1617-1980*. Hertogenbosch: Kerkbestuur Parochie Binnenstad, 1984.

Hartknoch, Christoph. *Preussische Kirchen-historia / darinnen von Einführung der christlichen Religion in diese Lande / wie auch von der Conservation, Fortpflantgung / Reformation und dem heutigen Zustande derselben Ausführlich gehandelt wird. Nebst vielen denckwürdigen Begebenheiten . . . aus vielen gedruckten und geschriebenen Documenten*. Franckfurt am Mayn und Leipzig: S. Beckenstein, 1686.

Hascher-Burger, Ulrike. *Singen Fur Die Seligkeit: Studien Zu Einer Liedersammlung Der Devotio Moderna: Zwolle, Historisch Centrum, Overijssel, Coll. Emmanuelshuizen, Cat. VI. Mit Edition Und Faksimile*. Leiden: Brill, 2007.

Hasper, Hendrik. *Calvijns beginsel voor den zang in den eredienst*. 's-Gravenhage: Nijhoff, 1955.

Hasselt, Gerard van. *Arnhemsche oudheden*. Arnhem: J. H. Moeleman, Jr., 1804.

———. *Kronijk van Arnhem (1310-1789)*. Arnhem: W. Troost en Zoon, 1790.

Hauer, Hendrik Adrianus. *Het afgescheurde kleed: Bijdrage tot de geschiedenis van de hervormde kerk te Oldenzaal en de reformatie in Twente*. Oldenzaal: De Bruyn, 1987.

Hayburn, Robert. F. *Papal Legislation in Sacred Music 95 A. D. to 1977*. Collegeville, MN: Liturgical, 1979.

Heimenbergius, Johannes. *Disputationis theologicæ expolitia ecclesiasticâ de organis & cantu organico in sacris* [sub praesidio Gisberti Voetii]. Ultrajecti: Aegidii Roman, 1641.
Heppe, Heinrich. *Geschichte des Pietismus und der Mystik in der reformirten Kirche: namentlich der Niederlande.* Leiden, 1879; Goudriaan, 19792.
Heringa, Jodocus (Eliza's Z). *Kerkelijke raadvrager en raadgever.* Utrecht: J. G. van Terveen en J. de Kruijff, 1826.
Herl, Joseph. *Worship Wars in Early Lutheranism.* Oxford: Oxford University Press, 2004.
Hertog, Jaap B. den. *De Haagse orgelstrijd: Enkele facetten van het kerkelijk leven rond 1641, naar aanleiding van het "Gebruyck of ongebruyck van 't orgel" van Constantijn Huygens en reacties daarop.* Master's thesis, University of Leiden, 1995.
Hervormde Gemeente te Deventer (1058, Collectie Overijssle). Deventer.
Hess, Joachim. *Dispositien der merkwaardigste Kerk-Orgelen, welken in de zeven Verëenigde Provincien als mede in Duytsland en Elders aangetroffen worden.* Gouda: Vander Klos, 1774.
———. *Korte schets van de allereerste uitvinding en verdere voortgang in het vervaardigen der orgelen, tot op dezen tijd: zijnde een aanhangsel op Den luister van het orgel.* Gouda: Wouter Verblaauw, 1810.
Hess, Joachim, and Jan Willem Enschedé. *Dispositiën van Kerk-Orgelen welke in Nederland worden aangetroffen. Vervolg naar het handschrift van omstreeks 1815 door J. W. Enschedé.* Amsterdam: F. Muller, 1907.
Hibben, Chris. *Gouda in Revolt: Particularism and Pacifism in the Revolt of the Netherlands, 1572–1588.* Utrecht: John Benjamins, 1983.
Higman, Francis. *La diffusion de la Réforme en France.* Geneva: Labor et Fides, 1992.
Hof, Willem Jan Op 't. *Het gereformeerd piëtisme.* Houten: Den Hertog, 2005.
Hofman, Hendrick Arie. *Constantijn Huygens (1596–1687): een christelijk-humanistisch bourgeois gentilhomme in dienst van het Oranjehuis.* Utrecht: HES Uitgevers, 1983.
Hofman, Teunis M. *Eenich achterdencken: Spanning tussen kerk en staat in het gewest Holland tussen 1570 en 1620.* Heerenveen: Groen en Zoon, 1997.
Hondius, Jacobus. *Swart register van duysent sonden: als een staeltje, dienende tot ontdeckinge, ende opweckinge, van den vervallen yver en godtvruchtigheydt der hedendaeghsche genaemde ledematen in de gereformeerde christelijcke gemeynten van Nederlandt.* Amsterdam: Gerardus Borstius, 1679.
Hooft, Pieter Corneliszoon. *Brieven: Nieuwe, vermeerderde... Uitgave III.* Leiden: Brill, 1857.
Hooft, Pieter Corneliszoon, and Hendrik Willem van Tricht. *De briefwisseling van Pieter Corneliszoon Hooft.* Culemborg: Tjeenk Willink/Noorduijn, 1976.
Hooijer, Cornelius, ed. *Oude kerkordeningen der Nederlandsche Hervormde Gemeenten (1563–1638), en het concept-reglement, op de organisatie van het hervormd kerkgenootschap in het koningrijk Holland (1809).* Zalt-Bommel: Joh. Noman, 1865.
Hoop Scheffer, Jacob Gijsbert de. "Korte geschiedenis van het kerkgezang onder de Doopsgezinden hier te lande; met naamlijsten van de dichters der onderscheidene bundels, thans nog bij hen in gebruik." *Doopsgezinde bijdragen* 5 (1865) 67–94.
Hospinianus, Rodolphus (= Rudolf Wirth). *De templis: hoc est, de origine, progressv, vsv et abvsv templorvm, ac omnino rerum omnium ad templa pertinentium libri V.* Tigvri: in officina Vvolfiana, 1603.

Huet, Damnes Pierre Marie P. *Over den gezangen-strijd in de Hervormde Kerk.* Helder: J. C. de Buisonjé, 1872.

Huizinga, Johan. *The Waning of the Middle Ages; A Study of the Forms of Life, Thought, and Art in France and the Netherlands in the Xivth and Xvth Centuries.* Garden City, NY: Doubleday & Co, 1954.

Huygens, Constantijn. *Constantijn Huygens, Gebruyck of ongebruyck van 't orgel in de kercken der Vereenighde Nederlanden 1641.* Edited by Frederic L. Zwaan. Amsterdam & London: Noord-Hollandsche uitgevers maatschappij, 1974.

———. *Constantini Hugenii De vita propria, sermonum inter liberos libri duo.* Harlemi: a. Loosjes, 1817.

———. *Gebruyck of ongebruyck van 't orgel in de kercken der Vereenighde Nederlanden.* Leiden: Bonaventuer ende Abraham Elsevier, 1641; Amsterdam: Arent Gerritsz. Vanden Heuvel, 1659.

———. *De gedichten van Constantijn Huygens, naar zijn handschrift uitg.* Edited by Jacob Adolf Worp. Groningen: J. B. Wolters, 1892–1899.

———. *De jeugd van Constantijn Huygens, door hemzelf beschreven.* Edited by C. L. Heesakkers. Rotterdam: A. Donker, 1946.

———. *Musique et musiciens au XVIIe siècle. Correspondance et oeuvre musicales de Constantin Huygens.* Edited by Willem Josef Andries Jonckbloet and J. P. N. Land. Leyden: E. J. Brill, 1884.

———. *Pathodia sacra et profana: unae voci basso continuo comitante.* Edited by Frits Noske and Noelle Barker. Amsterdam: North-Holland, 1957.

———. *Responsa Prudentum, ad Autorem Dissertationis de Organo in Ecllesiis Confeod. Belgii.* Leiden: Lugd[uni] Batavor, ex officina Elseviriorum, 1641.

———. *Use and Non-Use of the Organ in the Churches of the United Netherlands.* Translated by Erika E. Smit-van Rotte. New York: Institute of Mediaeval Music, 1964.

Huygens, Constantijn, and Caspar Streso. *De briefwisseling van Constantijn Huygens, 1608–1697.* Edited by Jacob Adolf Worp. Rijks geschiedkundige publicatiën. 's-Gravenhage: M. Nijhoff, 1911–1917.

Inglis, Jim. *The Organ in Scotland Before 1700.* Schagen: De Mixtuur, 1991.

Ioannis Calvini Opera Quae Supersunt Omnia. Edited by Guilielmus Baum et al. Brunswick: Braunschweig, 1863–1900.

Irwin, Joyce L. "Music and the Doctrine of Adiaphora in Orthodox Lutheran Theology." *Sixteenth Century Journal* 14 (1983) 157–72.

———. "Preaching About Pipes and Praise: Lutheran Organ Sermons of the Seventeenth Century." *Yale Journal of Music and Religion* 1 (2015) 21–34.

Israel, Jonathan I. *The Dutch Republic: Its Rise, Greatness, and Fall: 1477–1806.* Oxford: Oxford University Press, 1995.

Itterzon, Gerrit Pieter van. *Franciscus Gomarus: met een portret.* 's–Gravenhage: Nijhoff, 1929.

Iperen, Joshua van. *Kerkelijke historie van het psalmt-gezang der christenen, van de dagen der apostelen af, tot op onzen tegenwoordigen tyd toe; en inzonderheid van onze verbeterde Nederduitsche psalmberyminge.* Amsterdam: Loveringh en Allart, 1778.

Jaanus, Hendrik Johan. *Hervormd Delft ten tijde Arent Cornelisz. (1573–1605).* Amsterdam: Nordemann, 1950.

Jacobsz, Wouter. *Dagboek van broeder Wouter Jacobsz (Gualtherus Jacobi Masius) prior van Stein. Amsterdam 1572-1578 en Montfoort 1578-1579*. Groningen: I. H. van Eeghen, 1960.
Jakob, Friedrich. *Der Orgelbau im Kanton Zürich: Von seinen Anfängen bis zur Mitte des 19. Jahrhunderts*. Bern: Paul Haupt, 1969-71.
Janssen, Hendrick Quirinus. *De kerkhervorming in Vlaanderen*. Arnhem: Swaan, 1868.
Janssonius, Roelof Bennink. *Geschiedenis van het kerkgezang by de hervormden in Nederland*. Amsterdam: K. H. Schadd, 1863.
Jelsma, Auke Jan, and Owe Boersma. *Acta van het consistorie van de Nederlandse gemeente te Londen, 1569-1585*. 's-Gravenhage: Instituut voor Nederlandse Geschiedenis, 1993.
Jenny, Markus. "Der Genfer Psalter." *Musik und Altar* 18 (1966) 157-167.
Jerome, *Epistola ad Dardanum*. Patrologiae Cursus Completus: Series Latina. Edited by Jacques-Paul Migne. Paris: Migne, 1845-1902.
Jong, Otto J. de. "De Utrechtse Hymni van 1615." In *Utrechters entre-deux: stad en sticht in de eeuw van de reformatie, 1520-1620: vierde verzameling bijdragen van de Vereniging voor Nederlandse Kerkgeschiedenis*, edited by H. ten Boom, 263-92. Delft: Eburon, 1992.
Jongepier, Jan. *Toegang tot het orgel*. Utrecht: De Banier, 1998.
Junior, Eugenius. *Church-Pageantry Display'd*. London: Baldwin, 1700.
Kaajan, Hendrik. *De Pro-Acta der Dordtsche Synode*. Rotterdam: T. de Vries, 1914.
Kalb, Friedrich. *Theology of Worship in 17th-Century Lutheranism*. Translated by Henry P. A. Hamann. Saint Louis: Concordia, 1965.
Kalkman, Wouter. "Constantijn Huygens en de Haagse orgelstrijd." *Archief voor kerkelijke, geschiedenis inzonderheid van Nederland* 31 (1981) 167-77.
Kalma, Jacob Jetzes. *Een kerk onder toezicht: Friese synodeverslagen 1621-1650*. Leeuwarden: Ljouwert, 1987.
———. *Mensen in en om de Grote Kerk. Beelden uit de Leeuwarder kerkgeschiedenis*. Leeuwarden: Friese Pers Boekerij, 1987.
Kaplan, Benjamin J. *Calvinists and Libertines: The Reformed in Utrecht, 1578-1618*. PhD diss., Harvard University, 1989.
———. *Calvinists and Libertines: Confession and Community in Utrecht, 1578-1620*. Oxford: Clarendon, 1995.
Karant-Nunn, Susan C. *The Reformation of Ritual: An Interpretation of Early Modern Germany*. London: Routledge, 1997.
Kaufmann, Walter. *Die Orgeln Ostfrieslands: Orgeltopographie*. Aurich: Verlag Ostfriesische Landschaft, 1968.
Kerkhistorisch archief. Edited by Nicolaas Christiaan Kist and W. Moll. Amsterdam: P. N. van Kampen, 1857-1866.
Kersten, Gerrit Hendrik. *Kerkelijk handboekje*. Rotterdam: N. V. de Banier, 1937.
Die Kirchenratsprotokolle der Reformierten Gemeinde Emden, 1557-1620. Edited by Heinz Schilling and Klaus-Dieter Schreiber. Köln: Böhlau, 1989-1992.
Kindgon, Robert M. "The Genevan Revolution in Public Worship." *Princeton Seminary Bulletin* 20 (1999) 264-80.
———. *Register of the Consistory of Geneva in the Time of Calvin*. Grand Rapids: Eerdmans, 2000.
Kist, Florentius Cornelis. *De toestand van het protestantsche kerk-gezang in Nederland: benevens de middelen tot deszelfs verbetering*. Utrecht: L. E. Bosch en Zoon, 1840.

Kist, Nicolaas Christiaan. "Het kerkelijke orgel-gebruik bijzonder in Nederland: Een historisch onderzoek." *Archief voor kerkelijke geschiedenis, inzonderheid van Nederland* 10 (1840) 189–334.

Kleij, Wim D. van der, and Willem Hendrick Zwart. *Orgels en organisten in Kampen*. Kampen: IJsselacademie, 1995.

Kleijntjens, J. C. J. "Beeldenstorm in Groningen en in 'de Ommelanden.'" *Archief geschiedenis aartsbisdom Utrecht* 67 (1948) 171–216.

Klepperbein, Wilhelm August. *Die hundert und fünfzig Psalme und die Gesänge, welche bey dem öffentlichen Gottesdienst der mehrersten Gemeinen, die in den Vereinigten Niederlande[n] dem unveränderten Augsburgischen Glaubens-Bekentnis zugethan sind, auch in niederdeutsche Sprache gesungen werden*. Amsterdam: Hendrik Brandt, 1762.

Kler, Herman de, and Ton van Eck. *Zeven eeuwen orgels in Den Haag*. Alphen aan den Rijn: Repro-Holland, 1987.

Kluiver, Jan Hendrik, and Willem H. van Dort. *Historische orgels in Zeeland*. Sneek: Boeijenga, 1974–1976.

Knock, Nicolaas Arnoldi. *Dispositien der merkwaardigste kerk-orgelen, welken in provincie Friesland, Groningen en elders aangetroffen worden: kunnende dit werk verstrekken tot een vervolg van het werk van den Heer J. Hess*. Groningen: Petrus Doekema, 1788.

Knuttel, Willem Pieter Cornelis. *Acta der particuliere synoden van Zuid-Holland, 1621–1700*. 's-Gravenhage: M. Nijhoff, 1908.

———. *De toestand der Nederlandsche katholieken ten tijde der Republiek*. The Hague: Nijhoff, 1892.

Koch, Anton Carl Frederik. "The Reformation at Deventer in 1579–1580 Size and social Structure of the Catholic Section of the Population during the Religious Peace." In *Acta Historiae Neerlandicae/Studies on the History of the Netherlands VI*, 27–66. Dordrecht: Springer, 1973.

Koelman, Jacobus. *Sleutel ter opening van de donkerste kapittelen in de Openbaaringe gedaan aan Johannis op het eiland Patmos waar in kort doch duidelyk worden voorgesteld alle de voornaamste kerk- en waereldlyke veranderingen alles opgemaakt uit naarstige overdenking en onderzoek . . ., waar by te gelyk de schriften van Jurieu, van Wezel en Swart des aangaande, ter toets gebragt en wederleid worden door Jacobus Koelman*. Amsterdam: P. J. Entrop, 1688.

Kok, Johannes Antonius de. *Nederland op de breuklijn Rome-Reformatie*. Assen: van Gorcum, 1964.

Komter-Kuipers, Aafke. *Muzyk yn Fryslân oant 1800*. Boalsert: A. J. Osinga, 1935.

Kooi, Christine. *Liberty and Religion: Church and State in Leiden's Reformation, 1572–1620*. Leiden: H. J. Brill, 2000.

———. *Nieuw en ongezien: Kerk en samenleving in de classis Delft en Delfland 1572–1621*. Delft: Eburen, 1994.

———. "The Reformed Community of Leiden, 1572–1620." PhD diss., Yale University, 1993.

Kooiman, Willem Jan. *Luthers kerklied in de Nederlanden*. Amsterdam: 't Koggeschip, 1943.

Koslofsky, Craig. *The Reformation of the Dead: Death and Ritual in Early Modern Germany, 1450–1700*. London: MacMillan, 2000.

Kossman, Ernst Heinrich, and Albert Frederik Mellink. *Texts Concerning the Revolt of the Netherlands.* Cambridge: Cambridge University Press, 1974.

Kovács, György Gönczi. *Keresztyéni énekek.* Debrecen, 1592.

Krull, Aijelt Folkert. *Jacobus Koelman: eene kerkhistorische studie.* Sneek: J. Campen, 1901.

Kuyper, A. *Voetius' catechisatie over den Heidelbergschen Catechismus. Naar Poudroyen's editie van 1662 op nieuw uitgegeven, bij ons publiek ingeleid, en met enkele aanteekeningen voorzien.* Rotterdam: Gebroeders Huge, 1891.

Laing, David, ed. *The Works of John Knox.* Repr. New York: AMS Press, 1966.

Lament, Sterling A. "The 'Vroedschap' of Leiden 1550–1600: The Impact of Tradition and Change on the Governing Elite of a Dutch City." *Sixteenth Century Journal* 12 (1981) 14–42.

Lapide, Cornelii à. *Commentarii in Scripturam Sacram in Commentaria in 1. Epist. Ad Corinthios.* Lugduni: Pelaguad, 1854.

Larenus, Jodocus van. *Data pensa trahamus; seu ad Colum Flissing-anus, à larvato furente grallatore [Nicolao Vedelio], conviciorum, calumniarum, mendaciorum, ac putidorum sophismatum penso circumdatam, Jodoci Lareni responsio.* Mideoburgi: Jac. Fierens, 1649.

———. *Epinicium Ecclesiæ Dei ex peccati, mundi, ac Satanæ Tyrannide, per Christum liberatae. Seu meditatio in Canticum Esaiæ Cap XII.* Medioburgi, Zeland: Apud Jacobum Fierensium, 1647.

Lasco, Johannes á. *Forma ac Ratio tota ecclesiastici Ministerij, in peregrinorum, potissimùm ueró Germanorum Ecclesia: instituta Londini in Anglia, per Pientissimum Principem Angliae &c. Regem Eduardum, eius nominis Sextu: Anno post Christum natum 1550. Addito ad calcem libelli priuilegio suae Maiestatis.* Emden: C. Egenolff, G. van der Erven, 1555.

Lavater, Ludwig. *De Ritibus et Institutis ecclesiae Tigurinae opusculum.* Tiguri [Zurich]: Christoph Froschauer, 1559.

Le Huray, Peter. *Music and the Reformation in England 1549–1660.* New York: Oxford University Press, 1967.

Leichtentritt, Huge. "The Reform of Trent and its Effect in Music." *The Musical Quarterly* 30 (1944) 319–28.

Lenz, Rudolf. *De mortuis nil nisi bene? Leichenpredigten als multidisziplinäre Quelle unter besonderer Berücksichtigung der historischen Familienforschung, der Bildungsgeschichte und der Literaturgeschichte.* Sigmaringen: J. Thorbecke, 1990.

Lepoeter, Girard J. *Maria Coomans, ambachtsvrouwe van Wemeldinge.* Goes: De Koperen Tuin, 1998.

Lieburg, Fred A. van. "From Pure Church to Pious Culture: The Further Reformation in the Seventeenth-Century Dutch Republic." In *Later Calvinism: International Perspectives,* edited by W. Fred Graham, 409–429. Kirksville, MO: Sixteenth Century Journal, 1994.

———. "Het gereformeerde conventikelwezen in de classis Dordrecht in de 17e en 18e eeuw." *Holland, regionaal-historisch tijdschrift* 23 (1991) 2–21.

———. "Kleine professoren, halve dominees, fijne dokters. Oefenaars op de pastorale markt in de vroegmoderne tijd." *Documentatieblad Nadere Reformatie* 22 (1998) 1–25.

———. *De Nadere Reformatie in Utrecht ten tijde van Voetius: Sporen in de gereformeerde kerkeraadsacta.* Rotterdam: Lindenberg, 1989.

———. "The Participants at the Synod of Dordt." In *Acta et Documenta Synodi National Dordrechtanae (1618-1619)*, vol. 1:LXIII-CVII. Göttingen: Vandenhoeck & Ruprecht, 2014.

———. *Repertorium van Nederlandse hervormde predikantent tot 1816*. Dordrecht: N.p., 1996.

Een liedtboecxken tracterende van den offer des Heeren, in't welcke oude nieuwe liedekens wt verscheyden copyen vergadert zijn om by het offerboeck ghevoecht te worden. Emden: Nicolaas Biestkens, 1563.

Ligarius, Johannes. *Warhafftiger Gegenbericht der rechtglabigen Predicanten in Ostfriesslandt auff des D. Petzels Vorrede uber das Embdische Buch, Vom Handel des Abentmals: anno 1590 zu Bremen aussgangen*. Embden: Johann von Oldersum unter das alte Rathhauss, 1593.

Lindeboom, Johannes. *Austin Friars: Geschiedenis van de Nederlandse hervormde gemeente te Londen 1550-1950*. 's-Gravenhage: Martinus Nijhoff, 1950.

Lintelo, B. H. A. te. *Ketters en papen in Twente: De reformatie en de katholieke herleving in Twente 1580-1640*. Hengelo: Broekhuis, 1988.

Lorgion, Everardus Jan Diest. *Geschiedenis van de kerkhervorming in Friesland*. Leeuwarden: W. Eekhoff, 1842.

Lubieniecki, Stanislas. *History of the Polish Reformation and Nine Related Documents*. Edited by George Huntston Williams. Minneapolis: Augsburg Fortress, 1995.

Luidens, John P. *The Americanization of the Dutch Reformed Church*. PhD diss., University of Oklahoma, 1969.

Luth, Jan et al. *Het Kerklied: een geschiedenis*. Zoetermeer: Mozaïek, 2001.

Luth, Jan. *"Daer wert om 't seerste uytgekreten. . . ." Bijdragen tot een geschiedenis van de gemeentezang in het Nederlandse gereformeerde protestantisme ± 1550 - ± 1852*. Kampen: Uitgeverij van den Berg, 1986.

———. "Gemeentezang en orgelbegeleiding in de 19de eeuw: Een overzicht van de Duitse bronnen die de Nederlandse cultuur Beinvoloedden." *Het Orgel* 101 (2005) 24-31.

———. "Gemeentezang en orgelspel door de eeuwen heen." *Nieuw handboek voor de kerkorganist*, edited by Ingelse, van Laar, Sanderman, and Smelik, 7-13. Zoetermeer: Uitgeverij Boekencentrum, 1995.

———. "The Music of the Dutch Reformed Church in Sweelinck's Time." In *Sweelinck Studies Proceedings of the International Sweelinck Symposium Utrecht 1999*, edited by Pieter Dirksen, 27-56. Utrecht: STIMU, Foundation for Historical Performance Practice: 2002.

———. "Het Orgel als iconografisch en allegorisch fenomeen." *Het Orgel* 99 (2003) 32-38.

———. "Het orgelgebruik in de zeventiende eeuw." *Het Orgel* 95 (1999) 5-8.

———. "Psalmzingen in het Nederlandse gereformeerde protestantisme sinds de zestiende eeuw." In *Psalmzingen in de Nederlanden: vanaf de zestiende eeuw tot heden: een bundel studies*, edited by J. de Bruijn and W., Heijting, 185-199. Kampen: J. H. Kok, 1991.

Luth, Jan R., and B. Smilde. "De melodieën van het Geneefse psalter," in *Psalmzingen in de Nederlanden van de zestiende eeuw tot heden*, 215-31. Kampen: Kok, 1991.

Maag, Karin. *Seminary or University? The Genevan Academy and Reformed Higher Education, 1560-1620*. Aldershot, England: Scolar, 1995.

MacCulloch, Diarmaid. *Reformation: Europe's House Divided 1490–1700.* New York: Viking, 2003.
Marnef, Guido. *Het calvinistisch bewind te Mechelen, 1580–1585.* Kortrijk-Heule: UGA, 1987.
Marot, Clément, et al. *Les pseaumes de David mis en rime Françoise par Cl. Marot et Th. De Bèze / Wt den Fransoyschen dichte in Nederlantschen overgeset door Petrum Dathenum.* Amsterdam: Gillis van den Rade voor Joannes Commelinus, 1594.
Mastenbroek, T., and J. J. Bosman. *De Grote kerk Maassluis 1639–1989.* Maassluis: Maassluise Drukkerij, 1989.
Maxwell, William D. *A History of Worship in the Church of Scotland.* London: Oxford University Press, 1955.
McCrie, Charles G. *The Public Worship of Presbyterian Scotland.* Edinburgh and London: William Blackwood and Sons, 1892.
McGinn, Donald Joseph. *The Admonition Controversy.* New Brunswick: Rutgers University Press, 1949.
McMillan, William. *The Worship of the Scottish Reformed Church 1550–1638.* London: James Clarke & Company, 1930.
McNeill, John T. *The History and Character of Calvinism.* New York: Oxford University Press, 1962.
Meeter, Daniel James. *"Bless the Lord, O My Soul," The New-York Liturgy of the Dutch Reformed Church, 1767.* Lanham, MD: Scarecrow, 1998.
Meeuse, C. J. *Jacobus Koelman (1632–1695).* Kampen: Uitgeverij De Groot Goudriaan, 2008.
Meijer, G. A. "Missie-verslagen der Dominicanen, ingediend bij de propaganda fide." *Het Archief voor de geschiedenis van het aartsbidom Utrecht* 49 (1924) 129–74.
Meyjes, Egbert Johannes Wernhard. *Kerkelijk 's-Gravenhage in vroeger eeuw: Schetsen uit de geschiedenis der hervormde gemeente.* 's-Gravenhage: Erven W. A. Beschoor, 1918.
Meyjes, Guillaume Henri Marie. "Les rapports entre le Eglises Wallonnes des Pays-Bas et la France avant la Révocation." In *La Revocation de l'edit de Nantes et Les Provinces Unies, 1685. Colloque International du Tricentenaire, Leyde, Avril 1–3, 1985*, edited by Hans Bots and Guillaume Henri Marie Meyjes, 1–15. Amsterdam: Maarssen, 1986.
Mey, Petrus Johannes de. "De orgels en organisten van de St. Nicolaaskerk te Kampen voor en tijdens de reformatie." *Verslagen en mededelingen Overijssels Regt en Geschiedenis* 57 (1940).
Michels, Henrich. *Die wohlklingende Harmonie des Hoch- und Niederteutschen Gottesdienst der unveränderten Augsburgischen Confession zugethanen Kirchen in Niederland.* Amsterdam: Nicolaus Bürger en Johan van Heeckeren, 1713.
Micron, Marten. *De Christelicke ordinancien der Nederlantscher ghemeynten Christi, die ... in't jaer 1550. te Londen inghestelt was.* London: Collinus Volckwinner, 1554.
Millar, Patrick. *Four Centuries of Scottish Psalmody.* London, Glasgow & New York: Oxford University Press, 1949.
Milligen, Simon van. *De kerkzang van de eerste christelijke periode tot onzen tijd: (voorstel tot invoering van een nieuwe rhythmiek bij de protestantsche koralen).* Groningen: Noordhoff, 1908.
Milo, Dirk Willem Lodewijk. *Zangers en speellieden, bijdrage tot de ontwikkeling van een calvinistische kerkmuziek.* Goes: Oosterbaan & Le Cointre, 1946.

Minutes of the Indiana-Michigan Mennonite Conference, 1864–1929. Scottdale, PA, 1929.

Molhuysen, P. C., and P. J. Blok, eds. *Nieuw Nederlandsch Biografisch Woordenboek.* 10 vols. Leiden: A. W. Sijthoff, 1911–37.

Moll, Willem, and J. G. de Hoo Scheffer, eds. *Studiën en bijdragen op 't gebied der historische theologie.* Amsterdam: G. L. Funke, 1870–1880.

Mooij, Charles Cornelis Maria de. *Geloof kan bergen verzetten: Reformatie en katholieke herleving te Bergen op Zoom, 1577–1795.* Hilversum: Verloren, 1998.

Moseley, R. J. "The Marcussen Organ in the Nicolaïkerk, Utrecht." *The Musical Times* 100 (1959) 102–4.

Mueren, Florentijn Jan van der. *Het orgel in de Nederlanden: Verre traditie, gebruik in de kerkelijke diensten, meubel decoratieve houtversiering, orgelregistratie, orgelliteratuur: parallel-vergelijking tusschen al deze bestanddeelen.* Brussel: Standaard-Boekhandel, 1931.

———. "Rond het vokaal-instumentaal vraagstuk in de Kerkelijke Polyphonie der XVe eeuw." *Tijdschrift der vereeniging voor Noord-Nederlandse muziekgeschiedenis* 13 (1929) 20–28.

Müller, Joseph Theodor. *Hymnologisches Handbuch zum Gesangbuch der Brüdergemeine.* Herrnhut: Verl. des Vereins für Brüdergeschichte, 1916.

Murdock, Graeme. *Calvinism on the Frontier: 1600–1660. International Calvinism and the Reformed Church in Hungary and Transylvania.* Oxford: Clarendon, 2000.

Music, David W. *Instruments in Church, a Collection of Source Documents.* Lanham, MD: Scarecrow, 1998.

Mützenbecher, E. H. *Sammlung der geistlichen Lieder und Psalme, welche in den meisten Evangelisch-Lutherischen Gemeinen der Vereinigten Niederlande, und besonders in Amsterdam, beym öffentlichen Gottesdienste gebraucht werden.* Amsterdam: J. C. Roeder en J. H. Moeleman, 1789.

Nauta, Doede, et al. *De Synode van Emden, oktober 1571. Een bundel opstellen ter gelegenheid van de vierhonderdjarige herdenking.* Kampen: Kok, 1971.

Nettl, Paul. *Luther and Music.* Translated by Frida Best and Ralph Wood. Philadelphia: Muhlenberg, 1948.

Nierop, Henk Frans Karel van. *Beeldenstorm en burgerlijk verzet in Amsterdam 1566–1567.* Nijmegen: Socialistiese Uitgeverij Jijmegen, 1978.

Nieuwkoop, Johannes van. *Haarlemse orgelkunst van 1400 tot heden: Orgels, organisten en orgelgebruik in de Grote of St.-Bavokerk te Haarlem.* Muziekhistorische monografieën. Utrecht: Vereniging voor Nederlandse muziekgeschiedenis, 1988.

Nijenhuis, Willem. *Ecclesia Reformatia: Studies on the Reformation, Volume II.* Leiden: E. J. Brill, 1994.

Noske, Frits. *Music Bridging Divided Religions: The Motet in the Seventeenth-Century Dutch Republic.* Wilhelmshaven: Florian Noetzel, 1989.

———. "Rondom het orgeltractaat van Constantijn Huygens." *Tijdschrift voor muziekwetenschap* 17 (1955) 278–309.

Noske, Frits, and N. Barker. *Pathodia sacra et profana.* Amsterdam: North-Holland, 1957.

Nüscheler, Felix. *Magister Ulrich Zwingli, Lebensgeschichte und Bildniss.* Zürich und Winterthur: Johann Caspar Fuessli Sohn und in Commission bey Heinrich Steiner und Compagnie, 1776.

McCoy, Charles Sherwood. "The Covenant Theology of Johannes Cocceius." PhD diss., Yale, 1957.
Oldenhof, Herman Joseph. *In en om de schuilkerkjes van Noordelijk Westergo: Katholiek leven in Frieslands Noordwesthoek onder de Republiek (1580–1795)*. Assen: Van Gorcum, 1967.
Oomius, Simon. *Institutiones theologiæ practicæ*... Bolsward: Samuel van Haringhouk, 1672.
Oost, Gert. *Er staat een orgel in*. Baarn: Bosch & Keuning, 1983.
Oosterhof, Ant. P. and Engelke Jan Penning. *Orgelbouwkundige bijdragen*. Leeuwarden: 1938.
Oudenhoven, Jacobus van. *Beschryvinga der Stadt Heusden*. Amsterdam: Jan Hartig, 1743.
Overvoorde, Jacob Cornelis. "Advies van burgemeesters en gerecht van Leiden aan de Staten van Holland over de acta van de in 1578 te Dordrecht gehouden synode." *Bijdragen en mededelingen van het Historisch Genootschap* 9 (1912) 117–49.
Pareus, David. *Davidis Parei In divinam ad Corinthios priorem S. Pavli apostoli epistolam commentarivs*. Heidelbergæ: impensis Jonæ Rhodii . . . typis Johannis Lancelotii, 1613.
Parker, Geoffrey. *The Dutch Revolt*. Ithaca, NY: Cornell University Press, 1977.
Parresius, Theophilus (Koelman, Jacobus). *Historisch verhael van de proceduuren tegen D. Jacobus Koelman, predicant tot Sluys in Vlaenderen. Wegens zijn debvoiren tot reformatie ontrent het stuck der formulieren en feestdagen*. Rotterdam: Pieter Hendrick; Amsterdam: Mercy Brouwning; Vlissingen: Abraham van Laaren, 1677.
Peeters, Flor, and Maarten Albert Vente. *De orgelkunst in de Nederlanden van de 16e tot de 18e eeuw*. Antwerp: Mercatorfonds, 1971.
Petition to the Church Council of The Hague 1642. Koninklijke Bibliotheek. The Hague: Hs KA XLVIII, 630–631. 1642.
Petition that the members of the assembly (conventikel) submitted to the consistory of The Hague on 3 January 1642. Koninklijke Bibliotheek. The Hague: Hs KA XLVIII, 632–633. 1642.
Pettegree, Andrew. *Emden and the Dutch Revolt: Exile and the Development of Reformed Protestantism*. Oxford: Clarendon, 1992.
Pettegree, Andrew, et al. *Calvinism in Europe, 1540–1620*. Cambridge: Cambridge University Press, 1994.
Pidoux, Pierre. *Les origines des mélodies des psaumes huguenots*. Monthey: Cantate Domino, 1979.
———. *Le Psautier Huguenot Du XVIe Siècle*. Bâle, Switzerland: Baerenreiter, 1962.
Po-Chia Hsia, R., and Henk van Nierop, eds. *Calvinism and Religious Toleration in the Dutch Golden Age*. Cambridge: Cambridge University Press, 2002.
Poelhekke, Jan Joseph. *Frederik Hendrik, Prins van Oranje: Een biografisch drieluik*. Zutphen: Walburg, 1978.
Pol, Frank van der. *De reformatie te Kampen in de zestiende eeuw*. Kampen: J. H. Kok, 1990.
———. "Religious Diversity and Everyday Ethics in the Seventeenth-Century Dutch City of Kampen." *Church History* 71 (2002) 16–62.
Poll, Gerrit Jan van de. *Martin Bucer's Liturgical Ideas: The Strasburg Reformer and His Connection with the Liturgies of the Sixteenth Century*. Assen: Van Gorcum, 1954.

Polman, Bert. *Church Music and Liturgy in the Christian Reformed Church of North America*. PhD diss., University of Minnesota, 1981.

Pont, Johannes Wilhelm. *Geschiedenis van het lutheranisme in de Nederlanden tot 1618*. Haarlem: Erven F. Bohn, 1911.

Poppius, Eduard. *Aanteykeningen ofte historisch verhaal . . . .* Amsterdam: Cornelis de Leeuw, 1649.

Portheine, H. Jr., "Orgels, orgelbouwers, orgelgebruik en organisten in de voormalige St. Martinus—en in de tegenwoordige St. Eusebius—of Groote Kerk te Arnhem." *Bulletin van den Nederlandschen Oudheidkundigen Bond* 5 (1912) 183–202.

Post, Regnerus Richardus. *The Modern Devotion. Confrontation with Reformation and Humanism*. Leiden: E. J. Brill, 1968.

Praetorious, Michael. *Syntagma musicum; ex veterum et recentiorum, ecclesiasticorum autorum lectione, polyhistorûm consignatione, vanarum linguarum notatione, hodierni seculi usurpatione, ipsius denique musicae antis observatione: in cantorum, organistarum, organopoeorum, caeterorumque musicam scientiam amantium & tractantium gratiam collectum; et secundùm generalem indicem toti open praefixum, in quatuor tomos distnibutum, à Michaële Praetorio*. Vol. II. Wolfenbüttel: Elias Holwein, 1619.

Price, J. Leslie. *Holland and the Dutch Republic in the Seventeenth Century: The Politics of Particularism*. Oxford: Clarendon, 1994.

The principall acts of the Generall Assembly, conveened at Edinburgh upon the last Wednesday of May, the 29 of that month, in the year 1644. Edinburgh: Evan Tyler, Printer to the King's most excellent majestie, 1644.

Ramakers, Bart, ed. *Conformisten en rebellen: Rederijkerscultuur in de Nederlanden (1400–1650)*. Amsterdam: Amsterdam University Press, 2003.

Rambach, August Jakob. *Über D. Martin Luthers verdienst um den Kirchengesang*. Reprografischer Nachdruck der Ausgabe Hamburg 1813. Hildesheim, NY: G. Olms, 1972.

Rasch, Rudolf. "Some Notes on the Camphuysen Manuscript." *Tijdschrift van de Vereniging voor Nederlandse muziekgeschiedenis* 23 (1973) 30–43.

Rauschning, Hermann. *Geschichte der Musik und Musikpflege in Danzig von den Anfängen bis zur Auflösung der Kirchenkapellen*. Danzig: Quellen und Darstellungen zur Geschichte Westpreußens, 1931.

Reitsma, Johannes, and Sietze Douwes van Veen. *Acta der provinciale en particuliere synoden: gehouden in de Noordelijke Nederlanden gedurende de jaren 1572–1620*. Groningen: J. B. Wolters, 1892.

Reitsma, Rients. *Centrifugal and Centripetal Forces in the Early Dutch Republic: The States of Overijssel, 1566–1600*. Amsterdam: Rodopi, 1982.

Resolutieboek Sneek, 1580–1663. Oud Archief Sneek Invoice Number 1: folio 42. Sneek: n.d., 1602.

Reuver, Arie de. *Sweet Communion. Trajectories of Spirituality from the Middle Ages through the Further Reformation*. Grand Rapids: Baker Academic, 2007.

Revesz, Imre. *History of the Hungarian Reformed Church*. Translated by George A. F. Knight. Washington, DC: The Hungarian Reformed Federation of America, 1956.

Revius, Jacobus, and Wisse Alfred Pierre Smit. *Over-ysselsche sangen en dichten*. Amsterdam: Uitgeversmaatschappij Holland, 1935.

Riemsdijk, Johan Cornelis Marius van. *Geschiedenis van de kerspelkerk van St. Jacob te Utrecht*. Leiden: Brill, 1888.

———. "Het orgel van de Nicolaikerk te Utrecht." *Tijdschrift der Vereeniging voor Noord-Nederlandse muziekgeschiedenis* 2 (1887) 195-99.

Rogers, Charles. *History of the Chapel Royal of Scotland: with the register of the Chapel Royal of Stirling, including details in relation to the rise and progress of Scottish music and observations respecting the Order of the Thistle*. Edinburgh: Grampian Club, 1882.

Rogier, Ludovicus Jacobus. *Geschiedenis van het katholicisme in Noord-Nederland in de 16e en de 17e eeuw*. Amsterdam: Urbi et Orbi, 1946-1947.

Roman Catholic Church. *The Council of Trent: The Canons and Decrees of the Sacred and Ecumenical Council of Trent*, edited and translated by J. Waterworth. London: Dolman, 1848.

Romein, Thomas Adrianus. *Naamlijst der predikanten, sedert de hervorming tot nu toe, in de hervormde gemeenten van Friesland*. Leeuwarden: A. Meijer, 1886.

———. "De reformatie te Groningen, na de reductie der stad in 1594." *Kerkhistorish archief* II (1859) 56-64.

Roodenburg, Herman. *Onder censuur: De kerkelijke tucht in de gereformeerde gemeente van Amsterdam, 1578-1700*. Hilversum: Verloren, 1990.

Rooijen, Abraham Jacob Servaas van. "Huygens contra Calckman en vice versa." *Tijdschrift voor Nederlandse muziekgeschiedenis* 9 (1911) 170-73.

Rooijen, Abraham Jacob Servaas van. "Biographische bijdragen tot de muziekgeschiedenis van Nederland." *Algemeen Nederlands Familieblad, tijdschrift voor geschiedenis* (1895-1896).

Rooze-Stouthamer, Clasina Martina. *Hervorming in Zeeland (ca. 1520-1572)*. Goes: De Koperen Tuin, 1996.

Rose, Jacqueline. "John Locke, 'Matters Indifferent,' and the Restoration of the Church of England." *Historical Journal* 48 (2005) 601-21.

Royaards, Herman Johan. *Geschiedenis der hervorming in de stad Utrecht (1583-1598)*. Leiden: S. and J. Luchtmans, 1847.

Rutgers, Frederik Lodewijk, ed. *Acta van de Nederlandsche synoden der zestiende eeuw*. 's-Gravenhage: Martinus Nijhoff, 1889.

Rutgers, Frederik Lodewijk, and Jan de Jong, eds. *Verklaring van de kerkenordening van de Nationale Synode van Dordrecht van 1618-1619: college-voordrachten van Prof. Dr. F. L. Rutgers over gereformeerd kerkrecht*. Rotterdam: Libertas, 1918.

Rutherford, Samuel. *The Divine Right of Church-Government and Excommunication: Or a Peaceable Dispute for the Perfection of the Holy Scripture in Point of Ceremonies and Church-Government; in Which the Removal of the Service-Book Is Justifi'd . . . To Which Is Added, a Brief Tractate of Scandal; with an Answer to the New Doctrine of the Doctors of Aberdeen, Touching Scandal*. London: John Field for Christopher Meredith, 1646.

Sapalski, Antoni. *Przewodnik dia organistów* . . . . Cracow: W. Kornecki, 1880.

Schama, Simon. *The Embarrassment of Riches: An Interpretation of Dutch Culture in the Golden Age*. New York: Vintage, 1997.

Schannat, Johann Friedrich, and Joseph Hartzheim. *Concilia Germaniae*. 11 vols. Witwe Krakamp, 1775-1790.

Schering, Arnold. *Die Neiderlaendische Orgelmesse in Zeitalter des Josquin*. Leipzig: Brietkpf & Härtel, 1912.

Schilling, Heinz. *Niederländische Exulanten im 16. Jahrhundert: Ihre Stellung im Sozialgefüge und im religiösen Leben deutscher und englischer Städte*. Schriften des

Vereins für Reformationsgeschichte, Nr. 187. Gütersloh: Verlagshaus G. Möhn, 1986.

———. *Religion, Political Culture and the Emergence of Early Modern Society. Essays in German and Dutch History*. Leiden: E. J. Brill, 1992.

Schoeck, Richard J. *Erasmus of Europe: The Prince of Humanists, 1501–1536*. Edinburgh: Edinburgh University Press, 1993.

Scholes, Percy A. *The Puritans and Music in England and New England*. Oxford: Clarendon, 1934.

Schoock, Martinus. *Exercitationes variae, de diversis materiis, quae hac editione nova tum locupletatae et vindicatae*. Trajecti ad Rhenum: Gisbertus à Zyll, 1663.

Schotel, Gilles Dionysius Jacobus. *De openbare eerdenienst der Nederl. Hervormde Kerk in de zestiende, zeventiende en achttiende eeuw*. Haarlem: A. C. Kruseman, 1870.

Schrevelius, Theodorus. *Theod: Schreveli, Harlemias, of Eerste stichting der stad Haarlem . . . : Vermeerdert met historiesche aantekeningen tot den jaare 1750*. Haarlem: Joannes Marshoorn, 1754.

Seiffert, Max. "Cornelis Schuijt." *Tijdschrift van de Vereniging voor Nederlandse muziekgeschiedenis* 5 (1897) 244–59.

Seijbel, Maarten. *Orgels in Overijssel*. Sneek: Boeijenga, 1965.

Selderhuis, Herman J. *Handboek Nederlandse kerkgeschiedenis*. Kampen: Kok, 2005.

Sibelius, Caspar. *De curriculo totius vitæ et peregrinationis suæ historica narratio*. Deventer, 1658.

Sibelius, Caspar, and Ludwig Scheibe. *Zeittafel der Geschichte der Lateinischen Schule und des aus ihr hervorgegangenen Gymnasiums in Elberfeld: Und, Eine Probe aus der Historica narratio Caspari Sibelii de curriculo totius vitae et peregrinationis suae: Festschrift zur Feier des dreihundertjährigen Bestehens der zum Gymnasium ausgebildeten Lateinischen Schule und der Einweihung des neuen Gymnasialgebäudes am 9. und 10. Januar 1893*. Elberfeld: Sam. Lucas, 1893.

Sinnema, Donald W., Christian Moser, and H. J. Selderhui, eds. *Acta et Documenta Synodi Nationalis Dordrechtanae (1618–1619)*. Göttingen: Vandenhoeck & Ruprecht, 2015.

Sicher, Fridolin, and E. Götzinger. *Chronik. Mitteilungen zur vaterlandischen Geschichte*. St. Gallen: Huber, 1885.

Sigtenhorst Meyer, Bernhard van den. *Jan P. Sweelinck en zijn instrumentale muziek*. The Hague: Servire, 1946.

Slee, Jacob Cornelis van. *Catalogus der handschriften berustende op de Athenaeumbibliotheek te Deventer*. Deventer: Deventer Boek-en Steendrukkerij, 1892.

———. "De Gereformeerde gemeente van Deventer in de eerste veertig jaren na hare wederoprichting in 1591." *Nederlandsch Archief voor Kerkgeschiedenis* 19 (1926) 122–58.

Smid, Menno. *Ostfriesische Kirchengeschichte*. Pewsum: Deichacht Krummhörn, 1974.

Smit, Jacobus Wilhelmus. "The Netherlands Revolution." In *Vaderlands verleden in veelvoud: 31 opstellen over de Nederlandse geschiedenis na 1500*, edited by G. A. M. Beekelaar et al., 19–54. The Hague: Nijhoff, 1975.

———. "The Present Position of Studies Regarding the Revolt of the Netherlands." In *Britain and the Netherlands*, edited by J. S. Bromley and E. H. Kossmann, 11–28. London: Chatto and Windus, 1960.

Sowards, Kelley. "The Two Lost Years of Erasmus: Summary, Review, and Speculation." *Studies in the Renaissance* 9 (1962) 161–86.

Spaans, Joke. *Haarlem na de reformatie: Stedelijke cultuur en kerkelijk leven, 1577–1620.* The Hague: Stichting Hollandse Historische Reeks, 1989.

———. "Katholieken en de Vrede van Munster." *De Zeventiende Eeuw* 13 (1997) 253–60.

Spicer, Andrew. *Calvinist Churches in Early Modern Europe.* Manchester and New York: Manchester University Press, 2007.

———. "'So Many Painted Jezebels.' Stained Glass Windows and the Formation of an Urban Identity in the Dutch Republic." In *Public Opinion and Changing Identities in the Early Modern Netherlands: Essays in Honour of Alastair Duke*, edited by Judith Pollmann and Andrew Spicer, 249–77. Leiden: E. J. Brill, 2007.

Sprunger, Eva. *The First Hundred Years: A History of the Mennonite Church in Adams County, Indiana, 1838–1938.* Berne, IN: 1938.

Sprunger, Keith. L. *Dutch Puritanism. A History of English and Scottish Churches of the Netherlands in the Sixteenth and Seventeenth Centuries.* Leiden: E. J. Brill, 1982.

Staehelin, Ernst. *Breife und Akten zum Leben Oekolampads: Zum vierhundertjährigen Jubiläum der Basler Reformation.* Leipzig: M. Heinsius Nachfolger, Eger & Sievers, 1934.

Starr, George. "Art and Architecture and the Hungarian Reformed Church." In *Seeing Beyond the Word: Visual Arts and the Calvinist Tradition*, edited by Paul Corby Finney, 301–40. Grand Rapids: Eerdmans, 1999.

Statenberijming: Het boek der psalmen, nevens de gezangen bij de Hervormde Kerk in gebruik, door last van de Hoog Mogende Heeren Staaten Generaal der Vereenigde Nederlanden, uit drie berijmingen, in den jaare 1773, gekooren, met de noodige daarin gemaakte veranderingen. The Hague: Isaac Scheltus, 1773.

Sterkenburg, Petrus Gijsbertus Jacobus van. *Een glossarium van zeventiende-eeuws Nederlands.* Groningen: Wolters-Noordhoff, 1981.

Stouppe, Jean-Baptiste. *La religion des Hollandois: representée en plusieurs lettres écrites par un officier de l'armée du roy, à un pasteur & professeur en theologie de Berne. La religion des Hollandois.* Cologne: Chez Pierre Marteau, 1673.

Strengholt, L. *Constanter: het leven van Constantijn Huygens.* Amsterdam: Querido, 1987.

Streso, Caspar. *Danckpredicatie uyt den CXXII psalm, gedaen in 's Gravenhage den 21 augusti 1651 op de groote zaele, in de doorluchtige ende hooghaensienlijcke vergaderinge van de Hooge Machten der Seven Gheunieerde Nederlandtsce Provintien.* 's-Gravenhage, 1641.

Strietman, Elsa, and Peter Happé, eds. *Urban Theatre in the Low Countries, 1400–1625.* Turnhout: Brepols, 2006.

Swigchem, Cornelis Albertus van, et al. *Een huis voor het Woord. Het protestantse kerkinterieur in Nederland tot 1900.* Zeist: Rijksdienst voor de Monumentenzorg, 1984.

Symmes, Thomas. *Utile dulci. Or, A joco-serious dialogue, concerning regular singing calculated for a particular town, (where it was publickly had, on Friday Oct. 12, 1722.) but may serve some other places in the same climate.* Boston: Printed by B. Green, for S. Gerrish, in Cornhill, 1723.

Taylor, W. David O. "John Calvin and Musical Instruments: A Critical Investigation." *Calvin Theological Journal* 48:2 (2013) 248–69.

Tel, Martin. "*Gebruyck of Ongebruyck*: A Brief Overview of Historic Trends in the Use of the Organ in the Calvinist Churches of the Netherlands." *Princeton Seminary Bulletin* 24 (2003) 313–27.
Temperley, Nicholas. *The Music of the English Parish Church*. Cambridge: Cambridge University Press, 1979.
Thomas, Keith. *Religion and the Decline of Magic*. New York: Scribner, 1971.
Thompson, Bard. *Liturgies of the Western Church*. Cleveland & New York: William Collins, 1962.
Tideman, Johannes. "Bijzonderheden uit de geschiedenis der Amsterdamsche Remonstrantsche gemeente." In *Studiën en bijdragen op 't gebied der historische theologie*, 4:495–527. Amsterdam: Funke, 1880.
Todd, Margo. *The Culture of Protestantism in Early Modern Scotland*. New Haven: Yale University Press, 2002.
Tollefsen, Randall H. *Catalogue of the Music Collection of the Moravian Congregation at Zeist*. Utrecht: Rijksarchief, 1985.
Tracy, James D. *The Low Countries in the Sixteenth Century. Erasmus, Religion and Politics, Trade and Finance*. Aldershot: Ashgate Variorum, 2005.
Tydeman, Hendrik Willem. "Caspar Sibelius, in leven predikant te Deventer, volgens zijn onuitgegeven eigen levensbeschriving." *Godgeleerde Bijdrage* 23 (1849) 481–537.
Ungvary, Alexander Sandor. *Lutheran and Calvinist Influences upon the Hungarian Reformed Church in the 16th and 17th Centuries*. Master's Thesis, Michigan State University, 1962.
Veen, Willem Klaas van der. "Het koor van de Martinikerk." *Mededelingen van het Instituut voor Liturgiewetenschap van de Rijkuniversiteit te Groningen* 7 (1972) 15–45.
Velde, Abraham van de. *De wonderen des Alder-hooghsten, ofte aenwysinge van de oorsaecken, wegen en middelen, waardoor de Geunieerde Provintien, uyt hare vorige onderdrukkinge zoo wonderbaarlyk, tegen vermoeden van de heele wereldt, tot soo grooten macht rijckdom, eere, en onsaggelijkheydt zyn verheven*. Amsterdam: Jan Graal, 1707.
Veldman, Harm. *De beeldenstorm in Groningen: Reformatorische vrijheidsbeweging in Stad en Ommelanden*. Goes: Oosterbaan & Le Cointre, 1990.
Veluanus, John Anastasius. *Een cort onderricht van allen principalen puncten des christengeloofs, met claer ghtuijchgenisse der heijligher schriftueren ende geode bekentenisse der oude doctoren met aenwijsinghe wanneer, en door welcke persoonen die erreuren opghestaen ende vermeerdert zijn, bereijt voor den simpelen ongeleerden Christenen, ende is daeromme ghenaempt der Leeken wechwijser. Auth. Joh. Anastasio Veluano—I John I. Des Heeren Christus Jesus bloet reijnicht ons van allen sonden*. Ghedrukt (Straatsburg) big Magnus van den Mergerghe van Oosterhout, het jaer ons Heeren duijsent vijf hondert ende vijf en viftich. Wezel: B. von Klarenbach (= Lambrecht van Joos), 1554.
Vente, Maarten Albert. *Bouwstoffen tot de geschiedenis van het Nederlandse orgel in de 16e eeuw*. Amsterdam: H. J. Paris, 1942.
———. *Die Brabanter Orgel; zur Geschichte der Orgelkunst in Belgien und Holland im Zeitalter der Gotik und der Renaissance*. Amsterdam: H. J. Paris, 1963.

———. *Proeve van een repertorium van de archivalia betrekking hebbende op het Nederlandse orgel en zijn makers tot omstreeks 1630.* Bruxelles: Académie royale de Belgique, 1954.

———. *Utrechtse orgelhistorische verkenningen: bijdragen tot de geschiedenis der orgelcultuur in de Lage Landen tot omstreeks 1630.* Utrecht: Vereiniging voor Nederlandse Musikgeschiedenis, 1989.

———. *Vijf eeuwen Zwolse orgels 1447-1971.* Amsterdam: Frits Knuf, 1971.

Vente, Maarten Albert, and Christiaan Cornelius Vlam, eds. *Documentaet archivalia ad historiam musicae neerlandicae. Bouwstenen voor een geschiedenis der toonkunst in de Nederlanden.* Utrecht: Vereniging voor Nederlands muziekgeschiedenis, 1965.

Verkamp, Bernard Joseph. *The Indifferent Mean: Adiaphorism in the English; Reformation to 1554.* Athens, OH: Ohio University Press, 1977.

Een vermaeckelicke, doch eenvoudige, en bondighe predicatie, ghepredickt tot Edinburgh in Schotlandt, in de St. Gillis kercke, op den laetsten sondagh van april, by een geleerden predikant uyt Hitlandt: over het onderteyckenen van 't kerckelijcke verbondt, tegens de papistische ceremonien, die de bisschoppen aldaer sochten in te voeren. Leiden, 1642.

Vermij, Reink. *The Calvinist Copernicans: The Reception of the New Astronomy in the Dutch Republic, 1575-1750.* Amsterdam: Koninklijke Nederlandse Akademie van Wetenschappen, 2002.

Verrykt met allerhande edicten van keyzer Karel en Philips den tweeden, handvesten, privilegien, octroyen, instructien, reglementen, resolutien, en andere aanmerkelyke stukken. Utrecht: Jacob van Poolsum, 1729.

Visser, Derk. "Establishing the Reformed Church: Clergy and Magistrates in the Low Countries 1572-1620." In *Later Calvinism: An International Perspective, Volume XXII Sixteenth Century Essays and Studies,* edited by W. Fred Graham, 388-407. Kirksville, MO: Northeast Missouri State University, 1994.

Visser, Piet. "Litanie van een liturgisch stiefkind: Een korte geschiedenis van de psalm bij de doopsgezinden." In *Psalmzingen in der Nederlanden van zestiende eeuw tot heden,* edited by J. de Bruijn and W. Heitjing, 115-48. Kampen: Kok, 1991.

Vlagsma, Auke Hendrik. "Het Grote Orgel in de Grote of St. Laurenskerk te Alkmaar van 1638 uit 1723." *De Mixtuur* 58 (1987) 346-68.

Vlam, Christiaan Cornelis. "Hoornse organisten en klokkenisten van het midden van de vijftiende tot het einde van de achttiende eeuw." *West-Frieslands oud en nieuw— 21e bundel van het Historisch Genootschap Oud West-Friesland* (1954) 68-88.

Voetius, Gisbertus, and Cornelis Poudroyen. *Voetius' catechisatie over den Heidelbergschen catechismus. Naar Poudroyen's editie van 1662 opnieuw uitgegeven.* Edited by Abraham Kuyper. Rotterdam: Huge, 1891. Reissue of Poudroyen's *Catechisatie; dat is, een grondige ende eenvoudige onderwijsinge over de leere des christelicken catechismis.* 1662.

Voetius, Gisbertus. *Disputationes theologicae selectae.* 5 vols. Utrecht: J. van Waesberge (Vols. 1-3); Amsterdam: J. Jansonius van Waesberge and E. Weyerstraet (Vol. 4); Utrecht: A. Smytegelt (Vol. 5), 1669.

———. *Grondige eende pertinente verklaringe over de vrage wien de kerckelijcke macht toekomt. In drie onderscheydene disputatien voorghestelt, van den eerweerdigen ende hooghgeleerden D. Gysbertus Voetius, doctore ende professor der H. Theologie in de Universiteyt tot Utrecht. Wt de Latijnsche inde Nederlandtsche tale duydelijk overgeset.* 's-Gravenhage: Joost Jansz. Verheul, 1640.

———. *Politicæ Ecclesiasticæ Partis Primae Libri Duo Priores* (vol. 1). Amsterdam: Joannis à Waesberge, 1663

———. *Politicæ Ecclesiasticæ Partis Primae Libri Duo Posteriores* (vol. 2). Amsterdam: Joannis à Waesberge, 1666.

———. *Politicæ Ecclesiasticæ Pars Secunda.* Amsterdam: Joannis à Waesberge, 1669;

———. *Politicæ Ecclesiasticæ Pars Tertia et Ultima.* Amsterdam: Joannis à Waesberge, 1676.

———. *Thersites heautontimorumenos, hoc est, Remonstrantium hyperaspistes, catechesi, et liturgiæ Germanicæ, Gallicæ, et Belgicæ denuo insultans, retusus.* Utrecht: A. van Herwyck & H. Ribbius, 1635.

W. S. *Korte aen-wijsinge, dat het tegen-gift van den orgel-bestormer ongesont is.* Alkmaar: Jan van den Briel, 1641.

Wackernagel, Karl Eduard Philipp. *Bibliographie zur Geschichte des deutschen Kirchenliedes im XVI. Jahrhundert.* Frankfurt: Heyder & Zimmer, 1855.

———. *Das deutsche Kirchenlied von der ältesten Zeit bis zu Anfang des XVII. Jahrhunderts.* Leipzig: Bände, 1864–1877.

———. *Lieder der niederländischen Reformierten aus der Zeit der Verfolgung im 16. Jahrhundert.* Frankfurt: Heyder & Zimmer, 1867.

Wainwright, Geoffrey, and Karen Beth Westerfield Tucker. *The Oxford History of Christian Worship.* Oxford: Oxford University Press, 2006.

Water, Johann van de. *Groot Placcaatboek vervattende alle de placaten, ordonnantien en edicten der Edele Mogende Heeren Staten 's Lands van Utrecht . . . .* Utrecht: Van Poolsum, 1728.

Weiland, Jan Sperna, and Willem Frijhoff, eds. *Erasmus of Rotterdam: The Man and the Scholar: Proceedings of the Symposium Held at the Erasmus University, Rotterdam, 9–11 November 1986.* Leiden: E. J. Brill, 1986.

Weiss, Nathanaël. "Un portrait de la femme de Calvin." *Bulletin de la Societe de l'Historie du Protestantisme Français* 56 (1907) 222–33.

Westra, Evert. *Uit Sions zalen. Een kerkmuzikale handreiking.* Baarn: Bosch & Keuning, 1966.

Wheelock, Arthur K. *The Public and Private in Dutch Culture of the Golden Age.* Newark: University of Delaware Press, 2000.

White, James. *Introduction to Christian Worship.* Nashville: Abingdon, 1980.

Williams, Charles Francis Abdy. *The Story of the Organ.* London: Walter Scott, 1903.

Williams, Peter. *The European Organ: 1450–1850.* Bloomington, IN: Indiana University Press, 1966.

———. *The Organ in Western Culture: 750–1250.* Cambridge: Cambridge University Press, 1993.

Woltjer, Jan Juliaan. *Friesland in hervormingstijd.* Leiden: Leiden Universitaire Pers, 1962.

Worp, Jacob Adolf, ed. *De briefwisseling van Const. Huygens (1608–1687).* 's-Gravenhage: Nijhoff, 1914.

———. "De jeugd van Christiaan Huygens, volgens een handschrift van zijn vader." *Oud Holland* 13 (1913) 209–35.

Wotherspoon, Henry Johnstone. "The Present State of Church Music in Scotland." *Transactions of the Aberdeen Ecclesiological Society* 2 (1890–1893) 36–44.

Woude, Adrianus Maria van der, et al. "Numerieke aspecten van de protestantisering in Noord-Nederland tussen 1656 en 1726." *A. A. G. Bijdragen* 13 (1965) 149–80.

Woudstra, Marten. *De Hollandsche vreemdelingen-gemeente te Londen gedurende de eerste jaren van haar bestaan*. Groningen: J. B. Wolters, 1908.

Ypeij, Annaeus, and Izaak Johannes Dermout. *Geschiedenis der Nederlandsche Hervormde Kerk*. Breda: W. van Bergen, 1819–1827.

Zandt, Herman S. J. *Organisten, orgelspel en kerkzang binnen het Nederlandse calvinisme, inzonderheid in de Nederlandse Hervormde Kerk*. Bedum: Uitgeverij Profiel, 1995.

Zepperus, Wilhelmus. *Legum Mosaicarum forensium explanatio*. Herbonæ Nassorum: Corvinus, 1604.

———. *Politia ecclesiastica: sive, Forma, ac ratio administrandi, et gubernandi regni Christi, quod est ecclesia in his terris*. Herbonæ: Christophori Corvini, 1607.

Zwaan, F. L., ed. *Constantijn Huygens, Gebruyck of ongebruyck van 't orgel in de kercken der Vereenighde Nederlanden 1641*. Proceedings of the Royal Dutch Academy of Sciences, Literary division, new series 84. Amsterdam: 1974.

Zwart, Jan. "Hendrik Joosten Speuy, een tijdgenoot van Sweelinck." *Het Orgel* 54 (1958) 97–98, 129–32.

———. *Van een deftig orgel: Maassluis 1732–1932*. Maassluis: Maassluissche Boekhandel en Drukerij, 1933.

Zwingli, Huldreich. *Huldreich Zwinglis Sämtliche Werke*. Edited by Emil Eglie et al. Berlin-Zurich: C. A. Schewtschke und Sohn, 1905.

NAME/SUBJECT INDEX

Aberdeen, city of, 29
Abkoude, city of, 109
Accordian, 38n105
Adama, Jacobus, 79
Adiaphora, 69, 107, 129, 172, 187
Admonition to the Parliament, 34
Alkmaar, St. Laurens Church, 115
Alphen aan de Rijn, city of, 152, 154
Altinga, Menso, 83
Amalia, Princess, 132
Ames, William, 43
Amsterdam, city of, 54
    Oude Kerk, 56
    Nieuwe Church, 115
    Wester Kerk, 142
Andreae, Jacob, 187
Antwerp, city of, 52, 56
Arminian church, 54
Arnhem, city of, 89
Aspilcueta [Navarrus], Martin, 179
Augustine, Saint, 9
Aural iconoclasm, 27–28

Bach, Johann Sebastian, 11
Bacon, John, 131
Baerle, Susanna van, 131
Ban, Joan Albert, 149
Baptist church, 53
Bardowick, city of, 82
Barlaeus, Caspar, 142–46
Basel, city of, 16–18
Batelier, Jacobus Johannes, 172
Bells, playing of, 67, 84, 95, 109, 178
Benting, Jan Apkes, 116–17
Bergsma, Wiebe, 77

Bern, city of, 18
Beza, Théodore, 187–88
Blenkenburg, Quirijn van, 53n10
Book of Common Prayer, 33
Boorn, city of, 104–5
Boxhorn, Marcus Zuerius, 131
Boxtel, David van, 172
Brandenbourgh, Peter Joachim, 79
Brielle, city of, 54
Bruges, city of, 56
Bruinsma, Henry, 2
Bruno, Henricus, 166
Bucer, Martin, 18–19
Bullinger, Heinrich, 13

Cajetan[o], Cardinal, 179
Calandrini, Jean Ludovicq, 148
Calckman, Jan Jansz, 6, 129, 152ff, 201
    Antidotum, 152ff
Calderwood, David, 31
Callegari, Giuseppe, 39
Calvin, John, 5, 20–28, 44, 64, 133, 192
Canons of Dordrecht, 126
Cantors, 29–30
Capito, Johann, 197
Carleton, Dudley, 130
Chapel Royal, 30
Christianij, Petrus, 79
Chrysostom, Saint, 137
Coccejus, Johannes, 171
Coomans, Maria, 1–2
Confessio Hungarica, 42
Contafactuals, 11

NAME/SUBJECT INDEX

Cornet organ stop, 68
Council of Trent, 60
Cudsemius, Petrus, 173
Culmer, Richard, 35

Danzig, city of, 39–40
Datheen, Pieter, 66
David, King, 137
De Lier, city of, 59
Debrecen, Articles of, 44–46
Degens, Willem, 110
Delft, city of, 92
    1638 Provincial synod of, 3, 69, 97, 129, 187, 189
    Gasthuis Church, 115
    Heilige Geest Gasthuiskerk, 93
    Nieuwe Kerk, 93
    Oude Kerk, 93
Demetrius, Rev., 124
Den Briel, city of, 121
Descartes, René, 131, 146
Deutschmann, Jakob, 46
Deventer, Bergkerk, 104
Deventer, city of, 103–5, 192
Donne, John, 130–31
Dordrecht, city of, 6, 57, 92
    Augustine church, 123, 126
    Groote Kerk, 123, 126–28
    International Synod of 1618–19, 120ff, 131, 112n118
    Provincial Synod of 1574, 63ff, 110
    National Synod of 1578, 66–67, 77, 86, 90, 99, 110, 112n118, 189
Drenthe, city of, 86
Duifhuis, Hubert, 94
Dutch Reformed Church, 50–51

Eckhardus, Henricus, 173
Edam, city of, 65
Edinburgh, city of, 29, 32
Edward VI, King, 34
Elizabeth I, Queen, 34
Emden, city of, 81–82, 101, 153
    National Synod of 1574, 65, 77
England, Church of, 33ff
English Reformed church, 54

Engwierum, Catrinabandt Church, 80
Eramus of Rotterdam, 17, 25, 159, 181
Essenius, Andreas, 107, 191
Eubulus, Christophilus, 109
Evelyn, John, 71
Eyk, Steven Hermansz van, 168

Falco, Regenerus, 80
Farel, Guillaume, 20
Faukeel, Herman, 113–15
Federalists, 171
Fergushill, John 29
Flushing, city of, 54
Francken, Ægeidus, 197n91
Franeker, city of, 105–6
Frankfurt upon Order, city of, 192
Frederick, Count of Montebéliard, 187
Frelinghuysen, Theodorus Jacobus, 185
Frick, Christoph, 82
Friesland, province of, 77–81
Funeral customs, 97–98, 178

Gdańsk, city of, 39
Gelderland, province of, 89–91
Geneva, city of, 16, 20, 28, 43
Genevan Psalter, 26, 43, 58
Ghent, city of, 56
Glasgow, city of, 32
Gołos, Jerzy, 41
Gouda, city of, 88, 125, 172
    St. John's Church, 88
Gouw, city of, 80
Gregorius, Abbot, 159
Grippe, Gherrit van, 123
Groenenberg, Gijsbert van, 95
Groningen
    Martini Church, 83, 132
    city of, 82–84, 132, 192
    Provincial Synod of 1599, 102

Haarlem, city of, 102, 105, 149
Hague, city of The, 54
    Court Chapel of the, 133
    St. Jacob's Church, 163–65

NAME/SUBJECT INDEX   233

Hamburg, Synod of, 12
Harlingen, Synod of, 80
Harmensz, Gysbert, 116
Hartknoch, Christoph, 39
Heeres, Johan, 105
Heidelberg Catechism, 42, 150, 185–87
Heimenberg, Johannes, 174ff
Helmbreeker, Cornelis, 102
Henry VIII, King, 33
Herborn, city of, 182
Hernhutters, 52
Hessen, *Church Regulations*, 11
Heusden, city of, 170
Holland, province of, 91–93, 121
Holyroodhouse, 31
Hooft, Pieter Cornelis, 142–44, 166
Hoorn, city of, 71, 115
Hospinianus, Rodolphus, 15
Huguenot, 53n8
Hungary, 42–48
Husschin, Johann, 16–18
Huygens, Constantijn, 3, 6, 115, 129, 130ff, 173, 176, 201
   Gebruyck of Ongebrucyk, 131ff
   Responsa prudentum, 164ff
Hymns, use of, 9ff

Iconoclasm, 53, 74, 78, 91
Iperen, Joshua van, 71

Jacobsz, Hillebrant, 101
James I/VI, King, 30, 128
Janssen Ritscke, 79
Jelsum, city of, 196
Joachimi, Albert, 148
Jonas, Justus, 25
Joris of Venice, 159
Joseph II, Emperor, 46
Juhász, Péter Méliusz, 44
Julius III, Pope, 35

Kamerijk, synod of, 60
Kampen, city of, 85–87, 98, 116
   Bovenkerk, 85
   Broederkerk, 86, 195n78
   Church of Holy Spirit, 86
   meeting of 1581, 86

St. Nicolaas Church, 85
Kiespenning, Albert, 123, 126
Knox, John, 28–33, 34, 44
Koelman, Jacobus, 109–12
Kraków, city of, 36–37
Kruiningen, city of, 1

Labadists, 171
Lajos II, 42
Lapide, Cornelius á, 183
Laren, Joos van, 175
Larenus, Joducus van, 175, 176
Lasco, Jan á, 36–42
Lavater, Ludwig, 43
Leeuwarden, city of, 116
   classis of, 80
   Grote Kerk, 79
   Jacobijnen Kerk, 79, 116
Leiden, city of, 54, 87–88, 92, 98
   Hooglandse Kerk, 116–18
   Pieterskerk, 87, 115
Liebsemahle, 52
Liefhebbers, 51
Lingen, city of, 86
London, city of, 140n36
Lotius, Elezear, 141
Lublin, city of, 37
Lucasz, Gerrit, 86
Luth, Jan, 79
Luther, Martin, 9–11, 25
Lutherans, Dutch, 52
Lydius, Balthasar, 126
Lyere, Ambassador Willem van, 148

Maassluis, city of, 59, 88
Marbeck, John, 33
Marcellus II, 35
Mary I, Queen, 30, 33
Maxwell, William, 29
Mechelen, synod of, 60
Meester, Andries de, 124
Mennonite church, 18, 53
Merten, Abraham, 98
Meulen, Johannes van der, 179
Michaelius, Jonas, 47
Middelburg, city of, 93, 112–15, 125
Molano, Johannes, 179
Monnikendam, city of, 84

Montebéliard, Colloquy of, 187
Monteverdi, Claudio, 131
Moravians, 52
Morlet, Jan III, 93
Mostart, David, 142
Muiderkring, 142

Nadere Reformatie, 106ff, 200
Nassau, Jan van, 121
Nethenus, Matthias, 107, 191
New York, New York, city of, 47
Niehoff, Heinrick, 88, 93
Nijken, Johannes, 90
North Holland, province of, 84
Nymegen, city of, 71
    classis of, 71

Oecolampadius, Johannes, 16–18
Oliemolen, 104n94
Ommelanden Church Order of 1595, 83
Ooms, Simon, 19ff
Oost-Friesland, Count of, 133
Orange, Prince Frederik Hendrik, 131–32
Orange, William of, 121
Organists, church membership, 102
Organists, Roman Catholic, 102
Overijssel, province of, 85ff

Pareus, David, 183
Paul III, Pope, 35, 60
Paul IV, Pope, 35
Pella, Iowa, city of, 48
Perkins, William, 43
Pińczów, city of, 36
Pio, Alberto, 181n43
Pipe organ, Dutch, 67ff
Pirie Act, 32
Placius, Johannes, 153
Plato, 21
Poland, country of, 36–42
Polyander, Jean, 81
Poppius, Eduard, 126
Portative organ, 38
Postlude, organ, 63
Precentors, 29–30
Presbyterian Church, 28–33

Presbyterian form of church governance, 4
Psalter of 1773, 71ff, 199
Purmerland, city of, 195n78
Puritans, 34–35

Raalte, Albertus van, 48
Rekeingenboek of Friesland, 79
Remonstrants, 54, 146, 171
Revius, Jacobius, 68
Rievaulx Abbey, 59
Rijn, Rembrandt van, 131
Ripperda, Asinge van, 78
Rites and Institution of the Zurich Church, 43
Roman Catholic Church, Dutch, 55ff
Rotterdam, city of, 54, 146
Rutherford, Samuel, 32

Schaffhausen, city of, 16
Schendel, Jacob van, 95
Scholte, Hendrik, 48
Schook, Martinus, 174, 192ff
Schoonhoven, Jan Cornelisz, 92
Schuilkerken, 55
Schurman, Anna Maria van, 148, 166
Schuyt, Cornelis, 87
Scotland Kirk, 128
Scotland, country of, 28–33
Seijbel, Maarten, 85
Servaessen, Adriaen, 123–24
Sextons, 103, 109
Siefert, Paul, 41
Sigismond III, King, 37–38, 41
Simons, Menno, 18
Sluis, city of, 109–10
Sneek, city of, 79
    Martini Church, 79
South Holland, 1638 provincial synod of, 63–64, 69–71, 77, 87–89, 142, 162
Speuij, Abigael, 129
Speuij, *De Psalmen Davids*, 124
Speuij, Hendrick Joostenszoon, 120ff
Statenberijming Psalter, 71

NAME/SUBJECT INDEX 235

Stiens, city of, 79
Strasbourg, city of, 19
Streso, Caspar, 141–42, 150–52, 153
Stuyvesant, Peter, 47
Sweelinck, Jan Pieterszoon, 120, 142
Swiss Brethren, 18
Synod of North Holland 1586, 84
Synod, 1817 national, 73

Ten Commandments, 140–41
Tertullian, 178
Todd, Margo, 2
Tongeren, Cornelis Jansz van, 123
Torre, Raphael de la, 179
Trent, Council of, 35, 60
Trombone choirs, 52
Trouwbus, 104n94
Tübingen, University of, 187
Twenthe, city of, 86
Tympani organ stop, 38–39

Union of Utrecht, 51, 96
Utrecht, city of, 56, 94
    Catharijnekerk, 197
    Dom Kerk, 108
    Geertekerk, 95
    hymnal 101, 107
    illustere school, 171
    Minderbroederkerk, 94
    Nicolaaskerk, 56
    Oudekerk, 56, 95
    St. Jacob's Church, 95
    Theological Advice, 107–8, 191ff
    Walloon congregation, 95
Uyttenbogaert, Johannes, 146

Veere, city of, 110
Velde, Abraham van de, 113–45
Velsen, Dirck Jansz, 84
Veluanus, Johann Anastasius, 57
Verstegen, Joannes, 57

Vitalian, Pope, 45, 159
Vlijmen, city of, 170
Voetius, Gisbertus, 6, 41n121,
    48n138, 101, 107–8, 111,
    129, 148, 170ff, 201
    Appendix Apologetica, 173
    Politicae Ecclesiasticae, 170ff
    Thersites, 172–73
Vogelgesang organ stop, 68
Voorzanger, 58–59, 79, 194
Vox humana organ stop, 68
Voys [Vois], Pieter de, 116, 149

Walcheren, classis of, 109–11
Walloon church, 53
Waterloos, Hendrik Frederiksz, 166
Wemeldinge, city of, 1
Wender, Earl Gerrit Beunen van, 153
Wickevoort, Joachim, 142–43
Wiersma, Johannes Cornelius, 196
Wijckenburg, Theodorus, 153
Wijngaerden, Jacob van, 131
Winsum, city of, 77
Wirth, Rudolf, 15
Witten, Jacob Frans, 124
Wode [Wood], Thomas, 30
Woerden, city of, 52
Wurstisen, Christian, 17

Zeeland, province of, 93–94, 121
    church order, 93–94
Zepper, Wilhelm, 182
Zepperus, Guilelmus, 182
Zierikzee, city of, 71
Zurich, city of, 12
Zwingli, Huldrych, 9, 12–15, 17–18
    Gründe der Schlußreden, 14
Zwolle, city of, 87n42
Zymbelstern organ stop, 68

SCRIPTURE INDEX

Genesis
4:21　　　21, 177n27

Deuteronomy
4:2　　　160n93

Exodus
15:20　　　23

I Samuel
1　　　25
18　　　23, 25

Job
21:12　　　177n27

Psalm
150　　　151, 184
150:4　　　177n27
33　　　22, 137
45　　　113
71:23　　　22

Isaiah
5:12　　　21, 22n40
6:9　　　161
42:10　　　24

Ezekial
33:32　　　177n27
12:2　　　161

Matthew
13:14–15　　　161
15:13　　　45
18　　　45
6:6　　　14
Luke 18　　　45

I Corinthians
10:21　　　160n94
14　　　15, 45, 45n137, 46, 63, 64, 64n34, 122, 137, 138, 159, 180–85, 191

Ephesians
5:18　　　24, 193
5:19　　　193
5:20　　　193

Colossians
3:16　　　14, 193
4:6　　　193

I Thessalonians
5:21　　　160n95

Hebrews
2:12   24

2 Peter
2:22   185

Revelation
14:2   184
5:8   184